World Without Time

World Without Time

THE BEDOUIN

by *Edward Nevins and Theon Wright*

PHOTOGRAPHS BY EDWARD NEVINS

Foreword by Sir John Bagot Glubb

The John Day Company
New York

Contents

Acknowledgments

Launching a successful expedition such as the Nevins Bedouin Expedition 1967 involves years of preparation and the invaluable help of many persons. Among those that have been of special help and to whom we offer thanks are:

Dr. John E. Mack, M.D.; Mr. George Moore; Mr. Henry S. Evans; Mr. Bruce Becker; Mr. Bernie Ortiz; Mr. and Mrs. N. K. Sneed III; Miss Barbara Stempowski; and Dorothy Nevins.

The Jordanian Ministries of Information and Tourism, the Desert Security Police, and the Continental Hotel of Ammān, Jordan. Also, Mr. Mohammad Baghal, Mr. Antoine T. Hallac, Mr. R'Faifan ibn Hussein, all of Jordan.

A grant from the Explorers Club, under whose flag the expedition was conducted, is also acknowledged with thanks.

Foreword

Few "might-have-beens" are more depressing than the thought of what might have happened in the Middle East since the end of the First World War and what actually has has happened. How rosy the future appeared for these lands newly freed from Ottoman rule and how tragic and distraught their actual fate has been!

The principal cause of the disasters of the past fifty years may be attributed to the errors of policy committed by the Western powers, Britain, France, and the United States. The source of their mistakes was ignorance—the West knew nothing of the history or the peoples of the Middle East and could not be bothered to learn. Neither the language nor the history of the Arabic-speaking peoples was included in the curriculum of schools or universities in the West. A student could gain the highest academic honors if he possessed an intimate knowledge of the life of Greece or Rome before the time of Christ, but the most profound study of the Middle East since A.D. 700 passed academically completely unrewarded.

Even to this day, both the politicians and the public in Western countries do not possess sufficient background knowledge to enable them to arrive at correct political decisions.

Mr. Nevins' book is an account of a personal journey and contains no politics at all, yet he, almost inadvertently, conveys useful background knowledge. He has realized that the original Arabs were the nomadic tribes of the Arabian Peninsula. In the seventh century these nomads suddenly burst out of their deserts and conquered a vast empire from Spain and Morocco to India and China. But only a negligible number of the Bedouin settled in these countries, the ethnic composition of which remained virtually unchanged.

Some of the Bedouin who swept forward on the crest of the wave of conquest ended in Spain, Morocco, or Afghanistan. The remainder returned to their desert peninsula. The Berbers of Africa, the Egyptians, the Lebanese, and the Syrians remained separate and distinctive nations, with little or no Arab blood in their veins. Only in the twentieth century, and particularly since World War II, has the idea arisen that all these people are "Arabs," of an ethnically homogeneous race.

This illusion has rendered the Middle Eastern scene incomprehensible to the Western reader, who does not know whether to visualize an Arab as a wild tribesman riding a camel across the trackless desert, a Syrian lawyer with a degree from the Sorbonne University in Paris, or a dark-skinned Egyptian fellah toiling in the muddy fields of the Nile delta. All these peoples are, in fact, as different from one another as are, let us say, the Norwegians, the Spaniards, and the Greeks in Europe.

To have written this foreword to Mr. Nevins' book does not imply that I agree with all his views or his speculations. But one thing which I can guarantee is that this book is completely honest and truthful. The author did do all the things which

10

he claims to have done, and he did visit the places which he mentions. The men whom he describes are real, living people, many of them known to me personally.

I hope that Mr. Nevins' book will whet the appetite of many American citizens to visit the Middle East to meet the various Arab peoples at first hand and to study their history, so completely neglected in our schools. Only by this means will the people and the government of the United States be able to frame wise and mutually advantageous policies toward these ancient and charming peoples.

J. B. GLUBB

Preface

The germ of the idea that is the subject of this book first bit me during the summer of 1966, when I was in New York planning an expedition into the Eastern Desert of the old Hashemite Kingdom of the Jordan. My primary purpose in undertaking this journey was to run down some of the actual traces of T. E. Lawrence, the fabled English intelligence officer of World War I who is credited in some quarters with having raised the Arab Revolt and introduced the techniques of guerrilla warfare in modern military operations.

I had traveled through the Bedouin country for a number of years, and a friend, Dr. John Mack, who was preparing a psychological study of Lawrence, had asked me to try to find evidence of his passing among the old Bedouin of the Eastern Desert, some of whom must have known him well. I had planned to follow his tracks from Azraq, in eastern Jordan, down across the desert to Wádi Rumm and Mudawwara, on the Saudi Arabian border, where he had participated in the destruction of the old Turkish railroad from Medina to Damascus.

I was with three friends at the Overseas Press Club in New York, discussing these matters; to my surprise they seemed quite doubtful of the usefulness of the project. One of them reminded me that the Lawrence legend had been so chewed to the bone that very little was left—if, indeed, there had been much to chew on in the first place. Lawrence had largely created his own character, and his passing references to the ecstasy of Arab boys on the hot desert no longer stirred much interest, even as erotic literature. There was the added point that his alleged position in the Arab Revolt was dubious, if not fictitious.

I felt that Lawrence's character was still sufficiently obscure and misty to warrant some further investigation. Besides, I had another reason for wanting to travel into the Eastern Desert.

It was probably at this point that the bug really bit me. The idea was not original at the time; I had been mulling over it for several years. But suddenly in the course of this discussion, the comparative importance of T. E. Lawrence, who lived only 50 years ago, and the origin of the nomads of the Arabian Steppe which goes back more than 5,000 years, took shape in my mind.

"Do any of you happen to know where the Arabs came from?" I asked. "Not the races that speak Arabic today—such as the Egyptians and Berbers and so on—but the true Arab, the Bedouin?"

No one seemed to know. One of those at the table, an editor with fairly extensive knowledge of history and ethnology, suggested that they probably descended from Ishmael, which is the biblical account. The absence of any definitive theory, even among my friends, all of whom were comparatively literate, crystallized in my mind the point I was about to make.

"As a matter of fact," I told them, "there is no real history of the Bedouin. No one knows where they came from, including the Bedouin themselves."

This was quite true. Written history of the Arab peoples does not go back much further than the seventh century, the time of

Mohammed. Like the Tuareg of the Sahara, a dying race of white-skinned people who may have been the original "white people of the Mediterranean," the Bedouin past is shrouded in historic and racial mystery. The story of their descent from Ishmael, son of Abraham and half-brother of Isaac, who founded the Jewish tradition—thus producing a simplified explanation of Arab-Jewish hostility as a kind of family quarrel—is merely a legend of the Bible. Archaeological diggings west of the Jordan Rift, which divides the Holy Land from the Arabian Steppe, have failed to produce any significant traces of the original nomad, with the possible exception of the Nabataean Arabs who ruled a vast domain southeast of the Dead Sea during the millennium before the Christian era; and even this is largely confined to the ruins around Petra. My own theory of research into this matter was quite unorthodox, and I would hesitate to voice it among scholars, since it bears little resemblance to a scientific discipline.

During my travels among the Bedouin, chiefly around the border area of south Jordan, I had observed the characteristic that is perhaps unique among nomadic peoples: the traditional clinging to the remote past. Their customs were as changeless as the desert itself. My theory, if it could be dignified as such, was the belief that the habits of such people provide the best source of information as to their origin. Archaeologists may prop mummies against the wall and hope to determine from an examination of dead bodies and the bric-a-brac around them what they were like and how they behaved when they were alive. This, however, is merely raking over dead ashes to find out what the house looked like when it was burning.

In my own case, it was actually more than a theory. I had found a number of tangible clues to the beginnings of the Bedouin in my sojourns on the desert. One such clue was a line of abandoned wells whose antiquity was uncertain but which were nevertheless known to Bedouin who had traversed the Eastern Desert and the even more remote region far east of the desert. I had heard of these old wells from Bedouin *sheikhs,* sitting in their tents at night, and I was certain from what I had heard that a line of ancient watering places, long since gone dry, extended from the Eastern Desert down the Arabian steppelands to South Arabia, the fabled Arabia Felix mentioned by Herodotus. Fragmentary records found in epigraphic writings on stone along the Hadhramaut coast of south Arabia indicate traces of similarity between these inscriptions and relics of Semitic languages of Akkadian and Aramaic origin in the valley of the Euphrates, more than 2,000 miles to the north.

While I claim no expertise in these matters, it seemed logical to surmise that the peoples of ancient Arabia Felix and those who settled in Ur of the Chaldees and Babylon may have been branches of an older civilization that was ejected or had migrated from India, spreading out in two directions—one settling in the valleys of the Tigris and Euphrates, and the other along the littoral of south Arabia from Muscat to Yemen. These latter peoples were known to have traded with Africa and the Mediterranean, and perhaps they had overland camel routes into Mesopotamia.

There was a further possibility that the fables that compose *The Thousand and One Nights* may have originated in this land now lost in history. The earliest translations of these stories, from Persian legends as early as the tenth century of the Christian era, refer to their having taken place on "an island, or peninsula of the Indies," and they could have been brought north into Persia over this long since disused caravan trail.

I told my companions of this line of abandoned wells and added that I hoped to extend my expedition into that region in an effort to locate them.

"Do you know where the old wells are?" one of my friends asked.

I nodded. I had plotted a course on a map developed by the Saudi Arabian government's department of mineral resources.

16

The line extended from the lower part of the Syrian Desert southward across the frontiers of Saudi Arabia into the Eastern Desert and on down through the steppeland, somewhat to the east of the present-day route through Jauf and Buraida, into the lands of the Shammar and Harb tribes. It was quite possible it ran along the edge of the steppe, following a trade route between Arabia Felix and the ancient cities of Mesopotamia.

If I could trace these wells, many of which were undoubtedly buried in the sand, I felt I might find a clue to the original habits and activities of the Bedouin and thus obtain some indication of how the early Arabs emerged into the recorded history of civilization—perhaps further back than anyone has been able to trace them.

A passage from Gibbon bears on this point: "The same life is uniformly pursued by the roving tribes of the desert; and in the portrait of the modern Bedouin we may trace the features of their ancestors who, in the age of Moses or Mohammed, dwelt under similar tents, conducted their horses and camels and sheep to the same springs and the same pastures."[1]

One of my companions wanted to know how I expected to find out things about the Bedouin that had escaped other researchers with more scholarship than I possessed. This was a natural question, but I reminded him that all the research labors of Arab historians and their Western colleagues failed to turn up any substantial clues as to how the Bedouin originated. Besides that, unscholarly folks like myself frequently have contributed to knowledge of such matters. An America journalist writing for a humor magazine was first to focus world attention on the Dead Sea Scrolls, which then forced the experts of biblical scholarship to change many concepts of both Christian and Jewish theology.

There was also the point that I had traveled for many years among the Bedouin, and they regarded me as one of their own. A Bedouin of the Bani-Sakhr tribes, R'Faifan ibn Hussein, who would be my only traveling companion on this expedition,

17

called me his "little brother." This was the real secret of Lawrence's ability to work with Arabs: he was not considered a stranger.

I mentioned that the fact that current scholarship had failed to arrive at any common conclusion as to the origin of the Bedouin also was worth emphasis. The only knowledge of pre-Christian Arabs, aside from scattered diggings around the Dead Sea, seems to have been gleaned from the Old Testament, and even these legends are the subject of conflicting theories. The story of Ishmael as the founder of all Arab dynasties is matched by the legend of Joktan (the son of Eber), who was the great-grandson of Noah and is believed by many to have fathered the Arab race. Joktan, Ophir, and Hazarmaveth (Gen. 10:26), which may have been the names of individuals or tribes, were biblical ancestors of the people of Arabia Felix who lived on the southern coast of the Arabian Peninsula, although it seems doubtful that they were Bedouin, since they were merchants and traders.

However, all this confusion that exists over the origin of the Arabs has served to cloud the issue. Many Bible scholars, for example, believe the Arabs, as well as the Jews and Aramaeans, were all descendants of Shem, from whom the word Semite was derived; and yet this is not a racial designation but a linguistic concoction of eighteenth-century German scholars who used the word to establish a common language identification among the ancient Akkadians, Aramaeans, Assyrians, and others who spoke similar languages, although they bore no resemblance to each other physically or ethnically.

I then presented what I thought was my most convincing point: the single-hump camel. This durable animal was unknown outside the Arabian Steppe prior to the fifteenth century B.C., except for fossilized remains found in North America and in parts of Africa. The domestication of the single-hump camel, or dromedary, was the one factor which made possible overland transportation from

Arabia Felix to the Mesopotamian Valley, carrying rich spices and silks from Somalia and the Indies to the wealthy cities of the Euphrates.

As a matter of fact, I intended to trace this route, which I believed was not over the King's Highway—the ancient Roman road along the sloping hills east of the Dead Sea—but was an ancient camel trail far out on the Eastern Desert. It was my hope that I would locate this route, which must have been traveled by Bedouin centuries before the Romans, and perhaps before the time of Abraham, using the camel as the only means of transportation on the desert until the Rolls-Royce of World War I and the jeep of World War II.

If my expedition bore fruit, it might serve to untangle certain conflicting theories about the Arabs. The history of Israel, for example, is a welter of confusing traditions and tribal legends of both Arabs and Jews. The story of Ishmael, that "wild ass of a man, his hand against everyone, and everyman's hand against him" (Gen. 16: 12), cast out into the desert with his mother, Hagar, who was Abraham's concubine, runs directly counter to the scholarly theory that the Arabs erupted from the desert long before the time of the Patriarchs and overran half the Euphrates Valley. In addition, it may be noted that the accepted account is merely the Hebrew version in the Old Testament. The Arabs themselves have a much more sympathetic view of Ishmael.

As I look back on that discussion at the Overseas Press Club, full of enthusiasm on my part and skepticism on the part of my friends, I realize that I missed one reason for my journey; but it would have required the gift of prophecy to note this decisive point, which was in the making.

This was the gathering storm in the Middle East, which even then was rising to the whirlwind of fury which later caught me. Even as I was discussing my expedition with my friends, the intermittent quarrels between the Arabs and the Jews was boiling up along the borders of Jordan and Syria, and in the Negev where Bedouin were driven from their homes, forced to flee from a land on which they had lived for centuries.

The eruption of this constant feud was probably the one factor I had not taken into account in planning my journey; as it turned out, it was the most decisive. It burst into open violence while I was racing across the Eastern Desert, not knowing which way to go, and it gave immediacy to my adventure, although it left me somewhat short of the results I expected to achieve. However, it also provided a ringside seat at what may have been the last stages of a feud that began in biblical times. Very possibly it was a final encroachment of Western civilization upon the lands of the Bible, an act which started with the Crusades; and as such it may have been the beginning of the end for a people who have survived without real change for a longer period of time than the dynasties of Egypt, generally regarded as the longest single event in the history of the world.

EDWARD M. NEVINS

New York
June, 1968

World Without Time

I. *The Ancient Lands*

1

The Bedouin of the desert, in the words of T. E. Lawrence, are not given to "shades of thought" or halftones; their vision sees only black and white, "a clearness or hardness of belief, almost mathematical in its limitation . . . a dogmatic people, despising doubt."[1]

This undeviating adherence to simple conviction, as expressed not only in religion but in the living habits of the original Arabs, may have been the source of my own innate belief that their origin—an unexplored page in the history of the world—might be traced back from what they are today to what they were 5,000 years ago, and thus their actual source could be uncovered by a study of their character.

This might appear at first glance to be an inversion of the normal historical process, by which things are traced from their beginnings; yet the fundamental habits of mind of these nomads of the Arabian Steppe lend themselves to this kind of retrogressive study. For centuries wandering tribes of Bedouin have lived in much the same way, breeding camels and sheep on the sandy slopes and gravel ridges of the vast plateau called in ancient writings "the island of Arabia." The arid waste of the Steppe lies between two fairly well populated rims of fertile coastline along the west, east, and south of the "island." Within these edges lies one of the world's bleakest regions, stretching for hundreds of miles, and growing more barren and sterile as it rises toward the inland plain.

The wilderness of the desert is mirrored in the uninhibited poetry of the Arabs, which forms a manifestation of the character of these people who have no fixed place in history. It is not introspective poetry, as is often the case in the West; it is a cry of stubborn resistance to the land itself, a hardness of spirit as unyielding as the desert. The austere temper of Bedouin, and their deep sense of dignity, is reflected in the way they eke out their living raising camels and goats. I had suggested to my friends in New York that it might be possible to trace the origin of these people who lived and thought within the same framework their ancestors had lived in for century upon century, simply by living among them. While flying over the desert, I had become aware of the harsh and unchanging land; traveling over it by camel, as I have, brings this awareness to the point of physical acuity. The waste of sand is uncompromising. The ridges, swept bare of sand, are like scars that have grown so old in the burning sunlight that they no longer fester; they lie open and dry as they have for centuries, even millennia.

The Bedouin draws his life and his thoughts from this bitter land. His faith in God is not a faith that comes from within; it is a faith that comes out of the desert. For hundreds of years he had said: *"Inshallah!"*—God willing! All things come from Allah, and Allah comes from the desert! Allah is the eternal embodiment of the world around him, and to the Bedouin that world is not fragile and changing, but one of hard, changeless reality, a world where hot blood surges in the blazing sun and the wind, and hospitality to a stranger is not an obligation but

24

a creed; where man moves endlessly in a circle, from one hill to the next, changing homes but never way of life; where breeding camels and tending flocks is the aim and substance of all earthly existence.

My feeling that I could penetrate the mystery of the beginnings of the Bedouin did not grow out of fancies. As I have noted, I had a very tangible plan which—if it had not been for a totally unexpected turn of events—might have led to a fairly successful end. The line of old wells mentioned earlier, most of them dry and abandoned, stretched for more than 2,000 miles from the area of ancient Damascus and Tadmore down across the Arabian Peninsula to the fertile coast of South Arabia, where the old trading ports once existed, sending ships westward and eastward across the Indian Ocean to Africa and to the Indies.

I had been mulling this over in my mind all the way from New York, and by the time we were descending over the low hills toward the small, two-runway field at Ammān on a cold, drizzly afternoon on the first day of February, 1967, my speculations had become almost an obsession. I had become convinced by my own rambling thoughts that I could unlock the secrets of antiquity of the original nomads of the Arabian Steppe through the medium of psychology rather than archaeology, or even ethnology, in which I had neither experience nor aptitude.

As my plane, BOAC's flight 212 from London, circled over the small patch of airport just north of Ammān, I was acutely aware of the complicated task I had set for myself. I had originally planned my expedition for the purpose of tracking down what might be termed the "psychology" of Lawrence of Arabia. Dr. John Mack was a professional psychologist whose extraordinary purpose seemed to be to psychoanalyze a man long since dead. I had embarked on the adventure, in its earliest stages, with only this in mind: I intended to locate some of my old friends on the desert and collect such fragments of their recollections of

Lawrence as I might, hoping to furnish my friend with grist for his psychological mill, in which he planned to grind up the under-lying elements of Lawrence's personality and mold them together again in a posthumous character study.

However, I was becoming aware that my real interest was not Lawrence but the Bedouin themselves; and it would be necessary to keep the two objectives well separated in my mind. In this connection, it might be useful to outline here the geography of my proposed route over the desert, since it was designed to en-compass both missions—to search for traces of Lawrence; and after that to try to locate the line of old wells along the far side of the Eastern Desert.

My original plan had been to start southward from Ammān toward Rumm and Guweira, spending some time in the red-walled canyons of southern Jordan where Lawrence had raided the Turkish railroad line. Here I intended to collect what information I could about the personality of Lawrence and his actual participation in the Arab Revolt. Then I intended to strike southward into Saudi Arabia, traveling by camel over the ancient Bedouin trails. I would be riding through territory seldom if ever visited by Westerners. Two Englishmen, H. St. John Philby and Bertram Thomas, had crossed the Arabian plateau in the region of the dread 'Rab al Khali Desert, farther south, but I did not intend to go there. My intention was to turn eastward after I reached Buraida, a junction of camel trails in the central steppe, cross the Quasim Desert which lies in the northern part of the peninsula, and try to locate the line of old wells that might lead me northward toward Wádi Sirhan, along the border between eastern Jordan and Saudi Arabia.

However, the government of Saudi Arabia had turned down my request to travel by camel over these lands, so I had to shift my course eastward. I had written my friend Tony Hallac in Ammān, asking that he make arrangements with the Jordanian authorities to permit me to travel eastward from Jiza, a small village south of Ammān, entering the Eastern Desert at the remote outpost of Azraq.

Tony had recruited an old friend, R᾽Faifan ibn Hussein, with whom I had traveled in southern Jordan; since he was a member of the Bani-Sakhr tribes of northern Jordan he would know the routes and the people of the Eastern Desert. In order to accomplish my work on the Lawrence mission, I planned to turn southward from Azraq, following the routes Lawrence took when he was marshaling the support of the Howeitat and Bani-Sakhr tribes. The distance from Āzraq southward to Wádi Rumm and Guweira is about 250 miles over camel trails toward the southern border between Jordan and Saudi Arabia. To the east of this route lies the Wádi Sirhan, and beyond that extends one of the most untraveled parts of the Arabian Steppe, linking the peninsula with the Syrian Desert and the fertile lands of Mesopotamia.

The borderland between Saudi Arabia, Iraq, Jordan, and Syria is not always defined, even on official maps. There is one large blank area known as "neutral territory." While I had been refused permission to enter Saudi Arabia, I planned to skirt this border and perhaps cross it, circling northward after my Lawrence mission was accomplished, heading toward the lower end of the Wádi Sirhan at a point east of Bāyir, an ancient watering place on the rim of the Eastern Desert.

Much of the material I hoped to gather for Dr. Mack could be obtained in the area between Azraq and Rumm, and after that I would continue on my own private venture. Beyond Bāyir to the east lay the Wádi Sirhan, a wide valley, and beyond that the village of Kaf, once an important crossroads on the caravan route northward from Arabia to Damascus and Baghdad. This area, known as the Qurayyāt Depression, was reported to be the location of two old castles at Kaf and Ithra, a few miles to the east, that may have predated the Roman conquest of the regions east of the Holy Land. It was also believed by many Bedouin that this region was formerly the coastline of a vast extension of the

27

Persian Gulf into the Arabian heartland before the dawn of known history. My plan was to search for traces of the old wells, reported to be at regular intervals, not more than three days' march from one to another. Any man can travel three days by camel without water for himself, and certainly he needs none for his beast. The distance is only about 100 kilometers.

The wells are not well known, except to the Bedouin, and they are not marked on maps. However, their locations were known to many camel drivers, even though the wells were no longer watering places. They formed a string of small oases from the edge of the Syrian Desert all the way down the Arabian plateau, and I had marked them out on a map as *Q'a* (pronounced *gaa*), the Arabic word for place, designating them as Q-1, Q-2, and so on. Q-1 was about 80 kilometers east of Azraq and north of Kaf; Q-2 was 30 kilometers southwest of this point; Q-3 and Q-4 were somewhere along the border east of Bāyir. These wells, I believed, formed stopping places on a forgotten highway, connecting the Fertile Crescent of Syria and Mesopotamia and the land of Arabia Felix. For several millennia no caravans had traveled this route, simply because there was no commerce. Trade that once flourished along the coast cities of southern Arabia, from Yemen to the Muscat peninsula, had dried up, and since the time of the Queen of Sheba, who once ruled this area, there had been no commerce with cities of the north across the desert.

During several earlier journeys into southern Jordan I had talked with Bedouin *sheikhs* who knew something of this area. Some of the wells were still watering places, used by nomads ranging from one grazing ground to another, but the continuous chain of wells that may have marked the ancient trail had long since disappeared. However, the existence of this trail was not a matter of conjecture. I knew where the wells were believed to be located, and my only problem had been getting there. This search for traces of Lawrence on behalf of my psychological friend had furnished me with the motive and the means.

28

There is little doubt that I also entertained certain romantic notions about this theory of an old caravan trail. There may even have been a touch of parapsychological significance in my attitude toward the project of finding the wells. I had the feeling that if I could trace this old camel trail, and live among the Bedouin who still roamed these areas, I might dredge from their subconscious memories some hint of knowledge which they possessed, possibly as tribal legends or even as bits of subliminal memories that could be woven into the fabric of Bedouin history.

There is obviously a logical defect in this reasoning, because if the Bedouin of today have no real knowledge of where they came from, they cannot very well impart this lack of knowledge to another. Frankly, I am not sure what I hoped to find or how I expected to find it. I was simply going to ride out into the desert with the vague notion that in discovering reminders of a forgotten past, I might bring to light traces of their antiquity that could lead me to a better understanding of the Bedouin of today.

The fact that these origins, or memories of the past, may have escaped the notice of eminent scholars, no doubt less romantic about the whole thing than I was, did not greatly concern me. I believe the human mind has ways of knowing things that do not always lend themselves to the techniques of scientific research. In my own experience with Bedouin, I had observed a kind of inner perceptiveness that seemed to be intensified by the loneliness of the life they led. I had often closed my eyes, while jogging along, and been certain as I opened them that I saw a line of white-robed men crossing the sands. I could easily visualize these desert riders, their long riding robes flowing behind them, their head cloths, or *kaffiyah,* bound to their heads with ropelike *agáls,* trailing pinions in the wind, looking much as they do today. Yet these would be desert riders centuries before the time of Christ!

It may be that I had subconsciously accepted the notion that the Bedouin of today, living on the desert over which these caravans passed, might also be capable of re-creating this image

29

in some kind of subliminal communication with the past. As I have said, I am not quite sure what my "theory" was, except that it quite definitely was not scientific. Possibly I was trying to psychoanalyze people who had been dead for millennia, just as Dr. Mack was trying to dredge up similar secrets about Lawrence of Arabia, who had lived only a half-century ago.

2

Tony Hallec met me at the airport. He was a dapper man, dressed in Western fashion, dark and suave, with a warm glint in his black eyes. He had left Haifa a few years before, driven out by the Israeli, and he now owned the Continental Hotel, a large, old-fashioned stone building in the center of Ammān.

On the way from the airport I noticed a large number of trucks rumbling toward the military airfield, which lies alongside the commercial airport at Ammān. I asked Tony the reason for the activity, and he shrugged noncommittally.

"There is always activity," he said. On the way into town we discussed my plans for the expedition. Arrangements had already been made to secure letters and papers from the *badia*—the Jordanian Desert Patrol—which would provide me clearance in the remote outposts of the Eastern Desert. There are no marked trails east and south of Azraq, and I would have to rely on the "Camel Corps" for directions and guidance.

Tony Hallec was a Jordanian, although not a Bedouin, and he knew the officers of the *badia* quite well. He had arranged for me to meet the commandant at Ammān, and also the head of the security police, who controlled the movements of everyone on the desert.

Shortly after my arrival at the Continental Hotel, R'Faifan made his appearance. He was a thin, wispy man, with a sharp nose, warm eyes, gnarled hands and skin the texture of leather. His face split into a grin as he greeted me with an outpouring of

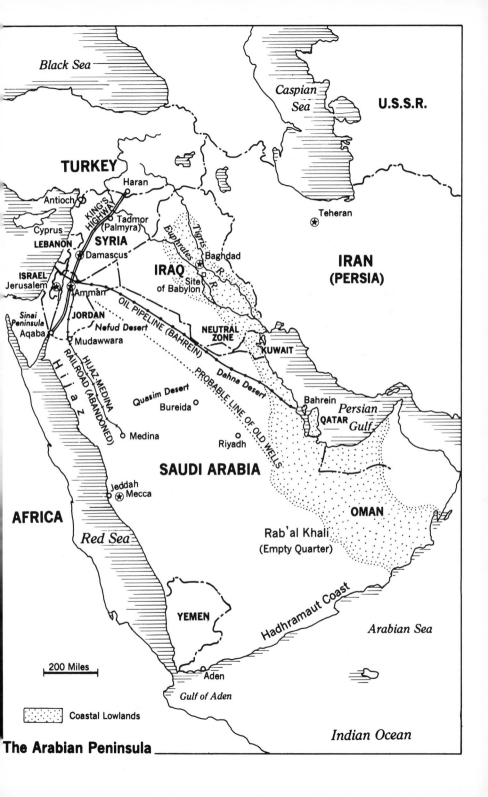

The Arabian Peninsula

Arabic that I hardly understood. I was his "little brother," and when I showed him a picture of my wife and year-old son, for want of a better means of communication he kissed it as if they were his own family. He then explained to me, in a medley of Arabic words and whistling noises that he made through his teeth, that he had literally abandoned his own family in order to join me. This, of course, was not strictly true; he had two strong sons and had left one in charge of the *bait sha' ar* to carry on the burden of tending flocks and watching over the family of women until R'Faifan returned.

Meanwhile R'Faifan reported on his efforts to obtain suitable camels for our expedition. This was a matter of no small importance, and thus far, he had not met with unqualified success.

No one who has ever traveled over the desert will underestimate the camel. As a beast of burden he has no peer, although his or her disposition usually leaves something to be desired. The camel's endurance is unbelievable, and its survival characteristics, including ability to travel for days without water, make it the most important single asset possessed by nomads, not necessarily excluding their wives. The Arabian camel is smaller but has slightly longer legs than the Bactrian, or "Asiatic," camel, and is able to carry heavier loads, up to 500 pounds. It can travel at a rate of 25 miles a day, or even more under pressure, but its usual speed is about 3 or 4 miles an hour.

The long, loping strides by which the camel traverses the sand and gravel surface of the desert, with legs moving uniformly on either side like a pacer, presents the ungainly swaying motion that appears awkward to the onlooker but eats up miles across the desert.

The Bactrian camel is seldom found below the Iranian plateau and is most frequently found in Afghanistan and along the Siberian steppelands. Prehistoric relics of the ancestors of the Arabian camel have been found in many parts of the world, notably in North America, where fossils of the Pleistocene Age indicate its existence as far north as Canada millions of years ago. Apparently it disappeared from the Western Hemisphere when sheets of glacial ice drove it southward into South America, and from there it migrated by some means into Africa and Asia.

Oddly enough, the camel was not known in the earliest historic times, except on the Arabian Steppe and in southern Asia. About the fifteenth century B.C. drawings of camels appeared in Egyptian tombs, apparently introduced by Bedouin nomads into the valley of the Nile about that time.

It is a strange circumstance that only the nomad of the Arabian Steppe knew of the single-hump camel and was able to domesticate it; and this, as I have noted, is a point worth more than passing interest. It may explain the manner in which the Bedouin first became known to civilization.

The camel market at Ammān is one of the liveliest animal trading places in the Middle East, although more camels are reported to be traded at Guweira, south of the Dead Sea, than anywhere else. I made several trips with R'Faifan around the markets near Ammān. Each time the camel traders quickly took him aside to offer various kinds of bribes, in the form of commissions or even an extra camel, if he would persuade me to accept their offerings, R'Faifan came to me each time and dutifully reported the amount of the bribe, which he figured into the price.

There are a number of points about a camel that need to be taken into consideration. R'Faifan was an expert at examining the breadth of chest, length of leg, indications of staying power, and particularly the various signs of mental attitude. A camel is more than a beast of burden; it has a personality. Even well-trained camels, who normally are quite docile, may burst forth in sudden rage, bite anyone near them, and snarl at drivers or trainers. Most camels have evil dispositions and are given to fits of moodiness, petulance, and outright anger.

Certain myths concerning camels are harbored by many Bedouin. They believe the camel stores "water cells" which enable it to survive for days without water. This is an old wives' tale; actually the camels conserve fat on their humps, and the oxidation of the fat supplies water for the body. A camel can travel as long as two weeks without drinking, lose 20 to 25 pounds through dehydration, and restore its water balance in ten minuted by drinking the amount it has lost!

We covered most of the Ammān market and the surrounding villages without success. The camels were too old, or too weak, or they had basic defects, such as being bone-spavined or insane. Finally R'Faifan told me of a village north of the Dead Sea, near Jericho, where reportedly there were many fine camels. We drove there in Tony Hallec's Volkswagen, taking not only R'Faifan but a corporal named Khalid Musa, representing the Desert Patrol. Tony and the corporal and I remained in the car while R'Faifan went into the camel-trading place, and after about an hour he came back surrounded by five Bedouin and three camels. I was sure R'Faifan approved of the animals, but there was now a system of Arab bargaining to undergo. After the Bedouin had paraded their camels—two females and a bull —before us, they mentioned the price. It was 100 Jordanian dinars, or about 280 U.S. dollars per camel.

This figure was so disagreeable to R'Faifan that he almost threw himself on the ground in anger and despair. He beat himself on the chest and waved at me, shouting Arabic words that I understood only vaguely; but I got the sense of them, which was a declaration that his reputation—past, present, and future— would be worthless as a trusted friend if he even mentioned the price to me.

The Bedouin traders began to shout back at R'Faifan. They were of the Jehalin tribes, driven out of the Negev by the Jews, and were known as hard bargainers. They thrust their faces to within an inch of R'Faifan's, waving their hands at him and me as if they had been insulted by his refusal to accept the first offer.

R'Faifan merely shook his head and stamped his feet, and when he looked at me I did the same. Tony Hallec nudged me, nodding also, and although the corporal who was with us made no sign, it was evident he approved our firm position. In bargaining with Bedouin it is essential not to exhibit any sign of weakness.

Meanwhile it had begun to rain. Tony and Khalid Musa and I huddled in the constricted interior of the Volkswagon while the Bedouin went off a little distance to confer among themselves. R'Faifan flashed me a knowing glance, and his quick smile indicated he was in no mood to surrender. Finally they came back from the huddle, a basic ritual in all camel trading, and offered a new price. R'Faifan came to me and reported the amount, 91 dinars per camel, but he assured me they could trample him into the ground before he would consent to such an outrageous price.

After he had shaken his head, they went off to confer again and came back with a new offer, only slightly less. R'Faifan shook his head again, and this seemed to drive them into a frenzy. One of the Bedouin became so excited he dropped the reins of one of the female camels—a small, light animal that seemed built for speed—and it ran off into the desert. A half hour or so was consumed in chasing the animal.

The pelting of the rain increased, and the wind came up, blowing across the ragged hills from the direction of Jericho. I was extremely uncomfortable and signaled to R'Faifan that he might as well break off negotiations, since there seemed no chance of arriving at a reasonable compromise.

This moved the Bedouin to even greater fury. With shrieks of protest, they gathered around the Volkswagon, and finally they made a "final offer"—80 dinars a camel! R'Faifan seemed to sense that they were nearing the trading point, and in spite of the rain he went back with them and pointed to various defects in the camels. One had a bony knee; another's chest was too narrow. The corporal remained quiet, watching me covertly yet not betraying his sympathies one way or another. Tony was enjoying the affair hugely, despite the rain; but I was about to call it all off and go home.

Finally R'Faifan made what was obviously a counteroffer— evidently much lower than the Bedouin price, although my limited Arabic prevented me from following the fluctuations in price. The Bedouin retired into a quick huddle. From the accelerated rate of bargaining it was evident that the affair was nearing a climax. R'Faifan finally indicated to me that a firm price had been arrived at—71 dinars per camel!

I nodded. I was so weary from listening to the jabbering that I probably would have settled for the first figure they had offered. Several traders who were watching my expression suddenly screamed their gratification at the price, which they had declared only an hour or so earlier would be ruinous to them and their entire families. Khalid Musa came over, smiling and nodding.

"I knew you would accept their offer," he said. "Your face showed it. The price is good."

I was not sure whether this was an accolade or merely his way of telling me I should never play poker with a Bedouin camel trader. It was now necessary to drive about a mile to a small *badia* station to have the official seal put on the trade, apparently a government precaution against foreigners' being too badly outtraded by the local camel dealers. The place where we concluded the trading was about a mile north of the Dead Sea, and the post was located on the new road between Jerusalem and Ammān. I signaled the traders to follow us, but instead they piled into the back seat of the Volkswagen, leaving one of their number to tend the camels.

We proceeded toward the little village, Tony Hallec at the wheel, I in the front seat with him, and R'Faifan somehow curled around the gearshift box. In the rear seat four Bedouin were piled one on top of the other, and in this fashion we jolted across the desert road toward the little village of Teil al Ghuzul, where the *badia* post was located.

The corporal had refrained from taking any position while the trading was in process, but now he joined in the general spirit of satisfaction, shouting from the rear seat: "You have fine camels, excellency! It was a good trade!"

It was like a celebration after a football game. Everyone smiled and cheered. When we arrived at the *badia* post, the officer in charge wrote out an agreement in Arabic, which I signed, also in Arabic. The owners not only had to sign, but they were fingerprinted, probably another government precaution against the possibility they had sold camels they did not own.

It was arranged that the camels would be delivered the following Sunday at Jiza, the village from which we would depart on our journey into the desert. I paid half the amount due, and the rest was to be paid upon our receipt of the camels.

R'Faifan was particularly proud of the white female, which he assured me, as we rode back to Ammān in Tony Hallec's little car, was as fine as any camel on the desert, of the best stock and strong enough to carry us both. As it turned out, our jubilation was a bit premature. It was not until several days later, when we completed the trade at Jiza, that I became aware that the white female was not only strong and fast but also slightly mad.

These quirks of temperament among camels are not unusual, particularly in the case of the *nága,* or female. The word actually applies to a state of being rather than the sex of the animal, since it refers only to camels that have borne at least one calf. It is quite possible, I suppose, that a psychologist specially trained in animal behavior might find this as evidence of postnatal depression, but for anyone riding or herding an insane camel, there is usually little time or disposition for a psychiatric diagnosis of the animal. You simply get rid of her.

3

Tony Hallec had done his work with the Jordanian government officials very well. In preparing an expedition with only two composing the expeditionary force—R'Faifan and myself—there were bound to be many questions, such as our ability to cope with problems of desert travel, and the likelihood that we would become lost and thus a responsibility of the government.

The Security Police force was headed by Brigadier Abu Nuwar, and he was the final source of permission to travel on the desert. He assigned this responsibility to Colonel Nayef Beyal Faez of the Desert Police, who not only gave me official permission but wrote a personal letter which I might use to assure friendly reception in the outlying forts of the Patrol in such remote places as Bāyir and Al Jafr. These two outposts lie along the southwestern route I had projected from the oasis of Azraq, the most northern point in my journey, down across the Eastern Desert plateau to Rumm and Guweira.

This element of official support of the expedition cannot be underestimated. R'Faifan and I were going into an area where non-Moslems seldom traveled. There would be no link between ourselves and the centers of civilization once we passed beyond Azraq. The only routes across the open desert were trails of *sheikhs* and camel drivers, moving their *buyût sha'ar*—the Arabic plural for the *bait sha'ar,* or "hair tent," the term used by the Bedouin to describe their desert homes—and these would be our only stopping places, except for our own campsites and the widely separated outposts of the Desert Patrol.

For this reason, we needed as strong an official endorsement of our presence in the desert as could be obtained, and this was provided generously by Colonel Nayef and Brigadier Abu Nuwar. Colonel Nayef was a tall, straight-limbed officer who bore the stamp of military discipline and genial good will and friendliness which I had long ago learned to admire in Jordanian officers. He seemed to regard my expedition as a trust, for which he assumed personal responsibility.

Colonal Nayef's office was a square room, built in a blockhouse on the roof of an old fort which served as headquarters of the Desert Patrol. It was sparsely furnished, with a single desk at one end, maps tacked on the walls, and the inevitable coffeepot bubbling on a small stove in the center. This coffee-drinking custom among Arabs is so general that a room would seem naked without a coffeepot simmering, its contents served at every opportunity.

The colonel and his aide, Captain Nae al Majali, led me over to the maps and with their fingers traced certain camel trails between watering places on the desert. R'Faifan, who had spent 20 years with the Camel Corps and knew the lands to the east, followed the tracing carefully, nodding from time to time.

Finally I pointed to the lower end of the map, indicating the area of Wádi Araba west of Rumm and Guweira, in southern Jordan, southeast of the Dead Sea. I looked at Colonel Nayef, but he shook his head.

"We are not sure that you will be safe in these areas," he said. "There may be border patrols. You will be able to travel on the Eastern Desert, but it would not be well to go too far to the west."

There was a kindness in his expression, and I knew he was making this point for my own welfare. Nevertheless, I pursued the point, "I hope to go into Wádi Araba, Colonel," I said. "It is part of the area I have planned to cover."

He said nothing more, and remembering the military trucks rumbling along the road at night, I did not press the matter.

It might be noted here that Jordan and Israel are divided by a great natural fault known as the Jordan Rift, which runs from the Sea of Galilee down through the Dead Sea and continues through Wádi Araba to the Gulf of Aqaba. It is a line of demarcation which for centuries has separated the Holy Land from the desert. The coastal lands of Palestine form the southern end of a sweeping arc of rich farmlands from the upper Euphrates River to the Mediterranean Sea. This has been known for ages as the Fertile Crescent, and its inhabitants have been divided from the desert by the Jordan Rift. Beyond the Dead Sea are areas once heavily forested but now stretching eastward in a rising barren plateau toward the back of the Arabian Steppe, while to the west of the Dead Sea are the well-known places of Bible history—the land of Canaan, Jerusalem, Bethlehem, Jericho, Mount Hebron, Beersheba.

I had traveled over many parts of the bleak desert country east and southeast of the Dead Sea, but I had not journeyed very far into the Eastern Desert, and on this expedition I wanted to traverse a region of little-known tribal lands and possibly go as far as the largely untraveled region that slopes down eastward into the Persian Gulf.

Several years earlier an English expedition, led by Guy Mountfort, with the great English scientist Julian Huxley among its members, had pushed as far as Azraq and then turned back, heading down through the Jordan Rift. However, there was an area of more than a million square miles beyond Azraq where few Bedouin ever penetrated. It was along this region that the line of wells had been plotted.

As I have indicated, my primary task was to follow the tracks of Lawrence from Azraq down to Rumm and if possible across to Wádi Araba, where I hoped to find traces of his hideout in that area. There were also ruins of old castles and fortresses, built by the Omayyad caliphate after the rise of Islam under Mohammed, which I wanted to investigate. Some of these were more than 1,000 years old, and the fortress at Azraq dated back to pre-Roman times. But even more alluring was the prospect of going further back in history, perhaps finding remnants of cities that may have existed along the rim of an inland sea.

The actual history of these places is extremely sparse, and the origin of such desert peoples as the Edomites of Moses' time and the Nabataean Arabs who lived in the lands east of the Dead Sea during the Roman conquest is almost unknown, even to archaeologists who have dug into this area. Nevertheless, the possibility of finding traces of these forgotten civilizations—which must have been Bedouin—had always fascinated me.

In this connection, while it is not the purpose of this book to engage in theorizing about the relative origins of the Arabs and Jews, it may be worthwhile to summarize briefly some of the elements of their beginnings, since this became quite an important part of my own adventure into the Eastern Desert. There has been for many years a more or less scholarly squabble over the origins of the Bedouin and the Israelites. The theory that they are of the same original stock, splitting into two separate clans of the same family, actually has no particular foundation outside biblical legends. The opposing theory, which holds that the Arabs are the forerunners of all Semitic peoples, arising out of the Arabian Peninsula before the dawn of written history, is of equally uncertain origin, and the argument may never be settled one way or the other.

There actually is little to substantiate either theory, and it seems quite probable that the second one grew out of an obvious parallel with Islamic conquests of the seventh century, when the Arabs, under the stimulation of Mohammed and the surging Moslem faith, overran half the civilized world.

Joel Carmichael, in *The Shaping of the Arabs,* has this to say about the two general theories:

There is scarcely any doubt but that the idea of ancient "Semitic" peoples bursting out of the Arabian Peninsula over whole millennia and establishing civilizations on the borderlands north of the peninsula is mere theory. It is based on no records at all and is, in fact, modeled modeled on the historic eruption of the Arabs themselves in the seventh century and then retrojected to fit an unknown situation.[2]

Carmichael then adds:

For generations it has been a popular theory that the Hebrews were merely Bedouin transformed in the conventional manner through settlement in agricultural regions. . . . The theory does not seem to have the smallest factual foundation. The one objective fact underlying it is generally taken to be the record of the ancient Hebrews having been divided into . . . the "Twelve Tribes." This is often taken to imply an originally Bedouin background behind the agricultural atmosphere of the people of Israel in the Bible. Tribal organization, however, by no means implies nomadic background.[3]

The word Bedouin is from the Arabic word *bedu,* meaning "outlander." My own experience with the Bedouin, and to a large extent the reported experience of many who, like Lawrence, lived among them and with them, is that they are indeed a people entirely unto themselves. Their unchanging way of life over 40 centuries of historic times is probably the best evidence of their origin on the Arabian Steppe, where they still live.

The very fact that the Bedouin have survived for so long, fending off every hammerblow the surrounding civilizations could deliver—the tides of Babylonian, Assyrian, and Persian conquest, and even the occupation of much of the Bible lands by the Romans—testifies to an endurance and rugged imperviousness to outside influences that has no counterpart in history, with the possible exception of the Eskimos and a few scattered tribes in the Andes.

While there are strong linguistic and cultural similarities among the people of South Arabia—the Sabaeans, Minaeans, Qatabanians, and Hadhrami, and perhaps even older societies —and the rich and powerful peoples at the upper end of the Fertile Crescent, no such connections are discernible with the Bedouin. If they had any ties with these ancient peoples, it must have been as carriers of goods who linked Mesopotamia to

Photo by Walter Mack

Street scene in Ammān, showing the Continental Hotel.

R'Faifan ibn Hussein.

southern Arabia, or as breeders who provided the camels that rendered this overland transport service.

My desire to penetrate the Eastern Desert beyond Azraq and the Wádi Sirhan, in an effort to locate the line of wells along the route from Tadmor to South Arabia, was based on this theory. I also hoped to find out from the Bedouin themselves whatever traces of knowledge they may have of the long-forgotten trail across the ridges and gorges of eastern Arabia that may have been the old caravan route. For centuries the Bedouin have been the only inhabitants of this arid and inhospitable land; if anyone knew the secret of the old trail, they would.

II. *All Roads Run East*

1

Ammān is a city much like San Francisco or Rome, built on hills. Its narrow, twisting streets, curving around the hills, with taxicabs and meandering livestock competing with pedestrians for moving room, are reminders that this city, with its blazing rows of flat-topped apartment houses and crowded marketplaces, and the modernized hotels and stores around the great mosque rising from the center, is a last link between the newest and oldest civilizations.

It has grown rapidly in recent years; even as late as the First World War it was a small trail-crossing, referred to by Lawrence as a "village." The Western-oriented rulers of Hashemite Jordan have added tremendously to its size and importance in the past three decades, and it now stands as a gateway not only between the West and the East, but between the New World and the Old World.

It is significant that the trails feeding into Ammān from the two directions are entirely different from each other. West and southward lie newly built highways leading to Jerusalem and

45

the rich lands of the lower end of the Fertile Crescent, while to the east there are no strands of asphalt but only faint trails over the desert, made by camels and later engraved more deeply in the desert floor by jeeps and Land Rovers. Beyond the gray hills are reminders of earlier peoples, the ancient fort at Qasr al Kharāna, built by the Omayyads in the eighth century to guard Damascus from the south, and the older castle at the Azraq oasis, a relic of Roman rule 2,000 years ago.

Before the Christian era Ammān was Rabbath Ammon, a crossroads of trade used by the Greeks and Syrians. Later under Greek rule it was called Philadelphia. Today it is a city testifying to the rebirth of the Hashemite kingdom, with nearly a half-million inhabitants and modern buildings mingling with the old. As I look across the few intervening yards from my hotel room to the Grand Mosque, listening to the strident call of the *muezzin* summoning all of Moslem faith to prayer, I could not help thinking that the trails to the east were the same as those followed by Arabs when Abraham led his tribal followers toward the Promised Land 4,000 years ago.

For several days I remained in Ammān, assembling equipment for the journey. During this time I was introduced by a local merchant, Mohammed Salim Koshura, with whom I was doing business, to one of the most interesting men I have ever met, in Arabia or outside it. This was Sheikh Faisal ibn Jazi, the titular head of the great Jazi clan, one of the two principal families of the Howeitat tribes. He was related to the famed Auda abu Tayi, who had fought with Lawrence; and my shop-keeper friend whispered to me that Sheikh Faisal "knew much about Lawrence."

I never ascertained how much he knew, because this question was not discussed in any of my talks with him. He was about fifty, with a face that looked as if it had been carved of stone. He was a bit heavy for a Bedouin and walked with a slight limp. When I mentioned that I was seeking traces of T. E. Lawrence—my only reference to that matter in all my talks with him—he merely smiled and said: "You must honor me by visiting my home. We will talk then."

Whether his failure to mention Lawrence again was due to the traditional schism between the Jazi and Tayi factions of the Howeitat I do not know, but I doubt it. I did eventually visit him, twice; but the second time he was not at his home because war was then breaking out all over Jordan. I was by then desperately racing up the King's Highway, not knowing whether to return to Ammān or escape into the Eastern Desert.

By mid-February we were ready to set out from Jiza, a small village of mud-walled huts and stores about 20 miles below Ammān. It was here that the camels we had purchased from the Bedouin traders near Jericho were to be delivered. R'Faifan had gone ahead to set up a tent at the southern edge of the village, and when I arrived with Tony Hallec I found my Bedouin friend in the throes of "camel trouble." The white female we had purchased was already displaying signs of temperament, and R'Faifan assured me the devil must live in the beast.

"She has bitten me twice," he told me, displaying a bruised arm. "Once she also kicked me."

Shortly after we set up camp in Jiza, a series of misfortunes occurred which seemed at the time unusual and frustrating but, as I later realized, were routine mishaps in the desert. We had hardly established ourselves on the outskirts of Jiza, in a small tent which R'Faifan had borrowed until we were ready to leave, when we lost one of the camels. It was the white female, the *nâga* that had displayed manic tendencies from the beginning. R'Faifan had suggested, when the camels were delivered, that we trade her for another female who would be better riding.

I wished fervently that I had taken his advice. The amount I stood to lose was almost $200, which would create a sizable dent in my budget. In addition, there was the problem of finding another camel or carrying all our equipment as well as ourselves on the two remaining animals. Fortunately, R'Faifan had a good friend in the village, Khames Mabruk, a Negro who had been a slave but lived now as a free man among the Bedouin. He knew every camel and camel owner in the area, and it was not long before the lost camel was tracked down.

This Khames Marbruk had a curious history. His ancestors had originally lived in Nubia, and although still regarded as a "slave," he lived among the Bedouin as an equal. His wife was even more than equal. She was an outspoken woman, who did not cover her face with a veil and seemed completely uninhibited. During her visits to the market, she often took her youngest child (she had five), and when the child was hungry, she simply sat down and nursed him in the most convenient place, without bothering to hide either her face or breast.

During the first night of our stay in Jiza, R'Faifan, in gratitude for Khames Mabruk's help in finding the camel, decided to spend the night in Mabruk's house, which was only a short distance from the place where we camped. I prepared to bed down in the tent alone for the night. Meanwhile I had accepted an invitation to have dinner with Sheikh Sami Mithgal al Faiz, a prosperous Bedouin whom I had met on the trip down from Ammān, and who lived nearby.

The house of Sheikh Sami was by far the most pretentious in Jiza. It was on the southern edge of the village, only a couple of hundred yards from our tent. The house was a two-story stone structure surrounded by a courtyard, and the *sheikh* insisted that I remain as his guest until our departure. I thanked him but declined at first, returning after dinner to my tent for the night. The wind had begun to blow fiercely, and shortly after midnight it rose to such howling fury that I thought it would rip our tent from its fastenings.

Fortunately, R'Faifan and I had dug a drainage ditch around the tent, and this was all that saved it from being washed away by the rain. Before daybreak the place had become such a miserable refuge from the storm that I gathered my Bedouin *thōp* about me and fled across the few yards to Khames Marbruk's hut, where I managed to huddle in with Khames, his wife Selma, R'Faifan, and the five Mabruk children, getting a few hours of sleep until morning.

The next day I was happy to accept Sheikh Sami's invitation to remain as a guest in his house until our departure into the Eastern Desert. The *sheikh* had two homes and two wives; the first establishment was in Jiza, and the second a few kilometers out in the desert, where he had set up his *bait sha' ar* with an assortment of camels, goats, and sheep. He insisted that I have a final feast at his desert tent before leaving on my journey.

A full-scale Bedouin feast is unlike anything to be found in the Western world. The *sheikh* first conducted me to the pen where the lambs were gathered and asked me to assist him in selecting the finest young lamb for the feast. This was roasted and placed on a platter piled high with rice. The lamb was mounted so that its head curled under one leg and the fat base of the tail rose like a plume from the top of the hill of rice. A massive bowl of grease from the roasted animal was poured over this arrangement, so that it slopped over the side of the platter. The host and his guests gathered around the platter and scooped up the meat and rice, eating from their hands as the grease poured down their arms and ran in rivulets from their elbows.

While we were feasting, I noticed a member of the household who seemed to wander around aimlessly with nothing to do, apparently not taking any part in the family activities. His hands seemed to be shaking unnaturally, and I concluded he was afflicted with some sort of palsy. He was darker than most Bedouin, and his features seemed alien.

When I spoke to him, as he passed by, he jerked aside and walked quickly away. At first I thought he merely disliked any

49

stranger in the house; but Sheikh Sami, apparently observing my embarrassment when the man did not speak to me, took me to one side and explained the situation.

"The poor fellow cannot speak," he said. "He had a serious accident some years ago when brigands set on him and beat him. Since then he has been afflicted with a kind of brain damage."

He then told me the man's history. He was from Tunisia and was on his way back from a pilgrimage to Mecca, passing through the lands of the Bani-Sakhr tribesmen, when bandits attacked him. He was apparently left for dead when Sheikh Sami found him. The man was brought to the *sheikh*'s *bait sha'ar* and had remained there ever since, as part of the household.

I expressed some surprise that he had remained this long, since he was not a member of Sheikh Sami's household, or even of the Bani-Sakhr. He shook his head, and after looking at me very intently, as if to discover the reason for my curiosity, he said: "It is Allah's will that he remain. He was injured on my land. He is now my responsibility."

This was a simple statement of a basic Bedouin creed. Anyone passing across the lands of a tribal chief, unless he is an enemy, is automatically a guest; and whatever happens to a guest on his land is as much the sacred responsibility of the chief as if it had happened in his home. I also realized why Sheikh Sami had hesitated before explaining this to me: he did not want me to feel, as one from another land, that my own perception of the traditional requirements of Bedouin hospitality were any less than his own. This is a matter of innate courtesy for a Bedouin. And yet, being a Bedouin, he was certain that his customs with regard to strangers were superior to ours in America, and they undoubtedly are.

This was not the first *mansef* I had attended, but it was one of the most notable. The front of the tent had been closed against the biting northeast wind, and as we squatted around the huge

Portrait of a ship: the *nāga*, or female camel, which was called Al-Gazala (the gazelle), ridden by the author.

Feast in the desert: the guests of Sheikh Sami enjoy the repast of lamb and rice; author is in center.

platter, watching the grease and butter cascade down the mound of meat and rice, I felt the delightful tranquillity that seems to be a part of living in the desert. Sheikh Sami squatted beside me, watching me with his warm, good-humored smile as if to make certain from the expression of my face that I was satisfied. As guest of honor, I had to partake of the food before anyone else would touch it; and in accordance with Bedouin manners, Sheikh Sami himself did not touch the food until he was sure all others had eaten.

Later he introduced me very briefly to his wife, an unusual departure from desert custom since I was not a member of the family or an intimate friend. Later in the evening, while we listened to the plaintive singing of a Negro slave to the music of the *rabába,* a single-string violin used by northern Bedouin, I caught a glimpse of her face as she peered from behind the curtain that separated the men's section of the tent from the women's quarters, known variously as *háram* or *muharram.*

She was a very attractive woman, with blond hair and an interesting face. Her forehead was covered with the inevitable blue tattoo marks, which are a feature of Bedouin beauty, and the lower part of her face was veiled up to the eyes. Whether it was curiosity or purely an accident that caused her to peek through the curtains I could not know, but I sensed from the way in which her unexpected appearance was disregarded by Sheikh Sami and his son, Mohammed, that it would have been considered ill-mannered for me to have looked at her, so I immediately turned in the other direction.

We spent the evening in luxurious comfort, lounging on pillows around the fire pit, which blazed pleasantly under the long-spouted brass coffeepots. They bubbled continuously as the supply of coffee was added from time to time from a round bowl in which the beans were ground with a long-handled pestle. Our conversational capabilities were somewhat limited by the fact that I spoke only moderately intelligible Arabic, and as a matter

52

of good taste I did not want to shift to English in deference to a couple of Sheikh Sami's guests.

Behind us, from the corner of the men's compartment, the Negro servant, strumming his one-string *rabába*, sang doleful songs of the desert in wailing quarter-tone notes. I was unable to follow the words, but Sheikh Sami explained that it was an old love song, in the chanting narrative style of Bedouin music.

Lying among the gaudy cushions, I sensed an unreality in the scene. Outside the cold northeast wind whistled through the tent guy ropes, while within the tent the coffee bubbled endlessly and our talk went on. It was as if I had suddenly found myself in a world of the past, unrelated to my present existence and perhaps more akin to that of *The Arabian Nights.*

2

I enjoyed the evening, knowing that in a few days R'Faifan and I would be trekking across the bare desert, camping at nights under bluffs with only our blankets to supply the barest cover from the winter winds.

We left Jiza the following morning, but we had not proceeded very far on the first short leg of our journey—which was only to the *bait sha'ar* of R'Faifan, halfway to Muwaqqar, the last village before we should be out on the desert—when camel trouble beset us again. The animals we had purchased at the village near Jericho were by no means of the best breed, and the white female, which R'Faifan had chosen to ride, was becoming so unruly that he had to dismount and lead her as well as the bull, which we used for a pack animal.

"We must sell her," R'Faifan told me. "A mad camel—particularly a female—affects all other camels."

I realized that this philosophical observation might be applied to creatures other than camels, including humans, but I said nothing to R'Faifan. We had many miles to travel together, and

I did not want to introduce an exposition of Western thoughts at the very beginning on as sensitive a subject as the relative temperaments of men and women. However, I agreed that we might try to bargain for another camel at Muwaqqar.

It might be worth noting that there are actually two basic breeds of camels in Arabia: the *'umaniyah,* or thoroughbred, of which one type—the *bátiniyah*—is the finest in Arabia for speed and riding; and the *jamal,* or pack camel, used the way mules are used in Western America. The *'umaniyah* is also known as the Oman camel, and it is found chiefly in Saudi Arabia, among eastern tribes, such as the *'*Utaiba, the Mutair, and the *'*Awazim, who breed these camels to specific colors, usually dark brown or black, although the Mutair breed fawn-colored or reddish coats.

The fine breeds of the south are capable of traveling long distances at great speed. Sheikh Naif ibn Hummaid, a *'*Utaiba tribesman imprisoned at Ryadh by Ibn Saud in 1925, reported that he escaped and traveled 800 miles in eight days on a light, fast *bátiniyah* camel in his flight eastward to his tribal home near Kuwait. There are many other reports of the unbelievable speed and endurance of these long-limbed animals.

The camels I had bought at the village near Jericho were of the poorer *jamal* breed, and I expected nothing very remarkable from them; but I certainly did not want to be encumbered with a mad female at the outset of our expedition, so I told R'Faifan to sell the animal.

We had a final stop to make before starting out into the desert; and that was at R'Faifan's own *bait sha' ar* near Muwaqqar. We approached his home over a slight rise. I was riding and R'Faifan walking, since he had not yet disposed of the *nága* and did not want to risk riding her. A three-pole tent was stretched across the slope of the hill, its lower side open and facing northeast, which was the direction of the wind. It is usually the custom to set the tent so that the prevailing breeze blows into the side when it is raised for ventilation, and since winds usually are from the northwest, known as *shamál,* the axis of the tent usually is slanted from northeast to southwest. If the wind shifts, usually to the east, the entire tent is changed so that the "face," or *wejh,* can be opened against the breeze for ventilation, or closed to protect those inside the tent from the rain.

R 'Faifan's family was fairly extensive: one wife, two sons, two daughters, one mother-in-law, and 30 sheep, 20 goats, 3 donkeys, and a miscellaneous assortment of dogs, cats, and chickens. As we rode into the valley, I observed—of all things—a tractor. It seemed that R 'Faifan had borrowed this modern convenience from Sheikh Sami Jiza to move his tent! I could not help wondering what this introduction of such a contraption did to my theory of the changeless Bedouin!

R 'Faifan had left it to his son, who tended the flocks while the other son was away in the Jordanian Army, to arrange for the moving of the tent. There were plans to shift it to a new location where spring grazing would be better. Meanwhile our mad *nága* was sent back to Ammān, and we prepared for our departure early the following day into the Eastern Desert. Our expedition consisted of just two people and two camels—I on the female and R 'Faifan on the bull.

Although R 'Faifan's *bait sha' ar* was not as large or complex as some I had visited on the desert, it was a typical Bedouin home. The open side had been lifted to afford plenty of air; during a period of heavy winds it would be lowered, leaving the lee side partly open for ventilation. The tent itself was made of heavy, woven goat hair, and not of camel hair as is popularly supposed. The goat hair fabric, heavy enough to withstand wind and rain, is woven in strips 50 to 75 feet long. While it varies in texture, according to the affluence of the owner, it usually wears for a lifetime and is often passed down from father to son.

The strips that form the tent are supported by poles, and the edges are held by long guy ropes which stretch out for several feet, giving the tent the appearance of lying close to the ground. The interior usually is quite roomy, however. Frequently when there is an encampment of more than one tent in a tribal group they are arranged in a semicircle or in rows. The *sheikh's* tent always is located in the most prominent position, arranged so that it will be the first tent to which an approaching visitor will arrive. In early days the tent of the tribal chieftain was identified by a spear struck into the ground; but in modern times this is usually omitted. In any case, his is always the largest tent in the compound.

Within the tent an informal, homelike atmosphere usually prevails; yet, there is never a relaxation of the basic courtesies, which include a profound sense of respect for the *sheikh*—and indeed, for all members of the household—and continual deference to the guest or visitor. Male children behave themselves with extraordinary poise in the presence of their elders, exhibiting both deference and self-respect.

The center section, or *muharram,* means forbidden. It is reserved for women and their *maksar,* or women's litter.

One end of the tent, known as the *raba'a,* is exclusively for men. Large piles of pillows are always stacked against the sides, and a fire pit in the middle usually burns merrily. These fire pits are often fueled with camel dung, which has surprisingly little odor in the tent. A *q'ata,* or curtain, separates each of the sections, affording a measure of privacy. This is usually brightly colored, with decorative strips of cloth. Sometimes long colored streamers are attached to the guy ropes.

R'Faifan's son, who had rushed out to greet us, quickly stirred up the coffeepot when we came into the tent and joined us in planning our journey. R'Faifan had called his wife and two daughters from the *muharram* when we rode down toward his tents, which occupied a roughly quadrangular area near the edge of a small *wádi,* or dry creek, that served as a drainage ditch, carrying off rainwater from the hard surface of the ground

Ordinarily only relatives are permitted to see the female members of a *bait sh'aar,* and it is a distinct violation of custom to address any of the women directly; but since R'Faifan regarded me as his "little brother," his wife and two daughters were allowed to greet me. However, they immediately retreated into the *muharram,* and I caught only occasional glimpses of them. During the following day, when I was left in charge of the camels while the tent was being moved by Sheikh Sami's tractor to the new location, the two girls sat on a hilltop a little distance away and watched me.

The shyness of Bedouin girls is inbred, perhaps a combination of the generic and environmental results of centuries during which the women of nomad families have occupied a place in the home that is removed from common association with men, yet remains a distinct and accepted way of living for them. The Bedouin certainly cannot be said to ignore the element of sex in their lives, yet in their domestic customs and traditions, they maintain a simple and logical attitude toward their women. On this score, Lawrence offers an interesting observation in *Seven Pillars of Wisdom.*

The Arab was by nature continent; and the use of universal marriage had nearly abolished irregular courses in his tribes. The public women in the rare settlements we encountered in our months of wanderings would have been nothing to our numbers, even had their raddled meat been palatable to a man of healthy parts. In horror of such sordid commerce our youths began indifferently to slake one another's few needs in their own clean bodies—a cold convenience that, by comparison, seemed sexless and even pure. . . . Several, thirsting to punish appetites they could not wholly prevent, took a savage pride in degrading the body, and offered themselves fiercely in any habit which promised physical pain or filth. [1]

Lawrence's rather limited perspective touches only tangentially on the character of the desert nomad with respect to the women of his family, since he was involved chiefly in riding and fighting, which included only men. Nevertheless, his comment serves to point out the indestructible status of women in the Bedouin household. Even in R'Faifan's small *bait sha' ar,* the place of his daughters was assured; without any intruding complexities of the city—to which they never traveled—they would grow old in the ancient tradition, and in their turn would become matriarchs of the household, ruling the kitchen and the *muharram* and all other phases of domestic life with inviolable security, just as their mother had ruled R'Faifan's home.

In the evening of our arrival R'Faifan prepared an elaborate *mansef,* or feast, killing his finest lamb. I understood how much this meant to R'Faifan and his family and that it was a real sacrifice compared with the wealthier *sheikhs'* offerings; yet he prepared it with lavish indifference to cost in terms of his limited flock.

During the evening an old friend, Slaman, a Bedouin camel driver whom I had known on earlier trips in the desert, arrived at the *bait sha' ar,* and I discovered that R'Faifan had invited him in my honor to be a house guest. He had walked 20 miles across the desert to be there, and in traditional Bedouin fashion, he bowed and extended his hands, saying, *"As salám ' alaikum!"* —Peace be with you, my friend! I replied, *"Alaikum as salám!"* which means, roughly, The same to you!

We sat by the fire, which crackled merrily under a brass pot bubbling with coffee, while R'Faifan's son pounded coffee beans in a brass mortar and continued to replenish the supply as we talked. At this time my command of Arabic was rusty, but

Typical Bedouin desert home: the *bait shaʾar* or tent home of R ʾFaifan near Jiza.

Around the fire pit at night: R ʾFaifan with white *kaffiyah* at left; Sheikh Slaman and his young son.

R'Faifan and Slaman, out of politeness, communicated with their own meager knowledge of English and many gestures. R'Faifan had acquired a tuxedo at some pawnshop in Ammān, and he wore this constantly, buttoning it around his flowing robe even when riding a camel! Later, as we plodded through blinding storms in the south, I would marvel at the durability of this transformed dinner jacket in the fiercest travails of wind and weather.

As we settled back among the cushions, I realized that I had already gone through a kind of psychological transformation. I found myself not only acting like a Bedouin but thinking like one. I had shifted from Western clothes to the Bedouin garments I would wear on our journey: the flowing *kaffiyah* with the *agál* binding it to the head; the long robe, known in southern Arabia as a *shillahat* but in Jordan called a *thōp*. This may be white or colored, and in my case it was vivid green.

Even in the *bait sha' ar* of poorer Bedouin, such as R'Faifan, every effort is made to provide bright decorations. The *raba' a*, men's section, was covered with strips of bright cloth, and the cushions were all made of the best fabric, with gaily colored designs. Late in the evening R'Faifan's son brought out his *rabába,* used throughout the desert to provide musical accompaniment to mournful songs.

Most evenings among the Bedouin are spent in interminable conversation, with discussions about all matter of things, including camels and women. The Bedouin has a deep sense of humor, but oddly enough he seldom uses wit to attack another, usually reserving it for adroit references to his own prowess, either in camel riding or fighting. R'Faifan, in this particular instance, told of his exploits with the Camel Corps, and I caught the notion that in these matters he was both proud and discreet.

"We will meet an old friend on the desert," he told me. "He is now living with only one wife, and in our time with the *badia* it was I who enabled him to escape from the post each night to meet the girl who became his wife.''

R'Faifan punctuated this intelligence with a quick, sly grin that I had come to understand was his way of saying there was more to this than met the eye; and as I later learned, when we met his friend—Saud-Jazi—on the desert, I found that R'Faifan was more discreet in his own *bait sha'ar* than he was in the home of his old comrade-in-arms.

During the latter part of the evening another guest arrived in the form of a small goat who seemed to sense in me the most likely bed companion and snuggled up beside me on the sheepskin mattress where I was sleeping. This practice is not at all unusual in Bedouin tents, particularly on cold nights, and any natural aversion may have to the intimate society of goats is quickly lost in the general feeling that on the desert every creature is entitled to a few small comforts.

On the last night of our stay at R'Faifan's home a neighbor, Sheikh Nayef, whose *bait sha'ar* was a day's ride beyond Muwaqqar, stopped by and spent the evening relating stories of earlier days. He was a gentle man, with a thin, seamed face and sad, brooding eyes characteristic of so many Bedouin, and the words he spoke softly in Arabic, although I could not understand them readily, seemed to flow from his lips like the low chant of a priest. He told me he had not known Lawrence personally; few Bedouin had. But there was an old man, Sheikh Argub al-Kurai-sha, who stayed at Sheikh Nayef's *bait sha'ar,* and might furnish some of the information I sought. He invited us to visit his home on our way out to the Eastern Desert.

We accepted, and when we arrived a day or so later we found not one but two *búyút sha'ar.* This was an indication of extraordinary affluence, placing the *sheikh* considerably above R'Faifan in the social order, but this did not seem to disturb R'Faifan's Bedouin aplomb. He called my attention to the fact that the second tent, although of standard three-pole construction, was used exclusively for animals.

The old man, Sheikh Argub al-Kurai-sha, apparently a relative of our host, was taking care of the place, and he greeted us warmly. R'Faifan drew me aside shortly after we had entered to sit down on mattresses and thick rugs spread over the *raba' a.*

"He is one hundred and ten years old!" R'Faifan whispered.

I looked at the old man as he squatted on a pile of rugs in the corner, smoking a long-stemmed pipe. At first I thought it was hashish—whish is illegal in Jordan—but later found it was *he-shee,* an Arabian tobacco. The bowl at the end of a long stem is lighted from a live coal taken from the fire, and this enables the smoker to puff continuously without having to relight it with matches. The tobacco is by no means mild; and the unwary smoker, after a few puffs, may find his head spinning and his stomach turning at the same time.

The old *sheikh* confided to me, as I questioned him with the limited Arabic at my command, that he was actually one hundred and two years old—which would have made his age at the time Lawrence was in Arabia somewhere over fifty. His narrow face, weathered from long years in the desert, looked as if it had been carved out of gray wood; his sight was poor and his voice thin and inarticulate.

I had hoped to glean some information from him about what the Bedouin thought of Lawrence, but he only knew of him as "a small, thin man" and had never met him. This was only the first of the many impressions of this evanescent "English Arab" that I received, until the shadowy character of the almost legendary guerrilla leader seemed to be that of a ghost rather than a man.

During the evening, after Sheikh Argub had retired, R'Faifan and I sat before the fire, plotting our journey on a large map glued to an oilcloth base so that we could use it on the desert. We estimated that it would require from four to five days to pass through the Azraq oasis. This was the largest outpost of the Desert Patrol in the Eastern Desert, although the *badia* had detachments at several more remote posts south of Azraq on the rim of the desert, such as Bāyir and Al Jafr.

Between our starting point and Azraq lay the ancient ruins of Oasr al Kharāna and Qasr Amra, where Lawrence had holed up during the time between his forays against the Turks. At Amra in particular there was a remarkably well-preserved Omayyad hunting lodge which Guy Mountfort had described after his expedition in 1962. Within it were murals of wild animals that the Omayyad sportsmen had hunted on the desert and some rather astonishing scenes, so I had been told, depicting events in the life of a hunter when he is not hunting. Some of these were bizarre, others exotic; but since they were part of an early Bedouin milieu, I was anxious to view them. I planned to spend a day or two prowling through these old relics of an Arabian past.

As we headed into the Eastern Desert, looking across waves of rocky ridges and flintlike sand glistening in the morning sun, it struck me that Westerners seldom distinguish the real Arab—that is, the original nomad of the Arabian Steppe—from the "city Arabs." All who adhere to the Moslem faith usually are regarded as "Arabs," chiefly because they speak a common Arabic language. Yet even in Ammān, teeming with people who regard themselves as "Arabic," the distinction between city-dwelling Arabs and the Bedouin of the desert is quite definite.

I wondered why there should be this wide divergence, both in character and customs, between the Arabs of the desert and the cities. In Western United States there are also deserts, but people who live on them do not differ materially from those who live in nearby cities, or on the farmlands of Iowa, Nebraska, or the Dakotas. In Jordan there was a wide difference. The

Bedouin of the desert were a people unto themselves: proud and sensitive, cruel and compassionate, clannish and yet hospitable to a stranger.

It occurred to me, as I rode along following R'Faifan, that the very sparseness of Bedouin history might furnish a clue to their origin and character. Even the Moslem faith did not actually define the Bedouin, since it was a religion superimposed upon their tribal customs by Mohammed. They did not accept the words of Mohammed because he uttered them; they accepted the Moslem faith because it could be fitted into their tribal habits and traditions without any deep change. Of even greater significance, when Islam, the political arm of Mohammed, grew beyond the Bedouin environment, spreading into Persia and westward across North Africa to Spain, the nomads retreated into the desert, retaining only so much of the Moslem creed as still suited them!

It seemed to me that the evidence of lack of change during centuries of fairly authenticated Arab history would furnish a strong indication that they had not varied very much prior to that. Unfortunately, little is known about their habits and customs among Western peoples, and even the modern history of the Arabs is clouded in misconceptions and misunderstandings. This applies particularly to the rise and fall of the Islamic empire.

Who were these denizens of the desert who erupted from the Arabian Steppe some 13 centuries ago? Were they in actual fact a horde of wild-riding religious fanatics who came pounding out of Arabia brandishing the Koran in one hand and a sword in the other? Or were they simply desert nomads raiding their outlying neighbors? Was the rise of Islam due to a sudden burst of Arabic military superiority over the rest of the civilized world? Or was it merely a minor chapter in a longer drama, the brief story of a people who appeared fleetingly on the stage of world events and retired to the desert almost as quickly as they came?

I realized that too little of this was understood outside the

Arab world itself, and that perhaps some history of these people, uncolored by the religious coloring of Christian or Moslem scholars, might serve to bring a clearer focus on the Bedouin character. For example, Christian historians in the Middle Ages portrayed the rise of Islam as an outrage visited upon Christendom, whereas Arab historians viewed the situation, particularly with respect to the Crusades, in an entirely different light. The Crusades themselves were regarded as the blundering interference by barbarians from the West in the affairs of the greatest cultural and scientific influence of its time.

To go further into this point, it would seem useful to digress briefly to scan the history of these people, at least since the time of Mohammed—which is about all the authentic Arabian history that is available.

3

So much of Arabic history has been overlaid with more than four centuries of rule by the Ottoman Turks, who held sway over Islam from the fourteenth century to the First World War, that much of the true character of the rise of the Islamic empire has been buried and virtually lost. If we add to this the fact that contemporary reports of this wave of conquest from the seventh to the thirteenth centuries were provided—at least to the Western world—by Christian scholars intent on proving the moral and spiritual value of the Crusades, it is understandable that one of the most massive movements in world history remains almost legendary in Western minds.

The mongrelized version of Arabic expansion, in which Berbers, Sudanese, Egyptians, and Bedouin are all lumped together as a single ethnic group, has made it difficult to identify the true Arab—that is, the Bedouin followers of Mohammed who launched a quasi-military movement after Mohammed's death that created one of the most dramatic shifts of power in the history of the world. Within a period of eight decades, the followers of the Moslem faith conquered a larger area than the Roman Empire had achieved in 800 years!

This was an extraordinarily complex change in world power structure—in religion, economic and military strength, and cultural advancement. Yet the total effect on the true Arab—the Bedouin of the desert, who started the events—was almost negligible!

Mohammed himself was a comparatively simple man, essentially a product of Bedouin environment and tribal background. He was born in Mecca approximately A.D. 570. The exact date is uncertain. Years are reckoned by Moslems from the birth of the Prophet, although the first historic date is A.D. 622, the year of the *hegira*. In a sense Arabic chronology hangs by its own bootstraps. Mohammed, an orphan, was reared by his grandfather. Although he was a member of the Kureish tribe, which ruled Mecca, he seems to have been impoverished in his youth. The story of his later life is known in more detail than that of Jesus of Nazareth, the founder of the Christian faith, since his followers were able to produce accounts that have been documented by Arab scholars, whereas available records of Jesus have been culled from Hebrew historical writings and reports of Christian followers, most of whom wrote of him long after his death. Mohammed was a known personality who never professed divine origin, and whose thoughts were plainly recorded in the Koran.

The fact that Mohammed, although he professed to be illiterate, was regarded as author of the Koran, as contrasted with authors of the New Testament who interpreted Jesus' teachings, provides an authenticity as to his own views that cannot be supplied, even by objective scholarship, in the case of Jesus. The Koran itself is not a historical record; it is a rambling sequence of chapters, or verses, arranged in their original order by accident rather than content. For example, the second, third, and fourth chapters—"The Cow," "The Imrams," and "Women"—are long and tedious, whereas three verses that go to the heart of Moslem faith—"The Earthquake, or Day of Judgment," "The Unbelievers," and "Help"—are only a few lines each. The historical material is inaccurate and garbled, apparently gathered from miscellaneous legends in the Old Testament and other Hebrew writings. Chapter 34 on "Sheba" has almost nothing to do with Sheba, and the stories of Noah, Joseph, Jonah, and others have none of the historical structure of the Old Testament, but for the most part consist of moral and ethical polemics.

There is some evidence that Mohammed wished to ameliorate differences with Jews, since they were an important element in Arabic society. Moses is mentioned several hundred times, and Jesus only about a dozen time. The Jewish fast of Yom Kippur was made a Moslem ritual, and the number of prayers was changed from two times a day to three (later increased to five) to conform with Jewish tradition. The theory that the Arabs and the Jews have always quarreled, commonly held in the West, may be discounted. It is not supported by history, and as a matter of record, Mohammed had far stronger alliances with Jewish tribes than with Christians. Many of his historical references are gleaned from the Old Testament and Hebrew Scriptures, and while Arabs and Jews have fought intermittently over land and borders since the time of Moses, they have not been traditional enemies as is often supposed. The present Arab-Jewish conflict dates from the events following the partition of Palestine.

The basic similarity among Moslem, Judaic, and Christian traditions lies in their common belief in monotheism. This was the essential message of the Koran: "There is no God but God!" And in it lay the strength of Islam, which ultimately was carried to every part of the civilized world. While this belief in a single God was at variance with earlier tribal convictions among Bedouin, who believed in *jinns, ghrôls,* and malign as well as

67

benevolent spirits, this did not constitute a real obstacle to their acceptance of the Moslem creed. The code of conduct set forth in the Koran was largely based on tribal customs, and was more suitable in the desert than in the cities.

At the time of Mohammed's birth, Mecca was a lively trading center in the Hijaz, along the west coast of the Arabian Peninsula. The town was run by traders, merchants, and bankers, who were chiefly members of the Kureish tribe to which Mohammed belonged; and around it were less affluent Bedouin nomads, carrying on their usual practices of camel trading and raiding small caravans.

At the age of about forty Mohammed received a "call" to carry a gospel to the Arab people. This message can be stated simply in the fundamental tenet of the Moslem creed: "There is no God but God, and Mohammed is His Prophet!" It is quite probable that Mohammed, although a Kureish, felt the need to broaden tribal affiliations into a "universal community," and he advocated a society in which the religious faith of the Moslem creed would bind together all Arabs under a common belief in the will of Allah, and thus resolve tribal disputes and extend the power of his following. It became his purpose and political destiny to organize the Meccan community along these lines, and to extend it to the whole Arabian Steppe. There is no particular evidence that Mohammed ever intended his teachings to be carried beyond the boundaries of greater Arabia, or even out of the desert.

In 622, after Mohammed had been preaching for a dozen years, he fled from Mecca to the town of Yathrib, later called Medina; and this became the first exact date on the Moslem calendar. From that point he began to carry the message of the Koran to the entire Arab world.

The phenomenon of the spread of Moslem faith in the form of political expansion, called *Islam*—which in Arabic means "surrender to the will of God"—is one of the most interesting in all history, but it is too large and involved a subject for this book. The significance of these events from the standpoint of understanding the Bedouin lies in the effect of Islamism on the true Arabs—the nomads of the Arabian Steppe—both immediately and ultimately.

Within a decade after Mohammed fled to Medina, he was dead and the surge of his teachings of a "universal community" had carried Islamic power beyond Arabia into Syria and Iraq, and into North Africa, and was destined to spread the new faith to all parts of the civilized world.

Mohammed died A.D. 632. No provision had been made for a successor, since, as the Seal of the Prophets and the only envoy of God, he occupied a position that was unique and not replaceable. The Islamic movement was thrust into a turmoil from which it evolved, more or less accidentally, into a vast empire that stretched from the Indus River to Gibraltar, a complex of peoples of diverse racial origins and national aspirations that due to the oversimplification of nineteenth-century historians has been called Arabic.

The only purpose of this brief digression into the history of Islamism is to clarify the point that the Bedouin role in history is not identical with the spreading power of Islam.

The eruption of the Arab from the desert, however, gave initial impetus to this new upsurge, beginning with the year of Mohammed's death. The mission may be compressed into a single verse of the Koran:

When you meet the Unbelievers on the battlefield, strike off their heads; and when you have laid them low, bind your captives firmly. . . . As for those who are slain in the cause of Allah, He will not allow their works to perish. He will vouchsafe them guidance and ennoble their state; He will admit them to Paradise He has made known (Ch. 47, "Mohammed").

The two men chosen to succeed Mohammed and carry on the Islamic movement were his father-in-law Abu Bakr, and another relative, ' Umar. They were known as *khalifa,* or successors, and this was westernized into the term "caliph," which designated those who reigned over the expanding Islamic empire for the next 600 years. Abu Bakr was the first caliph. During the years that followed the prophet's death he sent small armies—actually little more than large Bedouin raiding parties—northward from the Hijaz into what is now Jordan and Syria, consolidating Meccan rule over the Arab tribes in these areas.

No systematic campaign was planned by the Arabs. Certain border tribes along the Byzantine and Persian frontiers found it easier to align themselves with the advancing Arab armies under Khalid ibn al-Walid, Abu Bakr's field marshal, than to resist them. They had no binding allegiance to their Persian or Byzantine overlords and easily changed to allies of Islam. Thus, almost by accident, the Islamic forces moved forward, occupying Syria and Iraq and finally crossing the Euphrates River and capturing an outlying Persian provincial capital, where they seized a great deal of booty.

The prospect of rich rewards was undoubtedly more of a spur to the Bedouin tribesmen from the desert than any notion of spreading the gospel of Mohammed among alien peoples. In fact the Arabs, throughout their phase of expansion, seemed to have little interest in proselytizing the people they overran. For the most part they were content to gather spoils of war and collect tribute in the form of taxes.

The latter increment in Islamic expansion provides an enlightening insight into Bedouin motivation; as the Arabs continued to advance into the lands around the Byzantine and Persian domains, they displayed an unquestioned preference for unconverted infidels who paid sizable taxes rather than those who accepted the Moslem faith.

Within two years of Mohammed's death, Arab forces under

Khalid had advanced to the outskirts of Damascus after a march that is a legend of military history. Oddly enough, the non-Moslem tribes on the frontier of Syria, many of them Christianized, gave the most active help. Apparently some of these tribes had been receiving subsidies from the Byzantine rulers, who were essentially orthodox Christians, and when Emperor Heraclius of Byzantium found himself short of funds, he stopped paying these bribes to the border tribes, so they turned to the oncoming Arabs as allies.

Heraclius, hearing of the Arab advance northward, moved his armies into Palestine, hoping to cut off the intruders from Medina, and Khalid took possession of the undefended city of Damascus. After his desert raiders had harassed the northern forces sufficiently, he struck at their main forces in a succession of wild, savage raids along the mountainous Wádi Araba and utterly routed the Byzantines.

Meanwhile Abu Bakr had died, and ' Umar became the sole leader of Islam. For a number of months Khalid kept his Bedouin raiders busy striking quickly at Byzantine forces along the Yarmuk Valley, which lies east of the Jordan between Ammān and Damascus. This valley, incidentally, was the scene of some of Lawrence's raiding activities in the Arab Revolt nearly 1,300 years later.

The ruling caste that assumed control over the conquered areas, headed by ' Umar and his successor at Damascus, Abu Ubayada, under Caliph Muawiya became known as the Omayyad dynasty; and the Omayyad rule over the caliphate of Syria and later of Iraq continued for a century. Aside from the historical events that led to the Arab expansion into the Iranian plateau, the reign of the Omayyad caliphs was of considerable significance in tracing the rise and fall of Bedouin influence. The Arab advances, as most modern historians agree, was not due to acceptance of the Moslem faith as such—although all the conquered lands ultimately were "Islamized"—but it was the

71

result of a combination of decay of the Persian and Byzantine empires, coupled with disgust and contempt for these overlords on the part of many of the border tribes, who readily joined the Arabs in the hope of getting booty from their former masters.

The same forces of disintegration in the Persian and Byzantine empires that helped the Omayyad caliphate to gain ascendency also contributed to their own ultimate replacement by the Abbasid dynasty that overthrew the Damascene caliphate about A.D. 750, and to the ultimate obliteration of Arab influence in the Islamic empire. In tracing these events, it again becomes evident that the Bedouin had no particular passion for administration of the countries they conquered. They enjoyed the fruits of war, in terms of captured treasures which had been beyond the wildest dreams of the desert nomads before the explosion of Islamism; but they had little stomach for the sedentary occupation of running a government.

A system of bringing non-Arabic elements into their families was introduced by the Omayyads under Caliph ' Umar at Damascus. These were known as "clients," and they carried on much of the actual work of administration. The result was a political version of Parkinson's Law: soon there were more "clients" than Arabs, and the device that was supposed to have relieved the Bedouin of the burden of actual government finally undid them. The massive influx of these non-Arabic factions from the Byzantine and Persian lands bordering on the widening Islamic empire diluted the Bedouin influence and gave rise to the Abbasid rebellion that ultimately unhorsed the Damascene caliphs.

By A.D. 740, more than a century after Mohammed's death, the Omayyad rulers at Damascus had lost prestige and power, and certain extremist movements, led by a descendant of one of Mohammed's uncles in Mecca, Mohammed ibn Ali ibn al-Abbas, began a movement that undermined the Omayyad caliphate. In 747 the Abbasids declared open revolt against

Damascus, and sent one of their number, Abu Muslim, a Persian "client," to arouse the dissidents. This led to the overthrow of the Omayyads and establishment of the Abbasid dynasty at Baghdad, a city constructed on the site of an ancient village west of the Euphrates which had been a trading center for more than 2,000 years.

The new Baghdad caliph, known as Saffah—the butcher—was Abul al-Abbas, and with his advent came the transformation of the Islamic empire and the denigration of the Bedouin as rulers of the empire. Although the Abbasid revolt had been engineered from Mecca, it was accomplished by the infiltration of Persian "clients" and the ultimate "Persianizing" of the Baghdad caliphate. Thus in a span of a single century, the so-called "eruption" of the Arabs from the desert had completed its cycle, and a new non-Bedouin world of Islam emerged in full force.

For the next five centuries the Islamic empire—later called Saracenic—which had already pushed westward beyond Egypt and across Africa, would become the dominant force in Western civilization. Cultural and political influences from Persia and the Orient began to revise the character of the government. The easy-going nature of the Bedouin tribal chiefs under the Damascene caliphate was replaced by an Oriental despotism; and above all, the economy of the empire flourished as it never had under Arab tribal leadership.

Baghdad became a teeming center of world commerce, with ships plying the waters between the Persian Gulf and India, China and the East Indian islands. Trade was established as far west as the Gold Coast of Africa, and the Mediterranean became an Islamic lake. The Bedouin Arab was virtually excluded from this progress. Although Arabic was still the language of the Abbasid ruling caste, the Arab himself was regarded as a barbarian and treated with contempt. Even Arabic poetry, the pride of the Bedouin, was ridiculed and replaced with more formalized Persian verse. Aramaeans, who were of Semitic origin—that is, they emerged from the common source of Semitic languages—spoke of themselves not as Arabs but as Nabataens taking their ancestry from the more ancient Arab kingdom of Nabataea which existed during the first millennium before the Christian era in the lands east of the Dead Sea.

During the eighth century, following the ascension of the Abbasid caliphate at Baghdad, the Byzantine empire held a line roughly from the eastern shore of the Mediterranean at Tarsus and Antioch to the Caucasus; everything below and to the east as far as the Indus River was ruled by Islam. The world of Christendom, which viewed the rise of Islam as a menace to Christian theology, was in return regarded by Moslems as a group of barbaric upstarts, engaged in sporadic thrusts at the culturally superior empire of Islam. This difference of viewpoint, largely based on theological self-interest, is of importance in analyzing the later history of the Bedouin and the dismemberment of the Arabic world in the thirteenth and fourteenth centuries.

Christian historians largely held to the theory that the rise of Islam was a kind of scourge visited upon sinful children of the Christian God, as opposed to the Moslem view that failure to follow the precepts of the Koran had opened Islam to shafts of adversity, such as the Crusaders. In the Koran it is written:

Rich is the reward of those who obey Allah. But those that disobey Him, if they possessed all that earth contains, and as much besides, they would gladly offer it for ransom. Theirs shall be an evil reckoning. Hell shall be their home . . . (Ch. 13, "Thunder").

This diversity of viewpoints between Christian and Arab scholars has largely obscured the real perspective of history in which the Bedouin can be examined and understood. Each looked upon the other in terms of his own theological concepts and historical background. It is probably this factor that has also

74

obscured some of the basic characteristics of the true Arabs, such as their fundamental existence as tribal nomads—an ingrained element of Bedouin life that even Mohammed could not change. In the Koran it is written:

O man! We have created you from a male and female and divided you into nations and tribes that you might get to know one another. The noblest of you in Allah's sight is he who fears Him most (Ch. 49, Chambers").

In spite of this, as Joel Carmichael has pointed out in *The Shaping of the Arabs,* as Gibbon wrote before him, the Bedouin of the desert have remained unchanged. Carmichael wrote:

Ultimately, indeed, it [Mohammed's universalism] was to lead to the retreat of the Arabs from the Islamic society whose groundwork they had laid. They left that society flourishing, as it were, without them, and although the nomadic Arabs remained nominal Moslems and still are to this day, they never changed their own way of life, nor did tribal society in Arabia change substantially even after the impact of Islam.[2]

The most profound event in the history of Islam, except for its meteoric rise to power and its ultimate collapse, was the confrontation with Christendom in the twelfth and thirteenth centuries. Moslem faith differed from Christianity in two respects: the cult of personality, in the person of Mohammed, was never a part of Moslem faith, as it was in the case of Jesus; and the Moslem religion never required a priesthood. Mohammed did not regard himself as divine, and was not so regarded by his Bedouin followers; he was merely the last and greatest of the Prophets, of whom Abraham, Moses, and Jesus were the other three. And among Moslems, each individual was responsible to Allah alone for his adherence to the "true faith."

Christianity, on the other hand, elevated Jesus into the equivalent of God, as the Savior of Man and the Son of God. This

75

difference in theological concepts distorted both Christian and Moslem views of each other, and in the minds of the Bedouin it created an image of Christians as "pagan" and "idolatrous," while Christians have regarded Moslems as "unbelievers." While modern scholarship has tended to straighten out this conflict in viewpoints, it has not permeated the mind of the average Westerner, whose knowledge of Arabic countries and understanding of Moslem faith is limited largely to school histories and *The Arabian Nights.*

During the two centuries from 1100 to 1300 the invasions of the Crusaders, seeking to recover parts of the Holy Land and also to gather such spoils of war as might fall their way, applied new pressures on the Islamic empire which had extended through North Africa into southern Europe. In addition to theological differences, habits and viewpoints of Moslems and Christians came into conflict. The attitude toward sex was one: Mohammed had never underestimated the importance of sex in the doctrines he preached to his followers, and celibacy—for the most part a Christian innovation—was unheard of among Moslems. Thus, while the Moslems and Jews could tolerate each other's religious views, there was an essential incompatibility between the Moslems and Christians that led to open hostility, and to the Crusades.

Although the First Crusade, engineered by Pope Urban II in an effort to heal the breach between the Greek Orthodox Byzantines and the Roman Catholics, was regarded as a mere pinprick by the Abbasid caliphs at Baghdad, who were more or less indifferent to the fate of Palestine and the Arabian Peninsula, the capture of Jerusalem in 1099 and the subsequent massacre of Moslems and Jews alike by the Christian invaders struck terror into the hearts of many Moslems in those areas. The Second Crusade, which followed the fall of Edessa, one of the Christian strongholds in the Middle East, was a failure, and

Jerusalem was recaptured in 1187 by the rising military genius of the Saracen, Salah-al-din Yusef ibn Ayyub, known to the Western world as Saladin.

During the next century the Crusades dwindled into a series of sporadic efforts on the part of the Christian politicians of Europe, who made deals with various elements of the European and Saracenic world until the Greek Orthodox patriarch of Constantinople decided to risk invasion by the Ottoman Turks rather than depend upon the diplomatic vagaries of the Roman pope, who had even tried to make an arrangement with the advancing Mongols from the east.

Three historic events in the mid-thirteenth century contributed to the ultimate collapse of the Abbasids: the expanding surge of Mongol nomads under Genghis Khan, culminating in the sack of Baghdad; the growing power of the Ottoman Turks; and the rise of the Mameluke "slave-warriors" of Egypt, who also were Turks.

The last of the great Abbasid caliphs, the fabled Hurun al-Rashid, reigned in splendor during the corruption of his government by the Persian infliltrators, and the dynasty died with the influx of Ottoman Turks under Othman in the fourteenth century. Under this thick layer of political change the Bedouin continued to live under alien rule until the latter years of the eighteenth century when the Wahhabi revolt reestablished Arab identity in political history. The ascension of ’Abdul ’Assiz ibn Saud, a powerful *emir* of central Arabia, initiated a final effort to rid Bedouin lands of Turkish control, which ended in the Arab Revolt of 1916–18 and the destruction of Ottoman power in the First World War. Mecca was recaptured by the Wahhabi Arabs, and the kingdom of Saudi Arabia established under another King Abdul Assiz ibn Saud, a descendant of the earlier rebel leader, in the early 1900’s.

4

The purpose of this minor detour into Arabian history, as indicated earlier, has been to place the Bedouin in proper perspective. As R'Faifan and I headed out into the mystery of the Eastern Desert toward relics of the past that antedated by a thousand years or more, the events I have just described, we were in a very real sense going backward into a timeless past.

It was only a short march from the *bait sha' ar* of Sheikh Nayef to the fortress of Kharāna, the first of these relics. Since we were in no hurry at the start of our expedition into the Eastern Desert, we set a leisurely pace. R'Faifan rode at the head of our two-man caravan, now and then jarring the desert air with peals of song. His version of Bedouin music was loud, and I knew so little of the music of the desert that I could not very well criticize the performance.

Now and then R'Faifan looked back and grinned amiably at me. I had a feeling that he was testing me, to determine what kind of companion I would be out on the desert, and I forbore to make any showing of either satisfaction or displeasure at his music. In dealing with Bedouin, it is necessary to develop a sense of restraint.

The road from Muwaqqar to Azraq follows a crooked line along an unmarked border that for centuries divided the Arabian Peninsula from the Syrian Desert and the lands beyond, known as the Fertile Crescent. These regions are covered with camel trails, none of which are marked or even identified on maps. But the road from Ammān eastward to Azraq was fairly well traveled and had been used by caravans for several thousand years.

The word "road" is hardly descriptive of the route. It consisted of a series of trails fanning out across the desert in vaguely parallel lines, all going in the same direction but having no common course. The individual trails varied from a few yards to a half-mile apart; and the desert cars which travel over them usually make their own trail, regardless of any established tracks in the sand.

North of this skein of trails lay one of the most uninviting stretches of desert I had ever seen. It was a land of black gravel and lava, stretching up to the Jabal Druze, a mountain range that forms the southern barrier of Syria. The area had much of the appearance of the Badlands of the Dakotas in North America. During the period of the Omayyad caliphate, when the luxurious rulers of the early "Arab Kingdom" at Damascus were fending off upstarts from their own family, Yashid I had built the forbidding fortress of Kharāna, toward which we were heading, as a bastion to defend this area.

In later years it had been reported that Lawrence used this gray castle as a base for raids on the Turks between Ammān and Damascus; and although I felt little of value would probably be left as historic memorabilia, I was anxious to inspect the premises.

Meanwhile a more urgent problem intruded itself into my reveries. I had become aware, as we clumped along, that R'Faifan's bull camel was having some serious indisposition, and perhaps had gone mad. It would utter forceful noises now and then, and R'Faifan would yank at the bridle reins and scream at the animal. We had left the insane *nâga* with R'Faifan's son to dispose of as best he could; and now R'Faifan was riding the bull, which had been purchased originally as a pack animal. This imposed upon him not only the burden of directing the camel along the trail but also the problem of maintaining a decent distance between the two of us, since I was riding the female. In contrast with his many peculiarities, the bull showed quite a normal interest in my mount. He would turn his head now and then and glare at me, as if he regarded me as interfering with the course of events between himself and the female camel.

There were cisterns along the route to Kharāna which the

badia had built to hold water for travelers, but since I expected to make much longer marches after we passed Azraq I urged R'Faifan to continue past these watering places so that we could accustom ourselves to long stretches without water.

The unrelenting glare of the sun's rays, caroming off the glazed stones on the ridges and flashing into my face, created almost unendurable pain in my eyes until I began to draw the folds of my *kaffiyah* over my face, leaving only a slit to see through. Now and then we could see small herds of goats grazing on the scanty shrubs that dotted the hills, but for the most part, as we rode mile after mile, there was nothing but unrelieved flintlike gravel and black rocks, now and then softened by gray clouds that rose behind some motorized traveler hastening one way or another in a Land Rover.

The ascent of the trail was gradual and hardly noticeable until we topped a rise and looked down upon the square, grim fortress of Kharāna. This was my first look into the antiquity of the Eastern Desert: a rough bastion of stones, rising three stories from the desert floor, with only the small slits through which the defenders had shot arrows at invaders to mar the solid expanse of the castle walls.

The fortress stood alone upon the desert, a reminder for more than twelve centuries of the far-flung borders that had been defended by the Omayyads in the seventh century. Around the walls of the old fort spread a plain of gray gravel, almost black in patches. Oasr al Kharāna is the only fortified Arab castle in Jordan; it was built as an outpost of Damascus. Its forbidding walls offered little in the way of comfort as we rode up, but we immediately set up camp within them to provide protection from the cold winds. On the lower floor of the fort we found stables used by Arab horsemen, with most of the living quarters on the second floor. The walls bore traces of the Omayyads as well as countless inscriptions of later Bedouin who had carved their *wāsm,* or tribal insignia, into the surface of the stone.

80

These *wāsm* are like brand names, used mainly to identify camels. They are passed down from one generation to the next, and Bedouin know the original tribal homes of travelers on the desert merely from looking at the *wāsm* burned into their camels hides. R 'Faifan was able to locate the *wāsm* of a number of his old cronies of the Camel Corps and also to point out that certain of his relatives had passed by the Kharāna fortress.

Since the castle is surrounded by numerous graves, marked by piles of stones to prevent hyenas and desert foxes from digging up buried remains, it is also believed by the Bedouin to be the home of many *jinns,* ghostly spirits. This would normally be regarded as an old wives' tale, and would certainly have been accepted as such by most travelers, including myself, but R 'Faifan assured me that the stories were not to be taken lightly.

"There have been many reports of strange noises," he told me. "It is well to sleep near the entrance."

In deference to his wishes, and because the castle was huge, occupying an area the size of a city block, I agreed, and we laid our blankets under one of the main archways leading into the courtyard. We had finished a supper of bully beef and bread and were lingering over a final cup of tea when I heard a steady thumping from somewhere deep in the recesses of the castle.

R 'Faifan looked at me to see whether I had heard it.

"Probably the stones cooling after a hot day," I suggested. He nodded. However, just as we were ready to roll into our blankets, the thumps started again. R 'Faifan grabbed his blanket and headed for the open courtyard. I decided to gather up our teapot and move out with him, as a matter of social amenity. He came back into the archway and suggested that we leave our teacups for the *jinns!*

"It is well to show respect for them," he said. "They also drink tea."

I was not certain how this came to be known to R 'Faifan, but

I was in no mood to argue. We set our two teacups on a stone slab and hauled the rest of our equipment outside.

We slept near the entrance, so that no one could have passed us during the night and gone into the castle. Nevertheless, the following morning when I went back inside to pick up our two teacups, they were gone!

We had only one cup left, which we had to share until we could replace the lost teacups at Azraq.

R'Faifan offered no explanation of the lost teacups; he merely looked at me and smiled wisely. Again, I did not argue the point, mainly because I was not quite sure what I would be arguing about.

III. *The Black Desert*

1

We rode hour after hour across the dark gravel ridges that form long, sun-blackened ribs on the desert, ascending gradually over the high plateau toward the Azraq oasis, and for the first time I understood why the Bedouin call this the Black Desert. I had ridden once before from Jiza southward, diagonally across the desert from Ammān to Al Jafr; but this was my first journey into the bleak waste of north Jordan which leads eastward into the never-never land known as the Empty Quarter.

We were heading toward the castle of Qasr Amra, a glistening white-and-pink patch on the desert floor. The round turrets of the old castle could be seen for miles, and if one caught the glint of sunlight on the walls it appeared as an isolated palace in the sky. A monument to the grandeur of the Omayyad caliphs, it was made of pink stone and originally used as a hunting lodge for the Damascene overlords who ruled Islam in the seventh and eighth centuries.

Beyond Amra was Azraq. It had once been on the old route from Jerusalem to Baghdad, but the eastern part of the caravan trail had fallen into disuse, and today it is largely a crossroads for those traveling from Ammān and for pilgrims on their way from Damascus down to Medina and Mecca.

To the east of Azraq lay the Empty Quarter, which I proposed to visit as soon as I accomplished my mission in the south. The ancient watering place at Kaf, which had long ceased to be anything more than a point on the map, was more than 100 kilometers beyond Azraq, and it was here that the two ruined castles at Kabr es Said and Ithra, which I have previously mentioned, were supposed to be located. At one time these may have been on the main highway from Mesopotamia to Arabia Felix which I was seeking, but now it was a land of desolation, the western edge of an immense quadrant at the eastern end of which there lived a strange people known as the "marsh Arabs."

There is some doubt as to whether these people are actually Arabs. Some ethnologists believe, as Dr. John Van Ess has indicated in his book *Meet the Arab,* that the marsh Arabs may be remnants of Babylonians or Chaldeans, who were agrarian rather than nomadic.[1] The marsh Arabs, known as Madaan to Bedouin, speak a pure form of Arabic that oddly enough is only to be found elsewhere in the Koran and in classical Arabic, an anomaly that actually explains nothing. They are nomadic in a sense, by necessity rather than preference. As the flood waters seasonally pour down the Euphrates and Tigris, draining the mountains of Anatolia and the Iranian Plateau and joining at the Lake of Hammar just north of the Persian Gulf, these waters spread over a wide area inhabited by the Madaan, and they are forced to change constantly to higher ground. They live in huts, moving entire villages from one bog to another, an insulated people who hate the Bedouin and all strangers and are equally disliked by their neighbors.

Few Bedouin invade this area, and R'Faifan and I had no intention of going there. But on our swing back from "Lawrence country" in southern Jordan we hoped to penetrate beyond the Wádi Sirhan, which forms the western border of the Empty Quarter, in search of the line of old wells that I was sure ran through the area of Kaf.

The term Empty Quarter itself is subject to the usual number of Arabic variations. It is often used to refer to the Rab el Kháli in the southern part of Arabia, which forms one of the most perilous stretches of desert in the world, in which entire caravans are reported to have been swallowed up. The Arabic word *rab'* means place, and has been confused with *rub'*, which means quarter, and on many maps the southern desert is referred to as Rub' el Kháli, quarter of emptiness. However, the area into which R'Faifan and I intended to travel, some 1,200 miles north of the Rab' el Kháli, is a land of gravel, sand, and marshes that lies in a vast quadrant nearly 700 miles across between eastern Jordan and the Persian Gulf. In the context of this narrative, it will be referred to as the Empty Quarter.[2]

R'Faifan awakened me at the crack of dawn at the Kharāna fortress to announce the arrival of a truckload of Bedouin who were en route to Ammān from Azraq and had stopped for morning prayers. Since it required some time for R'Faifan to exchange amenities with the various Bedouin in the group, most of whom he seemed to know, it was well into the morning when we finally rode out of Kharāna.

As one man offered R'Faifan a water bag, he exclaimed, *"Salâm ideek!"*—Blessed be your hands!—and I was again impressed with the curious combination of courtesy and amiable good will that seemed to pervade R'Faifan's relations with other Bedouin. However, my impression was slightly marred as we rode eastward and R'Faifan, leaning across from his high wooden saddle, yelled at me: "They are Ruwalla!" This was said with a sarcasm tantamount to consigning them to oblivion. Ruwalla tribes from northeast Jordan live along the untraveled border between Jordan and Saudi Arabia. They are chiefly camel herders and are powerful neighbors of the Bani-Sakhr tribes.

This apparent conflict between traditional courtesy and the deep-rooted pride each Bedouin feels for his own tribe might seem incomgruous to a Westerner, but the Arab sees no conflict whatever. All strangers, or acquaintances, who are met on the desert must be treated with respect, and when they enter the home or even tribal lands they receive this tribute of respect; but they remain strangers to the end. I had discovered in my experience with Bedouin that these social customs are regarded not as hypocritical but wholly natural.

As we clumped over the gravel ridges and sloping *widyán* (Arabic plural for valley) toward the gleaming castle of Qasr Amra, which could be seen from high ground, I became aware of increasing difficulties of riding. I was not exactly saddlesore, but I found that the wobbling gait natural to a camel required some care on my part; and for R'Faifan the situation was even worse. His bull plodded along like a dray horse, jolting him from side to side so that he frequently dismounted and walked. I began to wonder what would happen when we were making marches of 30 and 35 kilometers a day beyond Azraq. The problem of camel riding is more difficult in north Jordan and Syria then it is in the more southern parts of Arabia. The pace of the *bátiniyah,* riding camels, is faster and easier than that of the *jamâl* of the north. The big-boned animals owned by the Bani-Sakhr and Howeitat tribesmen have neither the speed nor staying power of the light-footed southern camels, and they are harder to ride.

As we followed a long ridge and down into the valley, the sight of the old Omayyad hunting lodge at Amra burst on us with all its splendor. Its rounded roofs and stone embattlements, once red but now faded to pink, had the appearance of abandoned luxury, a once glorious resort for hunting and pleasure of the Damascene caliphs now reduced to lonely desolation.

We rode through the arched entrance into a courtyard which

An old desert resort: the castle at Qasr Amra, built by the Omayyads as a hunting lodge, is one of the best-preserved relics of the
early rise of Islamic power at Damascus.

Paintings in the desert: frescoes, worn by time, on the walls of the
Omayyad castle at Amra, depict hunting scenes of more than 1,000
years ago.

had undoubtedly been a beautiful garden in bygone years, and after tethering our camels, we entered the old palace. Inside were startling murals on the scaling walls, depicting animals that once infested this region, from the oryx to the ostrich. There was nothing in the castle that antedated the period of Islamic conquest, the appearance of this dead splendor in the barren desert was a striking reminder of how old the desert really was.

R'Faifan and I prowled through the dark interior of the place and found many signs of itinerant Bedouin of a much later day: stains of old fires against the walls, places where the fading murals had been scraped off. All this testified to the passage of years during which the old castle had been used as a stopping place, like the corner of a subway station, and the brilliant paintings had become shabby reminders of a derelict past. Several frescoes had been damaged by fires built by Bedouin who used the place as a shelter, and the accumulation of refuse and various kinds of debris presented an unclean reminder of how little regard the latter-day desert travelers had for this relic of lost glory. The decay wrought by later generations of Bedouin was in itself a symbol of the transience of their rule over this land. Even the scattering of goat and sheep droppings seemed in a way to reflect the passage of the Bedouin, as continuous and unchanging as the wind.

We intended to bed down in the old palace, as we had at Kharāna, but the accumulation of stenches that even the desert winds could not blow away made it desirable to seek open space for sleeping. R'Faifan set out across the hill to look for brushwood for a fire and soon came galloping back with a report that there was a *bait sha'ar* of an "old friend" not more than a mile away. I sent him off to reconnoiter and meanwhile roamed through the rooms of the old castle, observing exotic scenes as well as colorful animal pictures on the walls.

I was amazed to find indications of running water that once

88

flowed from cisterns that apparently were heated. Hot and cold running water in the middle of the desert was a luxury I had not anticipated, although the visible result of this bit of engineering had long since disappeared. The notion that I might have been reclining on gaudy cushions in a remote palace in the desert and watching dancing girls parade before white-pantalooned men of the Damascus caliph's retinue stirred my imagination—and to complete the imaginative luxury, I could have taken a bath in hot water!

My reveries were interrupted by R'Faifan, who came loping into the place, waving his arms and informing me that he had found a friend who would take us in for the night. I immediately accepted. Since we had few prospects of anything but cold nights on the open desert ahead of us, with dinners of bully beef and tea cooked over a brush fire, I was glad to accept Bedouin hospitality wherever we found it. We gathered our gear and moved across the ridge to the tent of R'Faifan's friends. If I had any idea of luxuriating in the splendors of an Omayyad hunting lodge, I was quickly disillusioned. When we topped the hill and looked down upon the home of our host for the night, we found only a small, rather ill-kept *bait sha'ar* with only a two-pole tent and half a dozen scrawny goats grazing about the place.

R'Faifan's friend, whose name I was told was Hamad-Ab, was one of the poorer nomads of this region. He came out and greeted us warmly and led us into the tent. There were fewer ornamental cushions than was customary piled around the *raba'a*, and if he had a wife I did not see her. The fire pit in the center was crackling merrily, with coffee bubbling in the brass pot, and from another kettle he poured tea, which was sweetened to a rather sickish taste but which warmed us after the cold wind.

In the morning the old man laid out bowls of *leban*, a slightly curdled form of camel's milk, similar to buttermilk, and bread for our breakfast. The slightly sour milk is standard diet for morning meals on the desert, and it is supposed to have nourishing properties which enable camel drivers to sustain themselves for long periods without drinking.

Hammad-Ab was profuse in his apologies for the poor fare, but we assured him we had passed a comfortable night and that his hospitality was excellent. The wind had picked up during the early morning hours and was beginning to carry the cold chill of the northern mountains. The warmth of the tent had provided an unexpected shelter for which I was thoroughly grateful.

We were only a half-day march from Azraq, the point at which we planned to turn southward into the back region of the Eastern Desert, where there were few trails and long marches between watering places.

2

Shortly after we ascended the trail from the shallow valley in which Qasr Amra raised its solitary bulk from the desert floor, I saw a plume of dust and realized that a desert car was following us, traveling at a high speed. It pulled up a short distance away, and a *badia* jumped out and came running toward us. R'Faifan quickly clambered down from his camel's back and walked over to meet the desert patrolman.

He was dressed in the striking garb of the Camel Corps, a heavy, olive-drab coat covering his trim, brown uniform, with brown belts crossed on his chest and the red arm sash of a member of the military staff circling his shoulder. His red-checked *kaffiyah* was wrapped around his head, bound with a dark *agál* worn at a slightly rakish angle. The silver badge of the *badia* was pinned to the front of the *agál*.

He followed R'Faifan as they walked toward me, R'Faifan waving his hands and exclaiming: "Everything is fine! He is my friend!"

I had begun to understand that the words, "He is my

friend," were a generic expression for R'Faifan, covering every encounter on the desert. At first I was uncertain as to whether the relationship had just been established or was an old friendship. But I soon realized that this was of no importance. R'Faifan's relations with other Bedouin, and particularly with members of the Camel Corps, were so universally amiable that it was of no significance how rapidly the friendship may have been cemented. His talents in this respect would have made the late Dale Carnegie seem like an amateur.

The farther we progressed into the desert, the more I was able to appreciate and understand this characteristic quality of the Bedouin, or *bedu,* as he is called in Arabic. He will fight with the determination and sometimes with the cruelty of a fanatic, yet he will offer friendship with a sincerity unmatched in my experience.

Hospitality, for example, is not merely a pleasant and civilized way of greeting strangers; among the Bedouin it is a sacred obligation, as important as maintaining a family. The adjuration of Moses to the people of Israel, "Love ye therefore the stranger; for ye were strangers in the land of Egypt" (Deut. 10: 19), was not written of the Jews alone. It is a password among the nomads of the Arabian Steppe.

When a guest is invited into the *bait sha'ar* of a Bedouin chief, he becomes the most important person in the place. As he enters, the best place among the cushions is cleared for him. When food is served, he receives the first portions, and before any member of the family partakes of the food, the finest bits of meat are first passed to the "stranger." Violation of this tenet of good manners is regarded as worse than stealing, a practice not regarded as wholly unsupportable by denizens of the desert. Many early Bedouin tribes made their living by pilfering from their neighbors, yet once the neighbor entered a Bedouin home, his personal safety and welfare were a sacred obligation of his host.

91

After the *badia* turned back, satisfied with our credentials, we continued eastward in the direction of the Azraq oasis. This was probably the most important crossroads of the Eastern Desert in the pre-Christian era. Few watering places on the chain of deserts extending south from Syria present the green grandeur of this isolated group of pools. They lie like great silver blotches on the desert floor, fringed by tufted date palms and lined with bullrushes.

Azraq covers an area of perhaps 30 square miles, lying in a depression formed by an erosion of land, apparently from waters that once poured down from the great plateau south of the Syrian Desert into the lowlands that extend all the way to the lower Euphrates River and the head of the Persian Gulf. The oasis is about 200 kilometers east of Ammān.

Early in the afternoon of the fifth day of our journey eastward since we had set out from Muwaqqar, we topped a small rise and saw beyond us the gray-green expanse of the oasis. R'Faifan, riding ahead, pulled up his camel, and I stopped mine beside him. His wrinkled face with deeply graven lines along the cheeks, was wreathed in a smile.

"This is where we start," he said, pointing to the array of glistening pools that gleamed like polished metal in the murky light. "Beyond this"—he waved at the horizon—"is only desert."

I could appreciate his point. Below us, on the near side of the lower village—there is a village at the north end and one at the south end of the oasis—was the tiny, white-walled *badia* "fort," with the green-and-red flag of the Jordanian Camel Corps flying from a watchtower at one end. The small stone buildings within the enclosure could be clearly seen, and behind these was a corral for the camels. This was generally made of barbed wire, and the care of camels which are bred by the *badia* for speed and staying power is far superior to that given by the general run of camel herders on the desert.

Beyond the little fort lay the gray mound of Azraq castle,

Bedouin at prayer: R 'Faifan at an improvised mosque, or temple, near Kharāna. Bulge points toward Mecca.

Guardians of the desert: *badia*, Desert Patrol troopers at Azraq; corporal at left, private at right.

the ancient ruins of a fortress that had served successively as a defense post for the Romans more than 2,000 years ago, for the Omayyads and Abbasids who ruled this area during the rise of Islam in the seventh and eighth centuries, and finally for the Turks who were thrown out by the Arab Revolt in the First World War. It was this crumbling fortress that had housed T. E. Lawrence and leaders of the Bani-Sakhr and Howeitat tribesmen during the bitter winter of 1917–18, when little bands of Arab guerrillas rode out into the wasteland north of Ammān in an effort to cut the Yarmuk Valley railroad and throw the Turkish retreat from Jerusalem into disorder.

As far as I knew, few expeditions had penetrated southeast of Azraq. Except for the crew that laid the oil line from Dhahran and Bahrein Island across the Syrian desert to Dera and Jaffa on the Mediterranean coast, it was a land unknown to any except the Bedouin.

The mud flats surrounding the oasis are a gathering place for birds of all kinds—ornithological and anthropological. Bedouin had ridden swaying camels down into this lush depression in the barren face of the desert for centuries and had watered at the pools which lay in irregular patches between the villages, surrounded by date palms and overhanging branches of willow-like trees. The southern village, Azraq ash Shishan, was the largest and nearest on our line of approach; and beyond that, about three or four kilometers distant, was the smaller northern town of Azraq Druze. We advanced toward the Desert Patrol post, which lay under the shadow of the massive walls of the gray castle where Roman, Arabian, and Turkish rulers for more than 20 centuries held sway over this dark corner of the desert.

Between the two villages a network of ancient conduits linked the pools, surrounded with clusters of trees that formed a strange pattern of green life on the otherwise barren waste. Below Azraq, to the south, spread the rusty sweep of the desert, ranging from tawny cliffs that lined the *widyán* to the crests of the mountains in the distance. These purple guardians of the past have unquestionably seen more cultures pass in review than we know in recorded history.

The Azraq swamp lies on the eastern side of a stream that connects the two villages, curving northward past the ruins of Azraq castle and eastward around the northern Druze village. The lower town—Azraq ash Shishan—is the larger, with a scattering of square mud houses surrounding a few government buildings and the store. The white parapet of the mosque, with its rounded turret, rises from the northern end of the lower village; from this high point the call of the *muezzin* to prayer may be heard every morning and evening and during the day. Around the mosque are grayish walls, with tall cypress trees lining the walks that bring the faithful to and from town.

The Azraq pools, formed in the depression beyond the villages, have been watering places for Bedouin for thousands of years, and today the ruins of mud huts along the edges of the pools are reminders of many generations of nomads who have come and gone in this ancient place.

The inhabitants of the two towns have almost nothing to do with each other. The northern settlement is occupied by Druze from Syria, a majority of whom are not of the Moslem faith. The southern village—Shishan—is inhabited by Circassians who were moved into Jordan by the Turks, deported from their original homes in the Caucasus.

Bedouin do not often stay long at the Azraq oasis. Except for the *badia* fort and the encampment just east of the fort, along a salt flat which is the dried shore of the old swamp, there are no settled Bedouin tents in the hills around the watering places. Within the Circassian village are the houses of a few Jordanian government officials, but for the most part the desert people do not mingle with either the Druze or the Circassians. They are

95

strange peoples from distant lands, who do not live there as guests but somehow have established a permanent residence and remain unwanted dwellers on Bedouin land.

The Druze are among the most mysterious peoples in the Middle East. They number only a couple of hundred thousand souls, but they remain religiously and culturally isolated from the Arabs as well as from the Circassians. Their religion seems to be obscure, even to themselves. It is not Moslem or Christian or Jewish, but it appears to combine all the mysteries of the earlier religions of Asia, including Zoroastrianism from Persia, Greek mysteries, the Hindu belief in reincarnation, coupled with touches of transcendentalism, Gnosticism and transmigration of the soul, not to mention neo-Platonism, Nestorianism, and the messianic doctrines of early Christian sects.

As we rode down through a split in the hills, the *badia* post lay before us, a short distance from both the town of Shishan and the castle which lay against the Druze village to the north. The tents of the army camp were just beyond the fort.

An officer of the garrison met us as we rode up. He explained in very slow Arabic that I was to consider myself and R'Faifan as guests of the Desert Police. Since it quickly developed that R'Faifan knew many—if not all—of the members of the patrol stationed at Azraq, the accommodations at the post were not only welcome but quite enjoyable.

We were quartered within the fort itself. I was never sure whether the immediate hospitality was a result of some secret signal conveyed by R'Faifan to his old comrades-in-arms, or the natural generosity of the Bedouin, or even whether I was under a polite form of house arrest. In any event, we were greeted with the greatest courtesy, and I was immediately directed to a store in the village of Shishan where we could procure necessary supplies.

We needed such things as coffee and tea and tins of bully beef. I also found it possible to buy flashlight batteries at the store. Since the next point where these supplies could be obtained would be the *badia* post at Bāyir or perhaps south of the Bāyir wells at Al Jafr, it was necessary to pack in enough basic staples to last us for a good three weeks of traveling. There is no fixed trail across the hills south of Azraq, and the only stopping places would be scattered *buyút sha'ar* of Bedouin camel herders and a few well-to-do *sheikhs,* if we were lucky enough to run across them.

By the time I returned to the fort, after being driven into the village in a Land Rover by one of the *badia* troopers, R'Faifan had established himself firmly in the hearts and also in the quarters of his old Camel Corps mates. He had arranged for a prisoner, who was the sole occupant of the prison compound, to see to our comfort. I was surprised to find that the prisoner, who spoke English, had the complete run of the place. He had been in the Jordanian army and had gone A.W.O.L. due to some pressing business that was never quite made clear to me; but in any event, he was picked up and was now serving out his term.

There was an astonishing lack of security in the post, a characteristic of most penal arrangements of the *badia* posts; and our man, whose name was Brahim, appeared to live among the men of the Camel Corps with complete freedom. Since he seemed to be assigned to see to our personal comfort, I saw no reason to question the situation.

It turned out that the corporal, who had been given responsibility for our well-being, was an old crony of R'Faifan from his Camel Corps days. He informed me that we were to remain as long as we wished as guests of the Desert Police. Since the weather had worked itself into an early spring storm, we decided to remain in Azraq at least until the storm passed.

Besides investigating the old castle where Lawrence had holed up with the Arab tribesmen, I wanted to study the desert routes eastward, where we planned to begin our search for the line of abandoned wells as soon as the Lawrence mission was completed. The *badia* were helpful and friendly; many of them had ridden long distances into the desert, and when they understood the purpose of my journey into that area, exploring old trails leading to Kaf, they marked places on my map where we would find watering places.

The desert south of Azraq is one of the loneliest stretches in the Eastern Desert, with no marked trails and few travelers. Between Azraq and Bāyir the only landmarks are the "three sisters" of Thulaythuwāt, columns of standstone that stand out on the bare face of the desert, rising above the plain, and the ruined castle at Qasr at Tūba.

Meanwhile, R'Faifan and I rambled through the post, which was built around the square, two-story fort with stone guest houses on one side and the kitchen and "prisoners' quarters" on the other. Behind the post was the barbed-wire stockade where the camels wandered around without anyone's paying particular attention to them. In fact, the entire post seemed to be operating with little surveillance and without the customary troops patrolling the place or doing routine guard duty usually required in military establishments.

The English-speaking prisoner, Brahim, seemed to have attached himself to R'Faifan and me. He came into the room assigned to us early the following day and began to clean up. I protested, but R'Faifan gave me a sly wink. Later he explained.

"The fellow is glad to help," he said. "He respects your position, and it will help his own conscience for leaving his post and getting himself arrested if he can help you. Do you not see the value of this?"

The value was not entirely clear, but realizing that in R'Faifan I was speaking to a man of experience in these matters, I made no further protest.

"You have a fellow feeling for all these people," I remarked. "Is it because you were a member of the *badia*?"

He shrugged. "Everything is as Allah wills," he said non-committally.

There was fatalism as well as a sense of resignation in this response. R'Faifan was bred on the desert, as were his father and his father's father. The code of the desert may appear cruel and unrelenting, but it is also implacably just. If one man has many camels and a larger *bait sha'ar* than his neighbors, it is because he was born as head of the tribe—which is all that the term *sheikh* really means. By the very nature of things, Allah controls all, and any individual protest would be a complaint against Allah and therefore senseless.

Shortly afterward, Brahim returned with tea and sheep's milk for our breakfast, and I found myself quite willing to accept the Bedouin viewpoint that everything is as Allah wishes and should be accepted with imperturbable calm.

Since the old castle lay somewhat closer to the Druze area than to the Circassian village to the south, R'Faifan and I decided to make a tour of the place before we went into the village to make our final purchases for the journey southward. From a distance the ground between the two settlements, covered with pools, looked like a green blanket dotted with large silver slabs, but as we approached the fortress, the palms and bullrushes surrounding the pools gave it the appearance of an ancient garden. The clearness of the water seemed to indicate the existence of an underground lake from which water flowed into the oasis, or a series of subterranean rivers that reminded me of Coleridge's lines:

> Where Alph, the sacred river, ran
> Through caverns measureless to man
> Down to a sunless sea.

We found a Druze caretaker living in a stone house outside the fort, and he took us into the place, pointing to rooms in which he said Lawrence of Arabia was reported to have met with the tribal chiefs of the Bani-Sakhr and Howeitat and planned forays upon the Turkish railroad. He was a friendly man, with sandy hair and light blue eyes, shy at first but finally voluble as he realized that I could understand his limited English.

I was quite curious about the odd relations that seemed to exist between the people of the two villages, living close to each other yet having no real community. He shrugged and explained that he was a Druze and therefore knew little of the others. This, of course, was true; Circassians were Moslem but not Arabic, having been brought down by the Turks from the Caucasus and having no common connection with Druze or Bedouin, in tradition or in habits. The Druze seldom mingled with either the Shishan villagers or the *badia,* living their separate existence in mud-walled huts along the scattered pools of the oasis. I had been told that the Circassians made good soldiers—probably due to their Turkish training—whereas the Druze had little to do with anyone but themselves.

As we prowled through the old fortress with our amiable Druze guide, I could not help trying to imagine the existence of Lawrence when he had huddled here during the winter months, plotting with old Auda ibn Jazi, the Howeitat tribal leader, during the intervals between raids in the Yarmuk Valley. I made a cursory effort to try to find traces of their having lived here, but it had been 50 years ago, and many visitors since then would have carried off any relics of their having hidden out in this place.

The interior of the fortress bore trademarks of the original Roman builders, 2,000 years ago, although there was an overlay of Arab construction. The vaulted arches, built of blocks of stone, were quite definitely Roman; and at the end of one room was a massive stone door made of a single slab, with projections at each end of the back edge that fitted perfectly into slots in the floor and ceiling. This had been accomplished with such

Across the Black Desert: R'Faifan and two Bedouin travelers who joined us, riding eastward toward Kharana.

Ruins of ancient Rome: the Azraq fortress where Lawrence and Bedouin raiders hid during Arab Revolt; window above gate is lookout from Lawrence's room.

precision that the door still swung easily on these pins of solid stone.

As might have been expected, I found little in the old ruins, including the rooms occupied by Lawrence, that would cast any light on his personality or traits of character. I doubted that the region around Azraq would provide me with any tidbits helpful to Dr. Mack in his effort to reconstruct the Englishman's odd character. It would be necessary to cull this information from the old Bedouin who lived in the southern desert, around Rumm and Mudawwara.

That evening Brahmin came into our room, and he and R'Faifan spent some time drawing their *wāsm*. R'Faifan showed me his *wāsm*—a single stroke followed by a mark similar to the Greek letter *pi*. Then he showed me the Bani-Sakhr brand, a square with a dot in the center.

"How about my *wāsm*?" I asked. R'Faifan grinned happily and drew one which he said depicted my Arabic name, Abu Ghaith. This name had a peculiar history on its own part. When I arrived in Ammān and told R'Faifan of the birth of my young son since I had last seen him, he raised his hands to heaven and announced that the name of my offspring should be Ghaith, which means Prosperity That Follows Rain. Since I was my son's accredited father, my own name thenceforth should be Abu Ghaith, or Father of the Son Whose Name Is Prosperity That Follows Rain.

R'Faifan transcribed this idea into the form of a *wāsm* so complicated in design—possibly because R'Faifan was improvising it—that I was unable to decipher it, much less describe it.

3

The wind had been blowing all day from the west—the *háwa gharbi,* the Bedouin call it—and this brought the chill of cold air and rain from the Mediterranean across the sand dunes of Jordan and Syria. In the general opinion of Arab weather prophets, a west wind always forecasts three days of rain. Since we did not have a tent, I was not anxious to venture out on the open desert under these conditions, so we remained for the next two days at Azraq.

I had managed to strike up a friendship with a Jordanian government official, Faīk Wazani, who lived in a small house on the outskirts of Shishan village. He was head of the government commission for preservation of natural resources and seemed to be the ranking civilian officer in the area; among other things, he was well grounded in a knowledge of the topographical and geological formations east of Azraq.

He was well educated, speaking English as well as Arabic quite fluently, and he loved the desert and the Azraq area as few men did. In some respects he reminded me of American forest rangers, dedicated to remote places and to the protection of forests and rivers.

He showed me a small bottle containing dried scorpions, one of his most prized possessions. Then he took me to his house, where I met his wife, a pleasant, plump woman who apparently was Austrian. The home in which they lived seemed more American than Arabic, with furnishings imported from Europe and the United States. Even in this remote outpost, they had hot water and a shower.

Faīk Wazani came to our quarters at the post and under a flickering light traced the trails to the east. I told him about my plan to locate the line of abandoned wells that I thought might mark the ancient caravan trail from Tadmor down the length of Arabia, and he nodded. There was much unexplored territory in the Eastern Desert, he said.

I explained that my original intention to travel into Saudi Arabia had been blocked by the government of that country, and I outlined my present plans.

103

I told him I had decided upon an alternative route, which was divided into four segments. The first leg would be southward, passing through Bāyir—or Bi'r as it sometimes was called, meaning "well" in Arabic—and through Al Jafr, the *badia* post in the southern part of the desert; and from there into the Rumm area where Lawrence and his Arab raiders had operated. Below Al Jafr was the old abandoned railroad station at Fasu'a, to which I had previously traveled from the west.

I expected to reach Fasu'a and from there descend into Rumm Valley, a place familiar to me. After spending some time seeking traces of Lawrence among old Bedouin in that area, I proposed either to turn northward to Petra and thence cross the desert again to Bāyir, completing a rough quadrangular course; or I would try to cross into the Wádi Araba, south of the Dead Sea, and from this area ride eastward into the unmapped area between southeast Jordan and northeast Saudi Arabia to try to find the line of old wells. I said I had heard many reports from Bedouin of ancient ruins near Kaf that may have antedated the Roman conquest of this area; and I hoped this might lead to traces of the ancient caravan trail.

Faĭk Wazani had also heard stories of the ruins near Kaf, and he believed they existed and might lead to important discoveries. He said there were also reports of crustacean deposits in the limestone rock in the area of the Qurayyāt Depression. This might indicate that there had been a great inland sea in this area at one time, or that the Persian Gulf had extended several hundred miles beyond its present limit and that cities may have existed along the shore of this ancient sea.

The possibility that the Persian Gulf once covered the flatlands near the mouth of the Euphrates and Tigris, perhaps as far as Ur of the Chaldees and Babylon, appears to have been debated by scholars with far more learning than I possessed, and the theory is generally discounted; but to me it offered romantic possibilities. This was a part of the Empty Quarter that had not been invaded, except for the crews that laid the oil pipeline from Behrein to Jaffa, and if the Bedouin reports of fossils of sea life found in this region were true, it might lead to discoveries of the remnants of a civilization that existed before the time of Abraham. With this notion in mind, I had plotted on my map the supposed locations of these wells, extending along the curving depression of the Wádi Sirhan, an ancient valley, now entirely dry, that lies along the border of Jordan and Saudi Arabia, apparently running from the Badeit Esh Sham, the lower part of the Syrian Desert, down into the Arabian steppelands. While it might have required crossing the border into Saudi Arabia to trace these wells, I was prepared to take that risk if I should discover actual signs of the dried-up watering holes along the old highway linking Mesopotamia and Arabia Felix.

Faïk Wazani was enthusiastic about my project with respect to the journey eastward. It was only when I mentioned going down into Wádi Araba that he seemed to tighten up. It seemed to me that when I mentioned anything remotely suggesting contact with the Jews—and Wádi Araba was fairly remote from centers of population in Israel—there was a sudden coolness among Jordanians. I suppose he believed travel across the Israeli border was not healthy, and so I gave the matter no further thought.

On the third day of our sojourn at Azraq, the wind shifted to the east—the *sharqui,* or dry wind that blows rain out of the sky. This cleared the clouds, and since it also coincided with the three days which, under the mystique of Bedouin hospitality, is the limit a guest should remain anywhere, R'Faifan and I decided to leave the following morning. Under Bedouin rules of receiving strangers, it is quite permissible—after the third day of the stranger's sojourn—for the host to inquire of his visitor where he is going.

In our case, the ritual was not urgent, and we probably could have remained longer if we wished. But I had no desire to test the custom; and our schedule called for us to push on. The sergeant and corporal both protested our departure, but the one most concerned was Brahim, the prisoner. He seemed disconsolate at our leaving so soon, and I finally discovered the reason. He lived in his tribal home somewhere to the south of Azraq, and he had planned to accompany us as far as his family *bait sha' ar*, but unfortunately his term in the *badia* prison did not expire until the following week, so he could not join us.

Our schedule required that we complete our work for Dr. Mack at least by the early part of April and turn eastward into the Empty Quarter before the desert heat became unbearable. Furthermore, I still was determined to explore the Jordanian side of Wádi Araba if possible in spite of the indications that there might be danger along the western border. Lawrence had spent a great deal of time in this mountainous region, and while it is largely uninhabited I felt it would be worthwhile to visit this area before heading eastward.

With these objectives firmly in mind, I set forth on a windy March day from Azraq, with R'Faifan in the lead, he riding the bull camel and I the female. Our track now lay over the open desert. Behind us the low, marshy area of the Azraq oasis appeared as a gray-green patch on the horizon; and as it gradually receded from view, I realized we were leaving the last remnant of what we are pleased to call "civilization." Henceforth we would travel as nomads of the desert had traveled for centuries past: riding on swaying camels, one leg slung around the horn and the other resting cross-legged over one's foot, the easiest position for accommodating oneself to the lumbering, rocking-chair rhythm of the single-hump camel as it follows instinctively an almost indiscernible track where some other camel had walked before, all trails seemingly in different directions but all winding up at the next watering hole.

The cold, dry *sharqui,* had lifted the momentary moisture from the last few days of rain off the surface of the ground, and the gravel was hard and dry. We rode southward from the lush marshlands of the oasis, with their 2,000-year-old complex of dams and drainage conduits, into the barren gulch of the Wádi Ghadaf. Ahead were miles of successive ridges, and between them the rocky beds of ancient streams, long since gone dry.

There is a subtle change that overcomes anyone leaving even the bare accouterments of civilization—such as represented by R'Faifan borrowing the tractor of Sheikh Sami to move his tent! —and setting forth into the open desert. Up to this point we had made one short day's journey after the next, with some habitable target ahead of us, but now we were going out into the Eastern Desert, with only the shifting presence of nomad families and the two permanent outposts at Bāyir and Al Jafr, far down on the steppeland plateau, to mark out goals for our traveling.

I watched R'Faifan, with his imperturbable acceptance of all that Allah wills, staring through the slit of his red-and-white checked *kaffiyah* at the shimmering gravel beds ahead, and wondered whether he felt the emotional surge that I was experiencing, riding out of the old into the new, yet knowing that the "new" was far older than anything I had ever known. I doubted it. Much as I had lived and traveled with Bedouin, I never could quite acquire that implacable attitude so fully portrayed in their single expression: "Inshallah!"—As God wills!

As we rode across the desert, I thought of the Jordanian army trucks I had seen in convoy near Jiza a few days before we left, and I recalled Lawrence's description of his swift ride on a Rolls-Royce across the Wádi Ghardaf from Bāyir to Azraq, covering in hours distances that required days and weeks for the Bedouin to travel on the "ship of the desert." It seemed that war and its accompanying conflicts were the only common ground upon which all peoples met. It was a curious commentary upon our advancing civilization that different breeds of the human race

107

never seemed to get together on a basis of mutual understanding or the intermingling of cultures; it was always on a basis of fighting each other.

Yet the land through which I was now traveling was one of the oldest inhabited places in the world, and perhaps the oldest. It was the cradle of our own Western civilization, the birthplace of all Occidental religion—Christian, Judaic, and Moslem. The desert over which I was now making my way, at a veritable snail's pace compared with modern speed, was the same track over which Bedouin nomads had traveled at the time of the Patriarchs from Babylon and Ur of the Chaldees. The ancient ruins at Azraq, and those I hoped to find at Kaf, were relics of a changeless existence, of people long since dead and forgotten in history. This all lent itself to a strange feeling that seemed to overpower me as we jogged along the dry bed of the Wádi Ghadaf, that might have been a river a thousand years before Abraham, coursing through a fertile land teeming with civilized activity.

There is a quality about the desert that is unlike anything else I have encountered. It creates the sensation of being utterly alone, with an extension of physical distance beyond which is the unlimited extension of time itself. In this environment, the human mind is lifted out of itself, above the level of mundane existence, until one has the feeling of being cast out into a limitless world of endless space and time.

108

IV. *In the Tracks of Lawrence*

1

The *badia* corporal rode with us to the edge of the oasis and pointed southward. "You will find Sheikh Suʿ an beyond the hills," he said in Arabic. I had shown him a letter from Sheikh Sami, directing me to visit Sheikh Suʾan En-Waran, a prominent leader of the Sebʾn family of Bani-Sakhr. His *bait shaʾ ar,* the corporal said, was about 18 kilometers to the south. There was also the question of water. Our camels were slow and heavy-footed, and could not travel more than four or five days at the most without water. If we missed Sheikh Suʿ an, the only certain watering place beyond that was Bāyir, where three large wells made this place a desert crossroads.

The March winds were rising, and this frequently was a time when desert homes were moved to new grounds. As we rode out of Azraq, past the ruins of ancient Roman dams built to collect water in the marshes below the Shishan village, I had the feeling that this might be the last water we would see until we reached Bāyir.

109

However, some 18 kilometers south of the oasis my fears were dispelled; we saw several brown patches against the hills which I was certain must be the *sheikh*'s encampment. As we rode toward the tents, pausing for the customary halting of the camels, until our presence was recognized, an old woman came out of the largest tent.

R'Faifan who, according to desert etiquette had stopped to fiddle with his saddle strap, rode toward her, and after talking briefly he turned and waved to me. When I came up, he explained that Sheikh Su' an was away looking over a site for his new camping place, since he intended to move the following day.

There were other women in the *muharram;* I saw one or two faces peering from the edge of the tent flap which covered their section. Veils over the lower part of their faces indicated that they were women. But Bedouin women are shy and seldom disclose themselves to strangers, even when the head of the household is present.

For the old woman, however, the situation was quite different. She was the *um al' ayál,* mother of the *sheikh,* and as the senior woman in the home it was not only her privilege but her duty to welcome visitors when her son was away. She invited us in, volubly and graciously.

It might be noted in this respect that the status of Bedouin women in the desert is quite different from that of those who live in the cities, and in many respects probably far more satisfactory to the women. Multiple marriages are common among Arabs, which might give the impression that woman are held in little esteem, but the reverse is true in the desert. The wife of a Bedouin possesses certain rights that are inviolable, contributing not only to her dignity but her sense of freedom. As the *sheikh*'s wife, she is the *rayat al bait,* mistress of the tent. She rules the kitchen and most phases of domestic life. When she is the mother of the *sheikh,* she has even greater rights. In the absence of her son, she is supreme ruler of the household.

110

By a curiously illogical form of reasoning, the woman is both superior and inferior to her husband. She usually wears a veil, or *milfa*, covering the lower part of her face, and in southern Arabia she wears the even more chaste *burqa,* a heavier veil covering the entire face, with holes for the eyes. In the north Bedouin woman appear more readily before strangers, but only when the husband is present. The *rayat al bait* seldom shows herself when a guest is in the tent, but she still rules the household from the *muharram,* protecting her husband's honor in the matter of food served. She must provide an impeccable menu in order to maintain his reputation as a host, and in some cases Bedouin traveling across the desert will map their route to assure passing the *buyút sha' ar* known to have the finest food.

In keeping with their status of separation from men, Bedouin women are seldom mentioned by name. A guest will ask: *"Schlan um al' âyál?"* which means in essence: How is the one who stands behind you? In contrast with the American housewife, who may have to maintain her position in the home by devious means, the Bedouin wife simply operates under the rules and expects everyone, including her husband, to observe them.

This simplicity of family life is illustrated by divorce procedures among the nomads of the desert. The male member simply says to his wife: *"Ma arid ikh!"*—I divorce you!—and repeats it three times. The business is completed.

In the Bedouin tradition, derived from Moslem rules of conduct, divorce is not a matter of humiliation or disgrace either to the male member of the marriage or to his wife. It merely means that the man and his mate (or one of them) cannot get along together, and it is much more reasonable for them to separate than to continue to endure each other's companionship. Since sex is the essence of Bedouin home life, it is patently illogical for people to continue to live together when they can no longer enjoy sleeping with each other.

When a man initiates divorce, he must also provide a *jehaz,*

111

or settlement, involving their children. The wife retains custody of all small children until they are eight years old, after which she turns them over to their father. She then looks around for another husband.

While we were waiting for Sheikh Suʿ an to return from his home-hunting trip, his mother chatted with us quite amiably, speaking Arabic which I followed as best I could and R'Faifan repeated her words slowly when he saw I was in difficulty. She was a delightful woman, and finding that I was an American, she assured me of the warmest welcome by her husband. Within an hour he arrived.

Sheikh Suʿ an was one of the finest examples of Bedouin tribal leaders I have met. Tall, handsome, and wiry, his hawklike face was the sort usually associated with the romantic *sheikh* of Arabia. Sheikh Suʿ an immediately repeated the welcome of his mother and explained that he had planned to move his tents about 10 kilometers to the west. The location of a new camp is important to a nomad; neighbors are protected by what is known as *qasir,* a neighbor's rights. A man who pitches his tent within a distance that can be measured by throwing a "camel stick" as far as possible automatically becomes a neighbor and must join a protective tribal group.

In cases where a collection of *buyút sha'ar* belonging to Bedouin of the same family are located within the same area, the chief of the family, or *sheikh,* assumes the responsibility of the *qasir.* In such instances as Sheikh Suʿ an's migration to a new location for his home, it would be necessary for him to see that he did not inject himself into the protective area of an existing *bait sha'ar,* or acquire new responsibilities of his own. For this reason, he had been quite circumspect about selecting the site for his new home, carefully checking the credentials of all possible neighbors.

Nevertheless, having done this, it was the Bedouin custom to waste no time in putting the project into action.

112

Moving day in the desert: scene in the life of the nomads of the desert; Sheikh Su'an's household packing up to move to a new watering place.

Pools of Azraq: R'Faifan cups his hands to drink from the ancient oasis, one of the great watering places of the Eastern Desert.

"We move tomorrow," he told us. "You will be kind enough to accept our poor hospitality."

R'Faifan, with a sweeping gesture, seemed to offer our assistance. I understood his gestures better than his words, and I was a bit disconcerted, since he seemed to have promised unlimited help in moving camp, which would delay our schedule. R'Faifan, noticing my expression, drew me aside and explained that there was nothing to worry about, since the women would do all the work.

He was right. The following morning, after a pleasant evening and sound sleep, I saw that the women had been up before dawn preparing to move. The goat-hair strips of the tent were rolled and packed, and the camping paraphernalia was stuffed in bags ready to be loaded on the *sheikh*'s ten camels.

Each strip was about 60 feet long and 3 or 4 feet wide, and the rolls could be readily loaded on the pack saddles. Before the sun was two hours up in the sky, the entire encampment was ready to migrate to the new homesite. Meanwhile, Sheikh Suʿ an invited us to enjoy the hospitality of a neighbor across the hill, who would entertain and feed us while the women were moving camp!

I was accustomed to Bedouin hospitality, but it was the first time I had joined in the actual move of a nomad family, and I was quite interested. "We must follow the watering places," the *sheikh* explained. "The wind will be from the west, and our tents must be placed so that they face the wind. We will also be sheltered from the sun until late afternoon."

I watched the strange caravan move slowly to the west, with the women driving the camels across the dry, sun-baked hills toward their new home. The ungainly *dhalla,* the women's litter baskets, a weird contraption that looked like clothes-drying racks, swayed on the backs of camels as they disappeared over the ridge, with the women leading them on foot.

We remained for luncheon at a neighboring tent to which one of the *sheikh*'s neighbors had invited us; and then followed with

114

Radio in the deser: Sheikh Su'an (on left with fire poker) and his sons with two neighbors listen to transistor radio.

Son of the *sheikh*: Frahan, oldest son of Sheikh Su'an, stands beside his donkey; note salt grass on which donkey nibbles.

Sheikh Su' an. When we were about a mile from the new location, I noticed a small shack some distance off our trail. I called R'Faifan's attention to this, and he immediately veered off the trail, so I followed him. The mud hut was the home of a Druze caretaker of a watering hole, apparently maintained by the *badia* for camels of desert travelers. R'Faifan talked briefly with the fellow, who seemed delighted that someone had stopped to see him. Because of the antipathy that existed between Bedouin and these Druze outlanders, who were neither Moslem nor Bedouin, visits were infrequent and those who stopped apparently did not even talk to the old caretaker. We filled out bags with slightly brackish water and headed back to overtake Sheikh Su' an. However, R'Faifan turned off the trail and headed across the hill, apparently to see someone whose tent he recognized. In a short time he was back, waving his hands excitedly.

"We can trade our bull!" he shouted. "It is the best thing that has happened!"

I knew R'Faifan was not happy with his bull camel, which snapped at him frequently. He had told me the camel was mad and would never be satisfactory either for riding or as a pack animal. The new bull offered in trade had been castrated, he said, and he assured me it would be as docile as a house pet. After thinking the matter over, I finally agreed to the trade, providing we didn't have to pay a premium in the exchange. R'Faifan jogged back across the hill and in a short time returned, grinning from ear to ear and leading the most disconsolate and dilapidated camel I had ever seen. The matting of hair that covered the camel's neck and chest in irregular splotches looked like badly worn doormats. The animal's eyes, dark and despondent, gazed ahead with a stolid, soul-weary expression that seemed to have been drained of all hope.

R'Faifan hopped down from the saddle and slapped the animal on the flank as if it were a prize.

"An even trade," he announced triumphantly.

116

I remembered his premature satisfaction at the purchase of the white female camel at the village near Jericho. It was my experience that an even trade among camel traders was virtually non-existent. However, R'Faifan seemed pleased with his bargain, and since he had to ride the animal I felt I was in no position to object. As things developed, it was a good trade. The new bull ignored the *nága* I had been riding, which was a relief, since I had never known whether the old bull was about to advance on my female or myself. The castrated bull seemed to have an indifference that might be expected of a male camel deprived of its natural capabilities, and the following day, as we rode out over the desert, I expressed a renewed respect for R'Faifan's shrewdness as a camel bargainer.

"You will see," he promised me. "The new bull is twice as strong as the old one, and only half as dangerous."

That evening Sheikh Su' an brought his children into the *raba' a* to meet his guests. One of the boys, Frahan, was so handsome I asked the *sheikh* if I might take pictures of him. Sheikh Su' an readily agreed and even insisted on posing with the boy. The festivities at the new *bait sha' ar* were like a reprieve. I had expected nothing but the bleak, open desert, with nights spent by our own campfire, all the way to Bāyir; and here we were lounging on cushions again, listening to the melancholy strains of the *rabába* and tales of hunting on the desert.

2

The Wádi Ghadaf is a long, snakelike depression, twisting through the black gravel ridges that descend from the high plateau west of Qasr at Tūba, one of the Omayyad ruins on the Eastern Desert, northeastward toward the Azraq marshes, where it loses its identity in the lowlands of the oasis. It apparently was an ancient riverbed that once fertilized an immense valley; and its winding course may have taken it to the edge of the prehistoric sea that at one time washed against the Qurayyāt Depression.

Today it is a dry, hard bed of gravel and sharp flinty stones that cut our camels' padded feet. A dozen kilometers south of the place where we first sighted Sheikh Suʿ an's *bait sha' ar,* the course of the *wádi* veers to the southwest and runs in a tortuous path upward toward the ruins of Qasr at Tūa. This was our first destination after leaving the comfortable surroundings of the *sheikh* and his vigorous womenfolk.

All day we rode through the clumps of salt grass known as *hamdh,* a coarse grazing food which camels vitally need when there is no water. The bottom of the *wádi* was barren of vegetation, although the sides were dotted in places with small tufts of lighter brush grass, *nassi* to the Bedouin, used chiefly to graze goats. Sheikh Suʿ an advised us that there would be no established watering place between his *bait sha' ar* and Bāyir, and therefore we must plan to camp at night in areas where the salt grass could be found for the camels. The winter rains had freshened the grass, and aside from our own requirements, we would not have need of water for several days.

Camels have a "homing instinct"; they seem to sense the existence of other camels miles away. For this reason the rider who may have little knowledge of the land over which he is riding will let the animal have its head, and usually it will lead him safely to the next habitable place. Of our two camels, the *nága* seemed to have the best sense of direction, so I rode for the most part ahead of R 'Faifan, whose bull plodded steadily behind me.

We reached the turn in the Wádi Ghadaf late in the afternoon, and from one of the ridges over which we rode we could see far to the west the dark spots of tents; but these were too far off our course for us to visit them. There was an old camel trail, some 30 kilometers to the west, which ran down from Kharāna through Tūba, and had once been a main route from Damascus southward during the times of the Omayyads, but it also was too far off our trail for us to seek it, and since we did not have any urgent need of water, there was no purpose in abandoning the dry stream-bed over which we were traveling.

By evening we were well up on the plateau, and I could easily see the sharp outline of a *jabal* (Arabic for a peak or column of rock) that jutted from the dark plain of the desert like an unexpected rock in the ocean. We had reached a point where a barely discernible trail crossed the *wâdi*, from west to east, and I was almost tempted to follow it in the hope of reaching one of the old wells on the Eastern Desert. However, at this point we were only a few miles from the Saudi Arabian border, the closest we would come on our journey southward, and I was not prepared to risk my Jordanian credentials by crossing from the Hashemite kingdom into the territory of Arabia at this point. Bāyir, the place from which I hoped to take off into the untraveled reaches of the Eastern Desert, was still four days' march to the south.

R'Faifan, who had ridden ahead briefly to exercise his camel, waved to me just as the sun was beginning to dip behind the peaks to the west, and I suddenly recalled that the time for prayer was approaching.

The Bedouin creates his own "mosque" or *masjid* on the desert—a small enclosure of stones, with one protruding loop facing toward Mecca—and in this tiny place of worship he utters his evening and morning prayers. I pulled up, climbed down, and stretched my legs, which were stiff from a full day in the saddle. While R'Faifan went off to set up his desert temple with a few stones scraped up from the gravel in the stream bed, I began to collect our gear to establish our camp in the *wâdi*. That night I smoked Bedouin *he-shee* tobacco in the long pipe R'Faifan had presented to me and listened to his tales of life with the Camel Corps many years before.

The loneliness of the desert seemed to press down upon us,

like a force coming out of nowhere. I began to understand the moods of the Bedouin, poetic and violent at times; and at other times as hard and serene as the pinnacles of the *jabál* that rose in sharp silhouette against the desert sky. R'Faifan, wrapped in his inevitable tuxedo jacket, which he wore over his flowing robe, squatted in front of the fire and in his slow Arabic, interrupted in moments of great feeling with sudden expostulatory explosions which I did not fully understand, explained his philosophy of life: All Bedouin were pure of soul and honest, whereas all those who lived in cities were thieves and scoundrels!

At first I argued with him; but soon the pleasant monotony of his words and the silence of the desert began to have their effect, like a subtle narcotic, and I found myself agreeing wholly with my Bedouin friend.

"Except Tony Hallec," I said. "He is a good friend, and not deceitful."

R'Faifan's attitude changed like a 180-degree wind shift. He assured me, with many sweeping gestures of his hands that seemed to brush away all doubt, that no finer person than Tony Hallec lived. If Tony had overheard us, his ears would have been red. As a sentimental gesture, I decided again to show R'Faifan the pictures of my wife and son. He seized these and kissed them several times. We soon found ourselves discussing families. My child, R'Faifan assured me, was like his own.

"A child," he exclaimed, speaking in Arabic very slowly so that I could understand him, "is the gift of God. Your son is like my son." He took the picture from my hands and kissed it again. The comparison was a bit obscure, since his two sons were grown men and my child was only a baby, but the mood of sadness, brought on by the realization that I would be away from my wife and son for many weeks, seemed to lend poignancy to his words. I nodded. If R'Faifan had shown me a picture of his son at that moment, I probably would have kissed it.

The mood of anyone traveling on the desert is timeless, and

120

Desert castle: the ruins of Qasr at Tūba, southernmost outpost of the Omayyads, was started but never finished.

Banquet hall at Tūba: the broken shell of a great banquet hall built by the Omayyad caliphs for their luxurious life in the desert. The building is 1,500 years old.

after jogging along all day on a camel, the distances covered from one place to another become virtually meaningless. At night the sense of remoteness and the lack of any realization of time is even more noticeable. As I gazed out at the empty blackness that surrounded us, and the immense bowl of darkness above, pierced by brilliant stars, I felt the closeness of the desert. It was almost as if time itself were telescoped and I had been tossed backward in time. The ancient Wádi Ghadaf, along which we had been riding since morning, suddenly became a highway into the past, and by closing my eyes I could imagine this bleak, empty place thousands of years ago, when it must have been teeming with life. I had to jolt myself into a conscious realization that my own time was controlled by a much later civilization with which I had only temporarily lost contact, but which nevertheless ruled my personal destiny. My wife and child, over whose picture R'Faifan had almost wept an hour or so earlier, were realities, and the lost cities of the Eastern Desert were the gossamer web of fantasy.

Early the next morning, after R'Faifan had completed his morning prayers, we set out again; and after four or five hours of traveling we came to the *bait sha'ar* of a Ruwalla family that had migrated across the nearby Saudi Arabian border. R'Faifan again went through the age-old ritual of causing his camel to kneel on the desert and tugging at his saddle straps until the old man who ruled the family came out and invited us to lunch. There was a depth of courtesy in his manner that I had grown to expect. He asked us in and offered me good Arabian smoking tobacco, which was a welcome change from the *he-shee* I had been smoking since we left Azraq; and he also produced a luncheon of tomatoes, bread, and onion salad!

It seemed to me as we set off over the dark graveled stream bed, heading toward the ruins of Qasr at Tūba, a gray outline on the horizon, that our brief visit with the Ruwalla tribesman offered another striking revelation of the character of the Bed-

122

ouin. In this desert, where the tides of Islamic conquest once poured into Syria and Iraq, there appeared to be no indication of these interruptions in the lives of nomads as they moved from one watering place to another, shifting seasonally along the old camel trails.

I thought of the fatalistic lines of Omar:

> The worldly hope men set their hearts upon
> May prosper, or turn ashes, and anon
> Like snow upon the desert's dusty face,
> Lighting a little hour or two, is gone!

The castle at Qasr at Tūba was an example of this historical evanescence. Originally intended as a hunting lodge, it was never finished, and now the crumbled walls, spilling over into the courtyard that had lost all semblance of a garden, offered mute testimony to the transience of the sudden rise of the Arabs to power, only to fade back again into the silence of the desert.

We jogged toward the old ruins, now deserted and apparently completely dry. I wondered what the alien world, now converging on this ancient land, would do to its people. It seemed that in spite of their retreat into the silence of the desert after the decay of the Omayyad power and the decline of the Abbasid caliphate, the Arab chapter in history was still unfinished. The tribal life and the customs that had persisted since the dawn of time were becoming the focus of a new contest for power among peoples who had no real interest in the Bedouin, and even less understanding of their way of life.

It struck me, as we rode toward the ruins and surveyed the broken relics of a dim chapter in Arab history, that perhaps these people were doomed forever to exist in a kind of limbo between the East and the West. They were neither mystics nor of the machine age. They had not been touched by the sensitivity of Oriental philosophy, the intellectualism of Confucianism, the

123

mysticism of Buddhism, or the simple good-and-evil preachings of Zoroaster among the Bactrian peasants; and they were equally unaffected by the morality of the Christians and the Jews. They had lived in an in-between world, born in the desert and nourished by the words of the Koran.

Their single significant accomplishment as a people was the domestication of the single-hump camel. Camel-herding and camel-breeding had anchored them to the one facet of their economy that was enduring. Was this essential to their existence or was it a matter of preference? Why should nomads remain nomads—as the Eskimos have remained Eskimos?

In some way it seemed to me the Bedouin were suspended between two tides of civilization—the pragmatic advances of the West and the mysticism of the East—and they have not moved in either direction. Would they be forever consigned to this role in history, an "arrested civilization" in a no-man's-land between the surging currents of Eastern and Western philosophies? Was it possible that the only real mark on the record of mankind that the Bedouin would leave would be the breeding of the camel?

We passed a deep well, 4 kilometers north of the old castle, and noticed that it had dried up; and I wondered if this was an additional reason for abandoning work on the castle. Whatever the reason, that night as we made our camp in front of the old ruins, smoking our pipes and contemplating the stars, I saw the last inhabitants of Tūba emerge from the dark interior—a horde of bats that circled out for whatever nightly activities may have been normal for them.

The trail from Tūba southward to Bāyir was almost nonexistent. In fact, there seemed to have been very little commerce between the bat-infested castle and the wells of Bāyir. The only real landmarks on this route—over which Lawrence had traveled on his mysterious journeys from Aqaba to Azraq, rallying Howeitat chiefs to the cause of the Arab Revolt—were the "three sisters" of Thulaythuwāt. We could see these shining peaks, from a distance of perhaps 30 kilometers as we departed from Tūba early the following day.

However, it was at least three days' march from Tūba to Bāyir, and we knew it would be the following day before we reached the peaks. We refreshed the brackish water in our bags, last filled by the old Druze caretaker near Sheikh Suʿ anʼs *bait shaʼar,* at an unusual watering place which the *badia* had arranged a few miles from our camping spot. A rubber bag was tied to some rocks in the *wádi* so that it would catch rainwater. The small water supply was undoubtedly intended for camels, but ours were not yet ready to drink, so R ʼFaifan and I used what we figured the camels would have consumed.

"I have a friend close by," R ʼFaifan suddenly told me as we climbed on our camels and rode on. "He is an old comrade of the Camel Corps."

It began to sound like a broken record. I recalled that the *badia* corporal at Azraq had mentioned to R ʼFaifan an old companion who lived some 25 kilometers south of Qasr at Tūba, somewhere near Jabal Khamkat, which I knew towered some 2,000 feet above the desert west of our route. I had paid little attention to the remark, yet sure enough, as we climbed a ridge, we saw a *bait shaʼar* ahead.

R ʼFaifan's friend, Saud-Jazi, came out to meet us, greeting both of us warmly.

"We must kill a lamb and have a *mansef* in honor of my guests," Saud-Jazi announced. He was a member of the Howeitat tribe, a tall, strongly built man with a tuft of hair on his chin and the eyes of an eagle; and although R ʼFaifan was a Bani-Sakhr, they embraced as old comrades-in-arms. At the killing of the lamb, I observed that Saud-Jazi laid the bloody knife against the neck of my camel, marking the figure *J* on the blotched fur. This was a sure sign that, although a stranger, I was completely welcome in the Jazi *bait shaʼar.*

The welcome was so complete that it included our camels. That night as I prepared to rest on the pile of cushions, after feasting on the satisfying *mansef* of rice, piled high on a platter with the roast lamb on top, Saud-Jazi actually invited our camels into the tent. The animals were finally maneuvered backward so that they slept in front of the tent instead of inside, but I found myself wondering when one of the camels, with its slobbering snout, would nuzzle against me for warmth during the night.

During the evening R'Faifan and Saud-Jazi regaled each other with tales of their youth, when both had been members of the Camel Corps. R'Faifan, cackling merrily at these recollections, reminded Saud-Jazi of the time he had helped him slip out of the *badia* post to meet a girl he hoped to marry.

Saud-Jazi laughed, but not quite as hilariously as R'Faifan. I later found that the girl he met was now his wife, and he undoubtedly did not want R'Faifan to pursue the subject of their youthful peccadilloes too loudly, since the *q'ata* separating the men's compartment from the female members of the family was thin and not likely to be soundproof.

The warmth of Saud-Jazi's welcome was so genuine that I allowed myself to be persuaded to stay another day, even to the point of enduring the intimacy of the animals who seemed to wander in and out of the tent as if it were their natural home, which it probably was. The baby camels often crowded into the far end, sometimes with their mothers, and slept among the cooking gear. I found that tossing a few stones at them when they peered through the flaps into the tent where I was sleeping at night would quickly discourage their interest. Goats, however, were another matter. On the morning of the second night I found three goats sleeping beside me in the tent, and in view of the long intervals between baths in the desert I decided two nights in this friendly *bait sha'ar* would be about all I could stand.

126

Comrade of the Camel Corps: Sheikh Saud Jazi, R'Faifan's friend of earlier days in the Desert Police; a typical Bedouin.

The "three sisters": scene from top of one of the peaks of Thulay-thuwāt form middle peak scaled by author.

When I advised Saud-Jazi that we were leaving, he expressed the most profound sorrow. How many times did he have an opportunity to see his old comrade, R'Faifan? How often did old friends come to visit him, all the way from Ammān?

The hospitality of the *bait sha' ar* had been a warm welcome into the land of the Howeitat, and when the morning dawned in murky coldness, with a hint of storms that might sweep over the desert, I found myself wishing we could remain for another day in these pleasant surroundings. However, we had already cut some of the time off our schedule—a phase of Western traveling technology utterly beyond the understanding of the Bedouin—and I knew we had to be moving. Saud-Jazi's farewell was so deeply moving that I felt, perhaps for the first time, that I really belonged among the Bedouin.

The weather had turned extremely cold, and behind us was the menace of gathering winds and freezing temperatures, a portent that I did not fully understand at the time. R'Faifan looked slightly worried and remarked to me, "The rains have stopped here, but they have not stopped in the north." He pointed at the dark sky, far to the north, but since it was clearing and we were heading south, I paid little attention to his ominous forecast.

Beyond the tent of Saud-Jazi, some 11 or 12 kilometers to the south, were the three pinnacles of Thulayithuwāt. They stood as naked columns in the desert, rising like Alpine peaks perhaps 1,200 feet above the floor. In the millions of years that the Eastern Desert had existed, through aeons of geological change, these three columns seem to have resisted the erosion of the desert floor and remained bare sentinels of the past, undisturbed by wind and water.

As we approached, the artwork of the storms and battering rainfall was evident on their scarred sides. I turned to R'Faifan and informed him that I intended to climb the tallest of the three peaks. He shrugged, which is the Bedouin way of dis-

128

claiming any responsibility for the outcome. I am not a mountain climber by profession or preference, and by the time I was halfway up the almost perpendicular slope I wished I had never made the attempt! The rugged ledges along the sides offered fairly secure footing, but the angle of cliffs made it necessary to crawl rather than climb. However, I finally reached the top and was almost blown off the summit as I rounded the final ledge and faced the furious gusts of wind.

I managed to plant the flag of the Explorers Club on the top of the peak and, for purposes of immortalizing the event, took several photographs of it. By this time I was thoroughly worried by the wind, and even more by the prospect of descent. The techniques of upward climbing and downward climbing are quite different; in the first case, I had clung to the ledges, facing the earth and crawling slowly upward, usually looking toward the peak. On the way down, I had nothing to look at but the escarpment downward and the flat desert floor more than 1,000 feet below. And I had to skid down, with my backside to the ground!

By the time I had reached the halfway mark and was able to breathe more easily, I was also exhausted, so I decided to rest. I moved around the ledge to get a view from the far side, and to my considerable surprise I found R'Faifan sitting comfortably on the ledge gazing out across the desert with our field glasses. He had crawled up the windward side, choosing it—quite logically, as he explained it—because the wind would blow him against the mountain and not away from it. He was neither tired nor scared.

That evening, as R'Faifan washed his hands in sand before prayer—a variation of Moslem ritual permitted on the desert, where water is scarce—I became aware of the infinite confidence he had in all things that arise from the desert. He had not worried about his ability to climb the peak of Thulaythuwāt, or even to get back down; he had only been worried about

129

my possible inability to sustain the exhausting ordeal. I am quite certain that it never occurred to R'Faifan that Allah would let him fall from the peak, but since I was unenlightened, not having placed myself wholly in the hands of God, something might have happened to me!

That night as we sat before our campfire, 7 or 8 kilometers south of the peaks, where there was better grazing for the camels, I reflected on the historic importance of this place. We were at last getting deep into "Lawrence country," in the area of Bāyir and Al Jafr where Lawrence had traveled half a century ago when he and his English comrades were playing their role in the Arab Revolt. There was little chance of turning up anything of importance on Lawrence around Bāyir or Al Jafr, which he had called Jefer, but I had the queer feeling that I was beginning to peer into the unturned pages of one of the most mysterious chapters in modern military history, only the barest outlines of which are known even now to historians.

Lawrence was better known in the region around Rumm and Mudawwara, in southwest Jordan, but he carved out his most brilliant record in his efforts to win the support of Howeitat tribesmen on the plains of Bāyir and Al Jafr. For the moment at least, as I looked into the blackness of the desert at night, my interest in Dr. Mack's project took precedence over my desire to explore the more ancient history of the Bedouin in the lands to the east.

3

The trail from Thulaythuwāt into Bāyir was almost un-marked, since few herders take this route and there are no roads east or west, and therefore we had to find our own way across the dun-colored hills, guiding ourselves by the direction of the sun. The Wádi Bāyir, a deep cleft in the gravel beds, courses in from the southwest, and it is only when we reached the edge of the watering place that the ground became hard and flat and easy for the camels.

I was deeply interested in the configurations of these old stream beds, because they seemed to converge toward the lowlands around Kaf; and this tended to confirm my belief that this was once a fertile valley, with rivers flowing from the high plateau in the center of the desert into the basin that must have formed the shore of an ancient sea. The land over which we traveled was dry and barren except for patches of brush, but I could see far below the sloping ridges and depressions that marked out the winding course of the rivers, all running eastward.

As we jogged down from the line of low hills toward the Wádi Báyir, I was startled by a sudden blasting noise in the sky. Looking upward, I saw four American-built Starfighter jets, with Jordanian markings, swooping across the blue desert sky. This sudden intrusion into the silence of the desert struck me almost as a shock: I had been pondering over the origin of this land and the people who may have inhabited it thousands of years ago, and there above me was a devastating reminder of the modern presence over these ancient plains. The jets, with their trailing feathers of darkened air, also reminded me that in passing beyond the outer limits of my own "civilized world," I had also passed beyond the stream of current news. The feeling of urgency that I had experienced at Jiza, when I saw a convoy of trucks rumbling along the road from Ammān, was revived in my mind. I wondered what ominous new events might have happened along the western border that could be associated with this new military activity in the sky.

I decided to ask R'Faifan to make a few inquiries among the *badia,* to whom I planned to report as soon as the camels were watered, and find out the latest news from the West. Meanwhile we headed for the Báyir wells. As we rode along the dusty trail, I could not help thinking that this watering place

131

might possibly be a western link in the chain of old wells I intended to locate on the Eastern Desert. It was at Bāyir that Lawrence and Joyce had the secret meeting with the Arab leader, Alwain—"a smooth-cheeked, oppressed, silent man"—when they were laying plans to destroy the Hijaz-Medina railroad; and the route over which we were plodding with our camels was the same hard, dry bed of the *wádi* along which Lawrence and Joyce sped through the night on a Rolls-Royce desert car, crossing the Wádi Dharmah over which we had just ridden and the Wádi Ghadaf that led into the marshlands on the way to Azraq. They covered in a single night a distance that R'Faifan and I needed seven days to negotiate by camel.

The wells of Bāyir are anything but modern. There are three of them, and usually an assortment of camel herders and other travelers surround the wells, exchanging the latest gossip of the desert. A rope and pulley is used in each well to draw up rubber buckets of water. Two men haul at the rope, and a third guides the bucket up the last few feet to prevent tilting and spilling the contents back into the well, and the water is poured into a trough.

The only permanent building in Bāyir is the fort. The rest is a transient village, with tents strewn irregularly over the desert and camels and other livestock penned up temporarily while their owners rest on their way to the north or south or west or east. Camel herders wander about, exchanging bits of news, or they sit before their tents smoking *he-shee*.

R'Faifan and I made our way to the headquarters of the *badia* and received a warm welcome. A messenger of the Camel Corps from Qasr al Kharāna, where we had stopped on the way to Azraq, had ridden in a few days before and told them of our expedition and its purpose. I presented letters from the Corps headquarters in Ammān and also a note from Mr. Wazani of the National Resources Authority in Azraq. The noonday meal was in process of being served, and R'Faifan and I were invited to join, but first we went to the small bath-house behind the fort to wash some of the dust and crust of the desert from our bodies.

This was the first time I had taken my clothes off since I left Jiza—a period of more than two weeks. The ablutive inter-lude was just about in time; I discovered several *grăd*—*Arabic* for the camel louse—in my clothes, and spent some time com-pleting a thorough inspection of the garments before I put them on again!

The sergeant in charge of the *badia* post—Fayad Da'san—was an old friend of R'Faifan. It seemed to me that my Bedouin friend's circle of acquaintances widened like the ripples of the sea at each stop on our journey. Fayad Da'san had traveled to the east, beyond the Wádi Sirhan, and when he under-stood our ultimate purpose of crossing the *wádi* to search for the ancient wells, he immediately outlined the routes we should take.

He also knew of the ruins of the old castle near Kaf, called Kabr es Said, east of the border between Jordan and the northern point of Saudi Arabia, some 50 or 60 miles from Bāyir. It was older than the earliest times of the Hashemite kingdom, he said, and from his description I believed it must be Roman or even pre-Roman. The location of the Kabr es Said castle was beyond the position on the map that I had marked out for the nearest of the wells—Q-4—which I believed lay within the Jordanian border. After talking with Fayad Da'san, I reworked my map, noting the route we should take on our return from the south; and I determined that even if it meant crossing into Saudi Arabia I would do so and say nothing to the *badia* since the question of my transgressing the border would be a matter for the government of Ammān and not within control of the Desert Patrol.

The possibility of finding this ancient ruin opened up a new theory: it would extend the border of Roman conquest farther east than had been hitherto believed, and it might also indicate signs of more ancient cities on the shores of the inland sea that may have been an extension of the Persian Gulf over what is now a barren land and largely uninhabited. If this were indicated by deposits of shells in rocks and along the cliffs, as reported by Bedouin I had talked with, it would offer further possibilities that prehistoric societies may have flourished along the once fertile valley of what is now the arid Wádi Sirhan and the Qurayyāt Depression.

We spent three days at Bāyir, resting our camels and ourselves for the long, dry journey down the plateau toward the Ra's an Naqb, where the desert drops off into the red gorges of Wádi Rumm. Here our search for Lawrence's tracks would be concentrated. I spent part of the time talking with the *badia* riders, seeking any knowledge they might have of the old trails to the east, since this was to be my takeoff point into the lands to the east when R'Faifan and I returned from our journey through the "Lawrence country" to the south. I also arranged, with R'Faifan's help, to visit some of the tents of Bedouin scattered around the wells. Bāyir is an important trail crossing, since it is a gathering place for nomads traveling from the south into new grazing lands in central Jordan. It marks the first big oasis on the trails between the Bani-Sakhr and Howeitat tribal lands, the two far-flung clans that form the most powerful tribal groups in Jordan, and the Howeitat have added strength through alliances with branches of their tribes in Saudi Arabia and the Sinai Peninsula.

There was little to be learned from the camel herders, however, that in any way bore upon the Lawrence legend. For the most part they were men of fifty or younger, who could not have known anything about the Arab Revolt or its leaders; and the most I hoped to glean was some knowledge of the older men of the tribes who might be found on the desert to the south, or perhaps could be visited on our return journey, on which we planned to circle back to Bāyir through the area of Ma'ān and Hasa, where the powerful chiefs of the Howeitat ranged.

R'Faifan was less knowledgeable in this part of Jordan than in his own tribal lands to the north, but he helped me to inquire among the Bedouin at Bāyir as to the probable location of Sheikh Faisal Hamd, one of the more influential of the Bedouin chiefs, whom I knew from previous journeys through southern Jordan.

One of the Bedouin who had arrived recently from the west told me of the location of Sheikh Faisal's *bait sha'ar* southeast of Hasa, and I determined to visit him. Although he was a man of middle age, he would know of older tribesmen who might provide information about Lawrence. R'Faifan, who had his own secret ways of obtaining intelligence, prowled among the Bedouin tents in the evening while I remained in our quarters at the fort and debugged my blankets, which had become infested with camel lice.

In the morning R'Faifan told me all he had learned, which was very little. He let me know, by devious suggestions, that there was still some sensitivity between the Jazi and Tayi branches of the Howeitat tribes which should be taken into account in dealing with either family. I knew from Lawrence's book that the long-standing feud between the Ibn Jazi Howeitat and the Abu Tayi Howeitat had been one of the problems that beset the English in trying to mount the Arab Revolt against the Turks in the First World War, and it was the settlement of this quarrel by Lawrence that enabled him supposedly to organize the Arab Revolt.

The current chief of the Tayi clan, Mohammed abu Tayi, the son of the old Auda abu Tayi, was known as a man of dignity and honor; and Faisal ibn Jazi, whom I had met at Ammān, had considerable political power. I planned to visit both *sheikhs* on our return across the desert.

135

At the moment I was concerned with our food supply. There was only one tin of bully beef and some stale biscuits to last us to Al Jafr, the next place we could obtain supplies. I suspected that Zuki, a *badia* prisoner who performed most of the handyman's chores around the compound, had pilfered our stores, but there was no way of proving this, and knowing the amiable relations that existed between the Desert Patrol troops and their prisoners, I did not want to offend Fayad Da'san, the *badia* sergeant who had entertained us at his *bait sha'ar*.

As a result, we were forced to hasten our departure for Al Jafr, and the following morning, in spite of the blustery March wind, we set out on the next lap of our journey. We had hardly enough food for half a day on a two-day trip, but fortunately our camels had grazed during the three days at Bāyir and would be able to make the journey without trouble. It was apparent, however, that R'Faifan and I would be on extremely short rations.

4

For two days the wind blew fiercely across the desert, from the north and west, and it was partly for this reason that we had delayed our departure from Bāyir. Our first stopping place was Jabal Quzima, a conical peak rising some 2,000 feet from the desert floor. The wind meanwhile showed no signs of decreasing, and there was a small gale blowing when we arrived at the base of the peak. It was from the north, and very cold.

"The winter is chasing us," R'Faifan told me with a wry smile.

We huddled in our tent, eating the last remnants of the stale biscuits and drinking tea—our only rations until we could reach Al Jafr sometime the following day.

The temperature had dropped to below freezing, and the

Wells of Bāyir: water drawn from ancient watering place, as it has been drawn for thousands of years on Eastern Desert.

Looking southward toward Al Jafr: Rʾaifan on his bull camel plodding down through the *wádi* north of the Desert Patrol outpost on the Eastern Desert.

chill wind whipping across the open desert seemed to drive the cold into our bones. The *wádi* along which we rode was an endless stretch of mud and sand, hard and flat as a tabletop, and in the distance the wind played tricks on our eyes, creating out of tumbling scrub bushes the semblance of houses in the distance. Even when we at last sighted the white walls of Al Jafr, I was not sure it was not a pile of tumbleweed blown against the banks of the *wádi*.

Al Jafr is an isolated encamplement far out in the Eastern Desert. Lawrence's vivid description of this place, which he called Jefer, was fixed in my mind: "We drove down the scrap to the Jefer flat, and skipped past it at sixty miles an hour . . . gazing back into the dappled waves of a mirage which streamed over the ground, a dark vapour below the pale sky, shifting a dozen times an hour . . . " It was like a weird city in the sky, balanced lightly on the shimmering desert haze that lies over the ground. As we approached the outpost, I thought of the odd contrast between the slow, plodding pace of the camel herder, driving his animals before him toward this remote desert oasis, and the swift approach of Lawrence, thundering across the dry Q'a Jafr valley in what may have been the first step in the later invasion of Western manners and methods into this outlying citadel.

The town itself consisted of the *badia* post and a prison compound, with a "government store" located in a particularly lush tract in the *wádi* about 4 kilometers to the north. Here the Jordanian government had built irrigation systems and established grain and hay farming in an effort to lure Bedouin off the desert into more agrarian pursuits. It was my observation that the project fell considerably short of success.

As R'Faifan and I rode down the *wádi* into the town, I observed the broken remnants of a mud-walled castle which the famed guerrilla leader Auda abu Tayi had built after the war and from which he held a brief feudal suzerainty over the

138

Howeitat tribes. The place was actually a kind of hunting lodge similar to those of the old Omayyad caliphs, and the chief recollections of Bedouin with whom I talked was that the place was more noted for its roistering parties, celebrating the overthrow of the Turks, than for any governing influence over the tribesmen. The two-story structure had crumbled in ruins, after the manner of certain low-cost housing projects in the United States.

During the two days at the *bait sha' ar* of Saud-Jazi I had been given a number of lessons in Arabic by my host; and in the ride from his camp to Al Jafr I had improved on this by constant exchanges in Arabic with R'Faifan, so that I now was fairly proficient in the minimum use of the language. Following our departure from Saud-Jazi's place, R'Faifan had insisted on changing my Bedouin name from Abu Ghaith to Abu Anz, which in free translation means Father of the Goat. This was undoubtedly due to the singular attraction I seemed to have for the goats who crowded into the tent to sleep with me.

As we approached Al Jafr from the northeast, R'Faifan called to me: "O Abu Anz!"

Since I had neither originated nor approved this new designation, I ignored his call; but he yelled even louder: "I have friends at the post, and we will be able to get out of this accursed storm."

I nodded. A sandstorm was now blowing so hard that I had to wrap my burnous across my face to keep the grains of sand from cutting my skin, and I had narrowed the aperture for my eyes to a slit. By this time my face was so blackened by the sun that only R'Faifan could have distinguished me from a Bedouin.

The mud flat over which we had been traveling was hard as cement, stretching for miles to the northeast and southwest, and along the bottom of the *wádi* as it passed through the corner of the town the trail was as smooth as a tabletop, beaten into an asphaltlike surface from the thousands of soft-footed camels that had passed this place. The tower of the *badia* fort, with the inevitable flag of the Jordanian Desert Patrol standing out stiffly in the wind, pointed out the location of the post.

In spite of the wind, the hot sun seemed to spread a layer of heat upon the dappled floor of the *wâdi*. We quickened the pace of our camels in order to reach the post as soon as possible. As we rode in, I noticed an atmosphere of festivity. There were streamers along the edge of the *badia* compound, and R'Faifan, leaning toward me and shouting against the wind, yelled that it was the feast of Id-al-Adha, the Moslem holiday marking the end of the month following the annual pilgrimage to Mecca. This is a sacred period among followers of the Prophet. It literally means the "end of the fast," and is not unlike the Jewish Passover or the Christian Easter following the period of Lent. It involves three days of uninterrupted feasting and celebration, and is a time when all Moslems devote themselves to uninhibited enjoyment of life.

The commandant came out to greet us, extending the usual warm hospitality we had encountered at all *badia* outposts, and in this case an officer of the Desert Patrol who spoke English joined us. He was administrator of the prison.

The commandant was a friendly fellow, and I soon found that the prisoners were equally agreeable. In that isolated place there seemed to be few barriers between men, and the prisoners—more than 70 of them—mingled freely with the troops of the patrol, performing chores cheerfully and apparently not even thinking about escape. There was a logical reason for this, of course; the wide, unending mud flats of Q'a Jafr surrounding the desert town contributed to this viewpoint, since it offered little encouragement in the way of an escape route. Any prisoner taking off across the desert would be easily caught.

There also seemed to be a strange fatalism among desert

140

prisoners. They appeared to have decided that having been sentenced to prison, it was the will of Allah and there was nothing to do but go through with the confinement—even if it was for life—with as little unpleasantness as possible. The English-speaking administrator told me there were seldom signs of trouble among the inmates. They accepted their lot as a kind of destiny they had no power to resist.

The lack of traffic through Al Jafr was quite noticeable. It was the time of year when the camel herders remained out on the desert, moving from winter to spring locations and grazing their livestock on such shrubbery as had grown up with the rains. In a month or so they would be moving farther into the desert for spring grazing and would only come into Al Jafr for such supplies as they needed in the endless circulation from one watering place to another.

Al Jafr itself was well supplied with water. It probably was located over an underground lake or streams that flowed below the hard, flat *wádi* in which the town was built, since there were numerous artesian wells that provided unlimited water. One of the *badia* offered some interesting information on this point; he had learned from R'Faifan of my plan to locate the old wells to the east, and he explained the simple geology of that region, in which flat surfaces extended in a kind of chain of dry lakes, southwestward from the Wádi Sirhan toward the great Nefud Desert.

The tribes that lived to the south and east—the Shammar, the Harb, the Mutair, and the 'Awazim—had circulated around parts of this chain for centuries, he said, each remaining within a loosely defined area, which was their tribal domain.

"Have they always lived in separate places?" I asked. The patrol rider nodded.

"Each tribe has its own watering places," he said. "They do not often cross into the land of another tribe."

This point interested me greatly. If the tribes circulated within their own areas, it might easily have been due to the breaking up of the ancient caravan route; and the most likely reason for this would have been that it was no longer necessary. I pondered over this. Certain roads crossed the Arabian plateau from east to west. The Al Batin road, for example, ran more than a thousand miles from Medina to Basra over the arid steppeland with only an occasional outpost, such as Buraida, Ajibba and Al Hafar. It was still used because there was commerce of a sort between Medina and Basra. The Moslem pilgrims followed this route from the lower lands of Iraq to Medina and southward to Mecca. But there were few such routes from north to south that did not ultimately end up at Medina and Mecca!

Why had the old camel route been abandoned? Probably because the reason for its existence—trade between the Hadhramaut Coast and Mesopotamia—no longer existed.

This was the basic purpose of my original plan to travel down into Saudi Arabia, through the lands of the Shammar tribes, heading eastward as far as possible toward the descending eastern coastal area, hoping that I might find in the habits and legends of the most remote tribes some evidence that the old line of wells was actually a desert highway, with some evidence of the existence of the old stopping places, perhaps desert caravansari or forts of an ancient patrol.

Were these early inhabitants of the desert a means of transport, who drove their camels northward from Arabia Felix to the Mesopotamian basin, loaded with costly silks and spices from Somalia and the Far East? Or were they suppliers along the way, who furnished water, food and camels for the actual travelers? There probably was no way of determining this, except by an examination of the ruins of caravansaries that served as way stations or forts along the ancient caravan route. Most of these probably would have been covered with sand or leveled by the winds that raged over the open desert.

It also seemed that nature and the rituals of the Moslem

faith conspired to give me ample time to ponder on this matter. The wind had continued to blow ever since we arrived at Al Jafr, immobilizing us at the fort; and the feast of Id-al-Adha continued to provide R'Faifan and me with uninterrupted eating. There was no end to the invitations to *mansefs* we received. Three members of the Desert Patrol—a sergeant and two corporals—who had left their families at their tribal homes to serve as *badia,* prevailed on us to spend a day at their mud-walled house, where they lived as bachelors. In addition to their own *mansef,* in which we had to join as a matter of courtesy, we were also invited to three other *mansefs,* which was like being invited to four Thanksgiving dinners on the same day!

I had reached the point where I felt that I was literally bursting: Although I had looked forward with some anticipation to release from our room at the fort, which seemed to catch all the eddies of sand blowing through the village, I reached such a degree of satiety from overeating, coupled with spasms of indigestion which I strove to conceal—since it would have been impolite to do more than belch occasionally—that I gave thanks to Allah when we finally staggered back into the fort late in the evening.

I reflected on the fact that only a few hours before, R'Faifan and I had been almost starving out on the desert, huddled under the lee of Jabal Quzima and nearly freezing as we drank tea brewed with brackish water and ate the last of our stale bread. It seemed that we had either a feast or a famine.

The wind continued to drive shifting veils of sand across the desert for two days, but it began to abate toward the end of the third day in Al Jafr, and we decided to start southward again. During the intervening hours I talked as extensively as my grasp of Arabic would permit with several of the Desert Patrol troops who knew this territory well. In addition to obtaining as much information as possible about the trail to various watering points, including the old railroad junction at Fasu'a and the location of a construction camp in that vicinity, now engaged in rebuilding the Hijaz-Medina railroad.

It is important to understand the topography of the Eastern Desert and its extension southward through the chain of deserts that form the Arabian Steppe. The entire plateau, possibly raised by a giant upheaval aeons ago, forms an elongated ridge of gravel and sand, at altitudes of some two or three thousand feet along a central ridge extending from the Syrian Desert (Bodiet esh Sham) down across the back of the Arabian Peninsula to the Indian Ocean. The littorals of the Persian Gulf in the east and the Red Sea in the west are lower than the central plateau, dropping off into the subsea level of the Jordan Rift and the Dead Sea, which form the line of faults that separate the desert from the Holy Land. Farther south on both sides of the central plateau, which actually consists of a chain of deserts —the Syrian and Eastern deserts, the Nefud, the Dahna and the Rab' el Kháli—are fertile coastal strips along the Red Sea on the west coast, and also on the east coast from Kuwait to the Trucial Coast and Muscat, the southeastern tip of Arabia.

Between these frames of fertility and population, the desert extends its mighty barrier to change: a vast domain covered with soft sand, gravel, and lava rocks with ridges swept bare by the winds. The Hijaz, lying along a higher line of mountains rimming the western side of the Peninsula, was the birthplace of Arab power in the seventh and eighth centuries. Medina and Mecca lie along this coastal area, where the *widyán* are watered and towns and villages are strung out along established roads. But the enduring existence of the true Arab, the Bedouin, was on the desert. There he passed centuries of changeless camel breeding and camel herding; his mind was not penetrated by alien injections from the rich lands of Africa and the Mediterranean, or from Persia and India, with which the peoples of the Hadhramaut Coast carried on their trade.

144

V. *Storm on the Desert*

1

The feast of Id-al-Adha lasted three days, and late in the third day R'Faifan and I sat in the cold guest room of the stone-walled *badia* fort and contemplated the prospect of heading out into the storm-swept desert. My Bedouin friend was sniffling and wiping his eyes, and I felt great pity for him. We had both contracted colds during that evening when we camped in the freezing wind at the base of Jabál Quzima, but my ailment was less severe than his. One of the prisoners had volunteered to provide medical aid, and upon my slight acquiescence he had raced to the dispensary and returned with every variety of pills in stock. His interest was so kindly and sincere that I felt obligated to swallow all of them, and as a result I had awakened the following morning completely cured of everything, including the indigestion I suffered from the multiple *mansefs* I had attended.

I might mention that the *badia* forts at Azraq and Al Jafr were almost identical: there was a wall surrounding a flagstone courtyard, with a watchtower at the right of the entrance gate

145

from which a considerable expanse of the surrounding desert could be seen. This parapet was not unlike the "blockhouse" outposts in the western United States, although I was never able to determine what they were watching from the watch-towers. There certainly were no Indians on the desert.

Along the walls were several small stone rooms, to the left of the gate; and in these were quartered the sergeant in command and the guests, such as R 'Faifan and myself. In the rear were the guardroom, water cistern, and storage room; and across the compound, under the barracks and the tower, was a combination kitchen and prison quarters. This might seem surprising, but it was logical: the prisoners performed most of the work in the cook shack. It was also handy for the sergeant, and for R 'Faifan and me, since we had constant attention from the inmates. This service was not compulsory; they seemed to enjoy serving us, as an outlet for what otherwise was a boring existence on the desert.

In spite of R 'Faifan's indisposition, it was necessary that we move on. My schedule was not fixed, but we had allotted a certain amount of time for each segment of the journey, and the three days at Bāyir and now at Al Jafr had cut into the time I had allocated for the journey from Azraq to Rumm.

"We must be ready to leave in the morning," I announced. R 'Faifan shrugged with resignation and sniffled audibly.

"As Allah wills," he said, and set about gathering our gear for an early departure. We had acquired sufficient supplies at Al Jafr, where the government store provided for all our immediate needs. The camels were well fed, watered, and rested.

Early the next morning we packed our supplies on the camels, climbed into the ornate saddles, and rode southward on the road to Rumm.

The sergeant in command of the post accompanied us to the edge of the village and indicated the direction of the trail we should follow to Fasu 'a. Beyond that were the red canyons of

Wádi Rumm, which lay some 80 kilometers beyond Al Jafr.

"Allah-i-'alaikum!" he called out as we rode off, which means loosely, "God be with you!"

As we left the little desert town, I felt again the pang of regret at leaving friends on the desert. Al Jafr in many ways was like one of the American frontier posts in the days of Indian warfare; it was an outpost where men led isolated lives, far from their families, and with no real tasks to perform unless some sort of fighting began—which was unlikely on the Eastern Desert.

South of Al Jafr the plateau of the desert slopes downward into the area of Bat'n al Ghūl and Rumm. The rim of this plateau is usually referred to as *Ra's an Naqb,* and riding toward it offers the astonishing sensation of riding *downward* toward a land of high mountains. That is because the floor of the desert below is actually cut away from the plateau, creating the kaleidoscope of color that makes this area one of the most magnificent in all Arabia.

I had traveled in this area many times, riding from the west as far as Al Jafr, but I had never traveled down this long, sloping plain into Rumm. This trail had been the main line of contact for Lawrence between the seaport link of Aqaba and the Bedouin tribes in the northeastern Jordan. It also may have been the route Moses took when he was driven back from the land of Canaan and forced to go around the land of Edom, turning out into the desert.

Whether Moses actually reached this part of the Eastern Desert over which R'Faifan and I were traveling on our camels is not easily determined from accounts in the Bible, and the Koran is even less explicit on that point. He apparently detoured from his first probe of Canaan, crossing Wádi Araba below the Dead Sea—which was where I wanted to go—evading hostile tribes until he reached Rabbath Ammon now the modern city of Ammän.

147

The route taken by Moses, however, was not material to my own purposes, and I did not worry about it. As R'Faifan and I jogged southward, the old spell of the desert came over me, I began to observe weird shapes on the horizon, strange trailings of vapor blown across the flat surface like strung-out, ghostly creations, and the red and purple spires of rock that rise sheer from the gray, mottled plain.

We had left Al Jafr on the day before Good Friday, a meaningless day to the Bedouin, and headed southwestward toward the little station at Fasu'a, from which the old roadbed of the Hijaz-Medina railroad curves westward toward Ma'ān, where it connects with the modern trunk line from Aqaba to Ammān and Damascus. R'Faifan was still suffering from a cold contracted during the night when we huddled under the scant shelter of Jabál Quzima before riding into Al Jafr. I seemed to have shaken off my affliction, largely due to the heavy doses of medication I had received from the prisoners at the fort, but Bedouin are more seriously affected by disorders of this sort. I looked with great sympathy at his thin face, almost concealed by the folds of his *kaffiyah*, as he shivered under the inevitable tuxedo jacket he wore over his robe.

Shortly after noon we topped a bare, windswept ridge and saw a *bait sha'ar* lying snugly against the mottled hillside. It was the tent of Sheikh Mufleh, and it was our first stopping place, since leaving the old Ruwalla tribesman, where R'Faifan did not know our host. However, this made little difference. Sheikh Mufleh came out in his flowing robes, greeting us warmly and welcoming us into his tent as if we were relatives or old friends. The hospitality of the desert was immediately extended to us, as to all strangers, and when we told him the purpose of our journey—to look for traces of the legendary Lawrence of Arabia in the regions where he had ridden and fought with Arab tribesmen 50 years ago—he raked his memory for recollections that might help us.

It is an odd characteristic of the Bedouin that they will even create aneodotes to provide a guest with things he wants to hear; I recall a later incident in which a *sheikh* in the area north of Rumm led me on a wild-goose chase all day looking for a cave in which he said Lawrence had hidden, near an ancient Nabataean castle, and of course neither the cave nor the castle existed, as I found out later. This was not a matter of duplicity or deceit; the *sheikh* was simply anxious to confirm my own expectations as a matter of hospitality.

Sheikh Mufleh insisted we remain for luncheon, and since this lasted well into the afternoon, he invited us to spend the night in his tent. It was not one of the better *buyút sha'ar* on the desert, and the *sheikh*'s flocks were scanty, but he killed one of his young camels and we were treated to a feast of camel meat! It was actually the first time I had tasted it, and it seemed to be something like strong beef.

While we lounged on the inevitable stacks of pillows in the *raba'a,* Sheikh Mufleh ransacked his thoughts for things he had heard about Lawrence, particularly from his father, who apparently had fought with Auda abu Tayi in the Arab Revolt. Finally, unable to dredge up anything specific or even concoct credible information, he brought his son, a boy of fifteen or sixteen, into the men's compartment to sing for us and recite Arab poetry!

I had recorded some of the *sheikh*'s stories on a tape recorder, which I had in my gear. This delighted our host, and he suggested I also record his son's poetry, which I did.

The Bedouin's acceptance of electronics as a matter of course, rather than regarding it as a modern intrusion into their ancient way of life, is one of the paradoxes of the desert that I cannot explain. It merely conforms with their simple directness in most things; the radio or the tape recorder is a fact of life which they never bother to dispute. Every *bait sha'ar,* including the most humble, has its radio and gets its newscasts from

Ammān. Most of these operate on batteries, which can be procured at the nearest *badia* post.

During the evening, as we squatted around the fire pit drinking interminable cups of coffee, I listened to Sheikh Mufleh's tales of hunting and fighting, and also to his son's poetry and singing of Arabic songs. Poetry and song, which is so deep in the life of desert Arabs that they would seem almost naked without it, is a special language for the Bedouin. It has been pointed out that the Arabic language lends itself to poetic expression, but perhaps the reverse is true: poetry lends itself to the temperament of the Bedouin.

Once during the evening I was startled to find myself thrust back into the present. The *sheikh*'s son had been reciting poetry with surprising feeling, and even passion, and I felt myself transported into the past again, as if I were on the fringe of an ancient world, when Sheikh Mufleh suddenly glued his ear to the radio. From a few scattered words of Arabic I understood that there were more reports of border skirmishes, such as I had heard in Ammān. At the end of the newscast he snapped his fingers, and I had the impression that he was more deeply concerned than he would like to admit, although he offered no comment on the matter.

R'Faifan was nursing his cold and did not appear deeply interested, so I refrained from asking questions. There is a delicate balance of social and psychological sensitivity in the relations of the Bedouin host to his guests that requires questions not be asked or matters discussed unless the host indicates a desire to do so. This is a form of politeness that might be of considerable use in the Western world.

The following morning as we rode across the desert toward Shedia, where we expected to make our first contact with the old railroad line, I asked R'Faifan if there was anything important in the news given over the radio. He shrugged and seemed unwilling to say anything, so I did not press the matter.

However, that afternoon we reached the railroad line and found a construction camp under the charge of an English engineer, Doug Manson, who supplied some interesting information.

He had recently been to Ma'ān, which was a main junction point in the north-south trails to the west of our route; and he said there was a good deal of concern over threats that had recently been made by President Nasser of Egypt to close the Strait of Tiran at the mouth of the Gulf of Aqaba in order to isolate the Negev.

"Trouble seems to be moving closer to us all the time," he said, shaking his head. "I do not like it, but of course it may not bother us this far out."

He became quite cheerful after a few minutes and showed me around the construction camp, which was located just north of Shedia, a small outpost on the desert which had once been the dividing point between trails that turned northeast over the Eastern Desert and the line of the railroad which the Turks had built from Medina to Ma'ān, where it connected with the main line between Damascus and Aqaba.

I was quite interested in Doug Manson's impressions of the Bedouin. He seemed to have an intuitive understanding of their feelings, and the laborers on the railroad bed appeared to be quite satisfied to be working under an Englishman. The construction project was largely to rebuild the railroad stations at Shedia and Fasu'a so that when the railroad was put into service again—if it ever was to be restored—there would be stations on the desert. It seemed rather hopeless to me, but he looked upon it with good-natured optimism.

"I'm riding into Ma'ān tomorrow," he said. "Stick around— I'll see you when I get back."

Doug Manson returned from Ma'ān the next afternoon, and we spent another night at the construction camp. Manson had received some definite news from the outside world, replacing rumors I had gathered over the past few weeks on the desert.

Ma'ān was linked to Ammān by telephone, and he told me: "There is some trouble brewing along the border. I'm not sure what it's all about, but whatever it is, it won't be good for my job." He spoke in a clipped, laconic tone, characteristic of Englishmen. I assumed he meant the Jordanian government might have uses for its available funds other than rebuilding an obsolete railroad. The construction camp itself was an odd combination of energy and indifference. The energy was supplied by Manson, but the activities—or lack of them—were largely the result of Bedouin indifference to both time and space.

The cook shack formed the center of the camp, and it was usually occupied. Near it were Manson's office and quarters, and along the roadbed were the tents of Bedouin workers. A bulldozer at the side of the roadbed did not seem to be in operation. As a matter of fact, nothing seemed to be in operation. It was another monument to the determination of the government to push forward in a pattern of progress against the insuperable obstacle of the inertia of an unchanging people.

I deeply sympathized with Doug Manson. He was trying to move the wheels of progress in a land that had known almost no progress for 5,000 years! As we pulled out the next morning and I waved to Doug Manson, I almost caught myself saying: "Carry on, old boy!"

2

We had been pushing ahead slowly for two days across the dry, sloping plateau, following a faint trail that twisted downward roughly parallel to the tracks of the old railroad, although we would not reach it again until Fasu'a, where there was an abandoned railroad station. I felt the cold rain against my back and noticed that R'Faifan turned now and then to cast a worried look in my direction. My cold had troubled me during the night at the construction camp, and in the morning it became worse, so I imagined at first that this was the object of R'Faifan's concern. I soon realized, however, that he was looking beyond me. I turned in my saddle and observed black clouds banking on the horizon. We had come through bad weather before, but this looked more ominous than anything I had previously seen.

Up to this point, the desert had been soundless except for the steady clop-clop of the camels. Now and then R'Faifan let loose an eerie scream, which was his way of communicating with his camel. It sounded like a cross between the skirl of a bagpipe and the shrill squeal of a professional hog caller. Apparently the camel understood, because at each scream, the ungainly animal quickened its stride for a moment or two, and then imperceptibly fell back into the same slow, rhythmic gait. Like everything else in this unchanging world, the lumbering camel refused to respond permanently to anything resembling the influence of civilization.

I had been thinking: How can anything happen in a world where there is no noise? The plateau, which led down toward an ancient caravan trail through Wádi Rumm was utterly silent. The tracks spread out over many individual courses, as Arab trails always do, imprinting a wide swath of faint marks on the desert floor.

There was still a nagging thought in my mind, put there by Doug Manson's last words the night he returned from Ma'ān, when he had told me quietly that there was "real trouble brewing in the west." His calmness and lack of alarm was characteristic of Englishmen in the Middle East, and it worried me more than it reassured me. It seemed to be a continuation of the rumors I heard in Ammān and the roaring of the jet planes R'Faifan and I had observed at Bāyir.

It may have been a subconscious resistance to this troubling notion that made me wonder now anything could happen in a world where there was no natural sound. Perhaps in further

153

response to this thought, I suddenly yelled at my companion: "R'Faifan! For heaven's sake, say something!"

R'Faifan turned, his dark, thin face split in a grin. His white teeth were in contrast to his black eyes, which flashed from the recess of his cowl-like *kaffiyah*. I also noticed that the lapels of the tuxedo jacket gleamed in a sudden slant of sunlight through the clouds. R'Faifan seemed about to accommodate me with a responsive scream, when another noise, like the thunder of damnation, burst upon my ears.

I glanced back again at the ominous clouds. Things were beginning to happen. Within a few seconds the stillness of the air was shattered with a violence that took me by surprise. Almost without warning, except for thunder, the sky opened up—as if in reply to my request for noise. It literally vomited its fury upon us. The rain came down in sheets, engulfing us so that it was not possible to see more than 50 yards ahead.

R'Faifan brought his camel close to mine and yelled into my ear: "We must get out of this. Where is the station?"

We had been heading toward the abandoned railroad station, located somewhere out on the desert beside the ruined tracks of the old Hijaz-Medina railroad. I knew the small, stone station was somewhere in the vicinity, since I had passed it years before on a journey into the Rumm area, but this was to the west of our present route. I also realized it would offer the only hope of shelter from the rising fury of the storm. However, I did not know its exact location, any more than R'Faifan did. I shook my head.

R'Faifan nodded, his mouth cracking in a quick smile, as if to assure me that he would produce the station. The storm had come up suddenly and was completely unexpected. There had been cold rain on the desert, but no intimation of this violence. It was quite possible that we were at least a day's ride from the station, and as I learned later, the storm was one of the worst in the memory of any Bedouin.

154

A storm on the desert is always a frightening experience. It swirls across the flat plain, sweeping sand and water with it. The lash of the torrent and the sting of grit in the air is enough to drive any sense of direction out of the mind, and even the bare instinct for survival can be lost in the confusion. Human beings, and even camels, are tiny bits of wind-whipped debris. Since we had been riding downward toward the rim of Ras'an Naqb, there was also the possibility that we would be blown over a cliff into one of the steep-walled canyons that fringe the northern border of the Arabian Steppe.

I realized that our hope of lasting out the storm without being literally demolished by it lay in finding shelter; and neither of us had any reasonable notion of the direction in which shelter was to be found. The rain quickly changed to sleet, and we were being driven along in a blizzard. The wind was from the north, and therefore behind us, so we hunched our backs against its mounting fury, keeping our camels as close together as possible.

The two animals continued their methodical gait, swaying through the semidarkness. They did not appear to be affected by the wind and the sleet, merely bobbing their heads a little lower to avoid the full impact of the wind, and since we had no idea of the direction to take, we gave them their heads. Even after the first violence of the rain, which had now become sleet and snow, we could not see more than a quarter of a mile ahead. Except for the instinctive sense of direction which camels have, we might have been traveling in a circle.

We had been plodding ahead for perhaps an hour when R'Faifan reached out and jerked at my robe, which was flapping in the wind like a loose Genoa jib. He seemed to be motioning for me to stop.

He put his face close to my ear and screamed: "We must walk ahead of the camels! We cannot ride!"

155

At first I thought he was trying to relieve the burden for the camels, which seemed a bit ridiculous, and I wondered if he was losing his mind. However, I soon realized the logic of his suggestion. The camels were able to withstand the buffeting wind and sleet and would form a windbreak for us. We clambered down and continued on foot, leading the camels. The freezing blasts raked us with gusts that at times seemed about to sweep us off the ground, but we clung to the saddle straps and plodded onward in what I fervently hoped was the direction of the old station.

Finally, after another hour which seemed an eternity, we almost stumbled over a strip of rusted rail. I gripped R'Faifan's shoulder.

"It is the old railroad!" I shouted. I doubt that he heard me, but he saw the short length of twisted rail at the same time I did and stooped to feel it, as if to determine whether it was real.

It might be mentioned that the old road had been torn up by Lawrence and his Arab raiders only in sections, with scattered rails left along the roadbed to rust away in the desert. This fragmenting of the railroad was Lawrence's tactical method of destroying the supply line but still keeping alive the Turks' hopes of rebuilding it. Lawrence, by his own account, deliberately wrecked parts of the roadbed and left other parts intact. This may have been shrewd strategy on his part, but it left R'Faifan and me adrift in the storm without any real clue as to the direction in which the rails ran; and this was our only hope of finding the abandoned station.

However, after crossing the apparent line of the railroad and recrossing it, we found several other rails and were soon able to plot a general line of direction.

We plodded onward, keeping track of the scattered rails as well as we could. Several times we seemed to have lost this bare marking on the desert, and at these moments the thought struck me that the roadbed would soon be skirting the precipice that fell away into the canyons of Bat'n al Ghūl, a name meaning ghoul's belly. If we should miss the old railroad station, we would have to stay close to the roadbed to avoid being blown off the cliffs into the deep gorges below the rim of the plateau. Each time we lost contact with the roadbed, marked only by intermittent rails that seemed to have been flung upon the desert at random, we crisscrossed the area warily until we found another rail.

By this slow, laborious process we moved onward, apparently hopelessly lost in the storm. Conversation between us had ceased, and R'Faifan no longer screamed at the camels. As I watched his round, white head, covered by a *kaffiyah* lashed to his skull with a brown *agál* and bobbing in rhythmic unison with each step, I began to feel a numbness, like mesmerism, creeping into my senses. This frightened me, and I slapped my face to keep my mind and senses alert. I had been in raging sandstorms before and was not unused to the unbridled force of the wind and sand sweeping across the desert, but this was worse than anything I had ever encountered. I began to wonder how long R'Faifan and I could hold out without finding some shelter or being battered into insensibility by the storm.

We had been pushing with our heads down for perhaps five hours, stopping only to get down on our hands and knees and crawl over the ground to find traces of the dissected railroad, when suddenly R'Faifan shouted. I looked up. In the driving sleet ahead I could make out the dim shape of what seemed to be a mound or hut. We stumbled ahead, and within a few seconds the shape became distinct. I screamed back at R'Faifan; it was the abandoned railroad station!

The sight of human habitation—even the remnants of some former occupancy—is always welcome on the desert; but in this case the vague lump of man-made creation, even without the aspect of organic life, was like harbor lights to a distressed

157

ship. We struggled forward, almost dragging the camels after us.

As we neared the dimly outlined station, which actually was a stone hut that had been badly battered by desert storms for half a century, we saw a moving figure.

"Someone is at the station!" I called out to R'Faifan. I could see his head bob. There is seldom any danger of attack from strangers on the desert, and in this storm it would be senseless. We approached the station without fear.

There were two people at the station, an old man, who came through the door to motion to us to come in, and a young boy, who crouched behind him. As I later discovered, this was the old man's son, a youth of about twenty.

"*Mabruk!*" he called out—It is written! His cracked voice could hardly be heard above the whistling wind. He held out his hands. "*Inshalla!*"

It was so typically Bedouin that I smiled, in spite of my misery. The old man helped us get the camels in the lee of the stone house, and we went inside. His simple remark was characteristic of the Bedouin. Man does not control his life or nature; all happens as Allah wills. Rain—even the blizzard, which had almost destroyed us out on the Ra's an Naqb—was part of the eternal passage of time, as Allah willed it. It is an old Arab saying that "rain will fall, pastures will spring up, our sheep will become fat."

As we followed the old man and his son into the warmth of the stone house, I listened to his exchange of characteristic phrases with R'Faifan: "*As salám 'alaikum!*"—Peace be with you! When the old man poured tea from the bubbling kettle, R'Faifan said, "*Salám ideek!*—Blessed be your hands!

We soon found out that the old man was the official keeper of the station, and his duties—for which he was paid about $15 a month—consisted of visiting the place occasionally to check on its condition. He had been on one of these official rounds when the storm struck earlier that day, and he expressed gratitude

158

to us—as well as to Allah—for our visit. He indicated this was a very fortunate thing for him, as he now had people with whom he could talk. I assured him it was fortunate for us also. We had a house to crawl into.

3

We learned from the old man that there was a great movement of pilgrims northward from Mecca and also refugees were leaving the border areas and traveling toward the central and northern parts of Jordan. He said there were many on the King's Highway, west of Ma'ān.

"At first I believed you were refugees," he said in Arabic. "In any case, you would have been welcome."

The old man had seen us before we sighted the station and had quickly built up the fire which had been smoldering at the rear of the room, piling on bits of brush and a few chips of camel dung. After caring for the camels as well as we could, we huddled around the fire, chattering explanations of who we were and why we were there.

The old Bedouin had put on a kettle for tea—the inevitable Arab greeting to strangers—and we dug into our saddle bags for some tins of bully beef and flour. R'Faifan poured water into the flour and soon had bread cooking on the fire. The four of us squatted around the blaze, the old man proffering bits of food before he or his son would touch any.

With hot bread and bully beef and tea we made a feast of it. Meanwhile R'Faifan had quickly established that curious relationship which seems to be like a sixth sense among Bedouin. The old man talked quite volubly about himself and his official position as keeper of the station. He had been on his way toward Shedia and Ma'ān; he and his son had stopped at the station on the routine checkup, in order to justify his pension, when the storm caught them. He explained in some

159

detail the trust and obligation imposed upon him by the "government" at Al Jafr, which was actually only an outpost of the Jordanian Desert Patrol.

That night the wind howled mercilessly around the stone walls of the station, battering it with a mixture of snow and sleet and mud! Desert storms are unlike any other forms of natural violence, except perhaps a volcano which pours molten lava upon the earth. As I huddled in the little station, I gave thanks to Allah that we were warm and safe. I also worried considerably about our camels. My own mount—the *nága,* or female—had been obstinate and unruly, and I was often compelled to kick her in the stomach to make her move. But now I felt a strange compassion for the animal, stubborn as she was. And R'Faifan's castrated bull, who was larger and more able to absorb the buffeting of the wind, also aroused my sympathy. I observed, as I peered through the door now and then, that he stared balefully at me in the flickering light from the fire inside the stone walls.

Both animals were humped against the wind, and since there was nothing I could do for them, and there was no likelihood that we would invite them to share the inside of the station, I returned to my blanket. R'Faifan, who had been watching me, uttered a short grunt.

"Do not worry, little brother," he mumbled. "They will be there in the morning. They have no better place to go."

This seemed to be philosophical, and logical. When morning came, R'Faifan was right; the camels were still there. I was impressed by the enormous stamina of these animals. Nothing seemed to dent their capacity for lumbering along, mile after mile, usually without water and for long stretches without food.

During the next two days the blizzard continued to rage across the plateau that extends from below the Syrian border along the eastern part of Jordan almost to the border of Saudi

Arabia. The Ra's an Naqb, over which we were traveling, descends gradually toward a cliff, or escarpment, that drops away into the mountainous area east of the great Wádi Rumm, where Lawrence headquartered. It was near Rumm, a scattered encampment of goat-hair tents surrounding a square mud-walled fort, that Lawrence had taken the short ride "straight up the gully into the face of the hill" and found a fresh spring, with water gushing from the mountainside into a pool near the ruins of an old Nabataean conduit.

I knew that below the old railroad station where we had taken refuge from the storm, the cliffs dropped for perhaps 1,000 feet or more into a broad valley of Bat'n al Ghūl. I had traveled this far on journeys made earlier from the southwest corner of Jordan, which is easily accessible on the King's Highway. But I had not previously crossed the Eastern Desert, and I had no idea where the old railroad began its descent into the valley. However, I was not anxious to attempt to find this precipitous route down into the valley floor in the midst of a storm, with the wind blowing behind us.

Meanwhile, I wanted to talk with the old watchman. He had a radio tucked among his duffle, and he told me he had heard over the radio before we arrived that this was the worst blizzard in many years and warnings had been issued in Desa and Guweira, two villages to the west, and even at the city of Aqaba on the Gulf, which was 100 miles southwest of the old station.

We managed to drive the camels out in the storm to forage from the scant vegetation around the stone station, but although camels will eat almost anything, they cannot eat rocks—and they returned still looking hungry. We fed them the last of the grain which we carried with us in saddlebags and settled down to await the cessation of the storm.

The old man continued to listen to his radio from time to time; while I was able to speak some Arabic, I was not proficient enough to understand the crackling noises that came

161

over the air. I was dependent on the old watchman's reports, and on the second morning he said to R'Faifan, who repeated his words to me: "I have understood you and the little brother are traveling to Guweira, and thence to the Wádi Araba."

I nodded and explained through R'Faifan that I wanted to go into the land where Moses had led his people. I was not certain whether the old man would know who Moses was, although he is mentioned frequently in the Koran. But he nodded.

"Musa!" he exclaimed. I wondered if he thought I intended to meet Moses in Wádi Araba, although I made no comment on this. The old man's perception was probably a bit rusty with age, and I felt it would only confuse matters if I tried to explain why I was going to a place where a man had traveled with his followers more than 3,000 years ago! R'Faifan meanwhile was aware of my embarassment, and he grinned at me.

Suddenly the old man said: "The *malak* is about to bite the devil!"

Malak means king, and I assumed he was talking about King Hussein. The remark made very little sense to me, until R'Faifan leaned over and whispered in English: "He is trying to tell you there may be trouble in Wádi Araba."

Since this probably had to do with the border skirmishes I had heard about in Ammān, I thought instantly of Doug Manson's remark about things "brewing up" in the west. The old man continued to watch me with sharp eyes, and I decided to let the matter drop for the moment. However, later in the evening I asked R'Faifan if the old man's remarks were based on gossip or information he had received over the radio. While our journey into Wádi Araba was not essential to the investigation of Lawrence, I wanted very badly to make the trip.

R'Faifan, apparently sensing my frustration, chose this moment to become mysterious. Most Bedouin seem instinctively to perceive the confusion or uncertainty of another, and they usually turn this to their own psychological profit, as if discomfiture of a foreigner—or even a guest—somehow established their greater prestige. When R'Faifan merely shrugged and said, *"Inshalla!"* I gave it up.

Later R'Faifan, apparently repenting of his effort to befuddle me, confided that the old man had undoubtedly heard reports that the border might be closed at Guweira. However, he added that since all things are as Allah wills, Allah might well choose to have the border open when we arrived there.

4

During the next two days I gave little thought to the old man's words. R'Faifan, squatting in front of the fire with his battered tuxedo drawn around him, kept things cheerful with the unfailing good humor that is the mark of the Bedouin disposition. I found more interest in listening to his talk with the old station keeper than in troubling myself over the political situation in Jordan.

The storm continued to howl across the plateau, battering the old station with such force that the walls seemed to shake. When I peered through the narrow door to look at the camels, huddled under the lee of the stone hut, I was almost moved by pity to invite them in. R'Faifan assured me this would be nonsensical. While the livestock were often brought into the larger *bait sha'ar,* segregated from the human inhabitants, the stone station offered no such exclusion—and it also provided no ventilation.

Now and then, when I looked out at the two forlorn animals, my *nága* gazed at me morosely from heavy-lidded eyes and appeared to be sneering at me for not stopping the wind. The old Bedouin's camel, partly hidden under an outcropping of rock behind the station, apparently was impervious to the storm, and R'Faifan's denatured bull hardly noticed me. The female, however, as if by an instinct peculiar to her sex, seemed to blame me for the whole business.

By the end of the third night in the station the wind had abated, and the morning dawned clear and cool, exactly right for traveling. Normally three days is the limit of hospitality that is expected of any Bedouin, but in this case we were not exactly guests of the old station keeper, and the storm presented an additional reason for remaining until it stopped, so R'Faifan and I did not feel we had overstayed our welcome.

The old man was profuse, however, in begging us to stay. When I explained, aided by R'Faifan, that we must continue toward Guweira to find out whether the trail to Wádi Araba was closed, he shook his head disconsolately, and then stated that he and his son were also leaving, heading north. He had been on his way to Ma'ān when the storm struck the station, and he indicated that he and the boy would continue on their way.

We said good-bye after the old man had prepared a final pot of coffee, and a short time later we were heading down toward the rim of the Wádi Bat'n al Ghūl. The edge of the plateau was only a couple of kilometers from the railroad station, and the sheer drop into the great valley below was rather startling, particularly when I realized we might have reached the rim during the storm in the darkness of night. The old roadbed followed a comparatively straight course down across the plateau from Ma'ān, where it formerly connected with the main line toward Ammān and Damascus. The old railroad passed through Shedia, and we had picked it up in the storm only a few miles south of that place. We would undoubtedly have followed it down toward the desert and might have been blown off the rim by the terrific force of the wind if we had not found the abandoned station.

The magnificent expanse of reddish desert became visible

as soon as we reached the rim. The roadbed could be discerned on a narrow, twisting defile, descending along the contours of a razorback ridge until it reached the valley floor. It was only a few miles from the rim, where we began our descent, to the base of the curved cliffs that surrounded the valley, but the drop was about 2,000 feet. I wondered how the antique engines of the old railroad could have made it up the grade.

We did not follow the roadbed, finding it easier for the camels to travel along the gullies, or arroyos, rather than on the ridge. As we rode along, the desert unfolded in a soul-stirring spectacle. Across the wide sweep of the valley numerous columns of sheer rock rose from the floor of the desert. They took every conceivable shape, some in crenellated columns that looked like battlements, rising hundreds of feet into the air; others in conical shapes, with striated layers of colored rock that looked as if they had been fashioned by hand. In the distance the towering *jabál* rose against a backdrop of hazy mountains; the spectrum of colors, with layers of pink and saffron, blue and scarlet and purple, melting into distant peaks, resembled a mighty mural against distant mountains and the blue sky. Comparison with the fantastic desert scenes of New Mexico and Arizona was inevitable; yet I believe nothing in the world can quite compare with the splendor of the Eastern Desert as it drops off toward the edge of the Arabian Steppe. The mountainous area actually is lower than the plateau, as if one had come upon a sunken panorama of a strange new world that lay below us while we jogged down toward the desert floor.

At the bottom of the narrow ridge we rode out across wide patches of *ghôr*, the Arabic term for the flat surface of the desert floor. Between the edge of the desert, at our feet, and the *jabál* that rose in the misty distance was a small dark splotch, which R'Faifan identified at the *bait sha'ar* of an old Bedouin who lived with his family in this lonely place In fact, his place was the "village" of Bat'n al Ghūl.

"He has the only teahouse in the desert," the station keeper had told us, with a dry crackle. I found that the old man was right. The Bedouin who lived there sold cups of tea to travelers. His price was the equivalent of about three cents a cup, and the outlook for business seemed bleak in this apparently untraveled spot.

R'Faifan quickly set me right on this point, however.

"He has lots of trade," he said. "During the times of pilgrimages many people pass this way. Many arrive in buses."

This seemed to be an exaggeration, but I quickly found that R'Faifan was right. As we rode across the *ghôr*, our camels' feet padding softly on the hardened surface, I spotted in the distance a rising cloud which at first seemed to be one of the sporadic whirlwinds that twist across the desert. But I soon realized that it was caused by a large number of buses, roaring across the flat *wâdi* like some weird desert charge in a demented De Mille spectacular. The last thing I expected to see in this remote region was a cavalcade of buses.

For several hours they careened across the unmarked desert floor, carrying hundreds of pilgrims, some bound for as far away as Yugoslavia, others to Damascus, Iraq, and Iran. Since there was no road, each bus traveled as best suited the driver, and how they avoided collisions I would never be able to understand. It was as if scores of rocking buses and trucks had been turned loose on a vastly widened New Jersey Turnpike, with no lanes or fences to guide their courses.

As R'Faifan explained to me, this was an old camel trail from Saudi Arabia northward; indeed, I could readily believe I had come upon the great overland road from Arabia Felix to Damascus and Tadmor, except that the modern form of transportation was infinitely faster and a great deal more dangerous. As the caravan wound its way up the narrow ridge, the buses miraculously converged into a single line that crawled toward the rim of the plateau and disappeared into the hazy distance.

At one point we passed a lonely grave, where some pilgrim had failed to make the return journey from Mecca and was buried in the desert as a *shahūd,* or martyr, his last earthly rest marked only by a small pile of stones. As we rode past the columns of buses, I wondered how many pilgrims, riding on slow, swaying camels or afoot, had passed this way in the 13 centuries since Mohammed had directed the first pilgrimages to Mecca.

The route across the Wádi Bat'n al Ghūl was actually a shortcut from the great caravan trails along the central part of Arabia, connecting at Ma'ān with the King's Highway, and it occurred to me that perhaps it would be better suited to the purpose of my expedition if we continued southward to explore the highlands toward Mudawwara, on the Saudi Arabian border. However, I had been virtually forbidden to travel that route, having no passport, and I decided it would be best to continue westward to Rumm and find out what was happening in the west.

As we approached the tiny hamlet, I saw that it consisted of a small two-pole tent and a sheet-metal shack, with a lean-to awning in front. It was in this somewhat dilapidated desert café that the old Bedouin sold cups of tea to his irregular trade of desert travelers. In spite of the scrubby atmosphere of the place, our welcome was assured. Even in such a commercial establishment, a guest—known as a *tha' if,* which sounds almost like "thief"—is assured of welcome. He seldom offers payment for a night's rest—and none would be accepted—but he must perform customary acts of courtesy by not soliciting an invitation.

The old Bedouin, who had been busy serving tea to the pilgrims, came forth personally to welcome us. It was obvious

167

that we could not share his tent, which was smaller than the three-pole tent the more prosperous Bedouin set up. The shack near the tent was useful only for brewing and serving tea, and it was our intention to establish our own camp wherever the old Bedouin should invite us to place it. The single *q'ata,* dividing curtain, separated the men's end of the Bedouin's tent from the place occupied by his wife. We did not see his spouse at first, since she remained inside, and when she finally appeared briefly, her face was veiled. But the old Arab's children gathered around us, watching with dark, curious eyes that were like black beads in their sunburned faces. R'Faifan and I accepted the gracious offer of hospitality, even though we knew his *bait sha'ar* was too small to accommodate us. We began unloading our camels, R'Faifan explaining in Arabic, with gestures, that we were traveling westward toward Rumm.

Bat'n al Ghūl was actually a crossroads on the old trail from the Hijaz, one branch turning westward toward Guweira and the other northward toward Ma'ān, the principal junction on the Turkish railroad system. The roadbed itself crossed our trail about a mile north of the old Bedouin's teahouse, after curving downward along the descending ledge from the rim of the great valley. There were piles of stone that once had been an old railroad station a short distance southward. Oddly enough, some Bedouin with an offbeat sense of humor had planted a handmade railroad crossing sign where the trail ran over the roadbed, although no trains had passed that way for half a century.

Behind us, to the east, rose the gray sandstone mountain that flanked the desert; and directly across to the west was the tall spire of Jabal Bat'n al Ghūl, rising directly from the desert floor to a height of perhaps 2,000 feet. The trail over which the buses had come charging down upon the tiny oasis— which was actually nothing more than a watering hole, filled by artesian water—faded away in the direction of Mudawwara, on the border of Saudi Arabia; and the trail westward curved through the red portals of the valley into the Wádi Rumm, some 30 or 40 kilometers beyond.

The red cliffs surrounding the valley were familiar to me, even though I had not been this far to the east before. The entire sunken region below the Ra's an Naqb, which rims the southern edge of the Eastern Desert, is similar in its contours and colors, extending from the western walls of Rumm for more than 100 miles eastward to the canyons beyond Bat'n al Ghūl, a tangled, illogical array of crimson gorges lined with mountains that from a distance look like purple drapery. We went into the little shack, where the Bedouin served tea, and when I offered to pay for it, he glared at me as if I had insulted him. At first I thought I had committed some irretrievable blunder in manners, but R'Faifan, who seemed to sense my indiscretions with the sharpness of a psychologist, or at least a politician, assured me that the desert tavernkeeper was not offended but merely wanted to show his sense of hospitality and perhaps his gratitude at our having stopped at his place.

During the evening I chatted with the old man, hoping to find out what strange motives caused him to remain in this isolated place, but his answers were neither responsive nor logical, so I assumed he either thought it was none of my business or did not want to explain his self-imposed exile from even the rudimentary society of the desert.

We set up our small camp near the café, warming tins of bully beef and brewing tea while the old Bedouin bustled about, offering us goat's milk from the ill-fed creatures he kept in his place, and clucking and crackling in a stream of disconnected Arabic, of which I caught only fragmentary bits of sense. We went over to his shack for evening coffee, out of politeness, and this time he graciously accepted the few pennies I offered, which left me even more confused as to the practices of desert etiquette.

169

He offered to make room for us to sleep in his tent, but since he was more of a tavern keeper than a nomad, I did not feel that the normal rules of desert hospitality should apply.

He was an interesting old fellow, with a small, wizened face, scarred by years under the glaring sun. His eyes, peering from the folds of the *kaffiyah* wrapped around his skull with a ragged *agál,* seemed sharp and intelligent as he talked, and I wondered again why anyone of even minimum sense would have chosen this remote spot as a place of business. His hands were gnarled and thin, with long fingers and a rather unexpected gracefulness to their movements as he gestured to emphasize his words. I had the feeling that he might easily have been one of the mysterious creatures out of *The Arabian Nights* and may have known more of the secrets of this desert than I would have suspected.

In fact, I would not have been surprised if R'Faifan, who understood these things better than I, had leaned over and confided in me that the old man had lived in this place since the times when camel caravans passed by carrying spices and incense from Arabia Felix to Damascus and Tadmor!

Later, as we sat around our fire, R'Faifan did tell me that the old man was of the Bani-Atiyah tribes, who ranged along the southern border of Jordan, and it occurred to me that we were now passing beyond the range of R'Faifan's social expertise into strange and unfamiliar country. I was not at all certain whether R'Faifan, in spite of his wide acquaintance in the north, would know many of the people along the border.

VI. *Ghosts of Wádi Rumm*

1

The wild complex of colored gorges, marked by pillars of sandstone that rise like dusty sentinels from the floor of the painted deserts surrounding Wádi Rumm, is in many respects—both geographically and historically—one of the most fascinating parts of the Arabian Peninsula. Charles Montagu Doughty, an early Western writer on Arabia, called these red-walled canyons "the brow of Syria."

The deep rifts in the steppeland spread out from R'as an Naqb, the southern rim of the Eastern Desert, down to the border of Saudi Arabia, forming a link between the northern and southern segments of Arabia. There are many camel trails, some marked and others only faintly discernible on the sacred surface of the *ghôr* (mud flats), but two main trails run across this area in somewhat parallel courses north and south, about 100 kilometers apart at the lower ends. One is the main route southward from Ma'ān, passing the old man's teahouse in Bat'n al Ghūl and continuing to Mudawwara on the Jordan-Saudi Arabian border and onward for 600 miles over the

Arabian Steppe to Medina and Mecca. The other is the big traffic artery known as the King's Highway from Damascus through Ammān and Ma'ān, where it branches off on a course east of the Dead Sea, until it reaches the head of the Gulf of Aqaba. It runs through Guweira northwest of Rumm.

Both trails are sometimes called *Béled al 'Arab* by the Bedouin; it is an old Arabic name meaning "the place going down into Arabia." The eastern route is also the pilgrim's road from Syria to Mecca, and it once connected the land of the Edomites with the central steppelands of Arabia more than 1,000 years before the Christian era. Camel drivers may have passed over this trail before the time of Moses.

At the Bat'n al Ghūl station, near the old man's desert restaurant, another trail, even fainter, branches to the west, and it was over this route, connecting Bat'n al Ghūl with Rumm and Guweira, that R'Faifan and I were now heading. It is not even marked on most maps. Threading across the baked mud-flat and on into the canyons that form a weird labyrinth of passages upward toward the edge of Rumm, it changes from a straight course across the desert to a twisting trail that winds through an illogical sequence of colored colonnades, finally emerging on the long mud flat of Q'a Desa and dropping down again into Rumm Valley. It was here that I hoped to complete the first phase of my expedition, seeking traces of the true character of Lawrence of Arabia among the old Bedouin chiefs of the Rumm area, where Lawrence had operated in 1917–18.

Some geographical knowledge of this region is necessary in order to understand its significance in the fighting between the Turks and the British in World War I. The chain of deserts, from Syria down to the southern coast of Arabia, was fairly remote from the interest of the Turkish rulers of the Middle East, but the western coastal lands of Arabia, from the Hijaz to Palestine, was essential to the Turks if they wished to retain

The Brow of Syria: looking southward from rim of the Ra's an Naqb toward Wádi Rumm, as described by Doughty.

Ship of the desert: the single-hump camel, the Bedouin gift to civilization, waiting out a sandstorm near Al Jafr.

control of the Mediterranean ports that flank the Suez Canal. This was the vital ground for which the British were wrestling.

The mass of vermilion deserts and canyons that formed the complex around Rumm was a bastion from which Lawrence's raiders could strike out in any direction—toward Mudawwara to the southeast, or against Ma'ān in the north. It was from these red-walled gorges that the forces gathered by Faisal and Zaid, two of the sons of Hussein ibn Ali, the *sharif* of Mecca, first began to harass the Turkish forces protecting the Hijaz-Medina railroad, either led by or under the tutelage and direction of the wily Lawrence.

I had approached Rumm from the west many times, but this was my first ride into this historic region from the Eastern Desert. As we clumped along on our camels—I on the *nāga* and R'Faifan still cheerfully riding his castrated bull—I had the sensation that both Lawrence and Doughty described; I was entering a strange new world of fantastic and almost unreal splendor.

From time to time I felt the hurt in my camel's feet, almost as if a shiver ran up her leg into mine, as her padded hoof struck on a sharp edge of flinty rock. Now and then I called to R'Faifan to halt, and we dismounted to examine the animal's soft feet. The dry, rough *ghôr* was hot, and the shortcut trail over which we were traveling had not been smoothed by the passage of millions of human and animal feet over the centuries, as was the trail through Bat'n al Ghūl. It was almost 30 kilometers before we struck a branching road running southwest from Guweira to Mudawwara, a low area called an Ahl abu Suwanna, where the trail was not so rough.

I did not realize it at the time, but a short distance beyond this junction was the *bait sha'ar* of Sheikh Sab'al La-Ji, who had known Auda abu Tayi, the Howeitat tribesman who was Lawrence's closest ally. However, we turned northward at this point, and missed Sheikh Sab'al by half a dozen miles. I visited his home several weeks later.

We had 60 kilometers to travel from the old man's teahouse to Desa, the small settlement near Wádi Rumm which was our immediate objective. The trail, over a flat stretch of hard-packed *ghôr* and up to the rim of Rumm Valley, could not be covered in a single march, and we stopped overnight at a place called Khreme, which seemed to have no significance as a name. It was simply a wide spot in the road.

We made a quick camp, scraping up brushwood from a nearby gulch to build a fire over which we brewed tea and warmed tins of bully beef. This, and sardines, was our staple diet on the desert. Early the following day we pushed on through the narrow gorges lined with columns of rock that leaned over us like lowering shadows, almost cutting off the sky. A few miles beyond Khreme we saw a queer figure, sitting on a small hillock of sand beside the trail: an ancient Arab, thin and diseased, with fingers extended upward like talons as he called out in a thin, cracked voice, *"Anna mayyat!"*—I am dying!

Whether he was a pilgrim whose sickness had caused him to be dropped off one of the buses traveling over the eastern road through Bat'n al Ghūl and who had then wandered to this lonely spot, or whether this was his way of living, I could not determine.

My first impulse was to stop and help the old man, but R'Faifan waved at me peremptorily, as if to inform me that this was not the thing to do. I quickened the pace of my camel, riding up to R'Faifan, and asked if we could not do something for the poor fellow, but my friend dismissed the matter with another wave of his hand.

"It is his wish to live this way and to die this way," he said with a flash of his teeth. *"Inshallah!"*

The cruelty of the desert struck me with sudden force; I

175

could not accept in my own way of reasoning this act of leaving the old man on the trail. Yet he had turned away and was looking again southward, toward Mecca. I knew it was a conviction of the Moslem faith that pilgrims who die on the trip to or from Mecca are *shadūd,* martyrs; and perhaps the old man wanted to die this way. He apparently had forgotten us as soon as we passed beyond him on the trail, for he did not look back at us again.

In retrospect, it was obvious that R'Faifan's attitude was neither reprehensible nor unfeeling. Those who are bred in the desert do not often display the sophisticated morality of more populated parts of the world, but their customs are more suited than ours to the environment in which they live. It is we who are the outlanders.

I thought more about this matter as we rode along, wondering how much of what I thought was philosophizing and how much rationalizing. I had seen a great deal of the gentler side of the Bedouin: the warm hospitality and the dignified manner in which the stranger is greeted in their homes. This incident with the old man was the harder side. The desert breeds men who can live on its barren breast, husbanding the scanty nourishment of life scraped off gravel beds of dry rivers and along the brown, windswept ridges. They ask no quarter of life, and give none. R'Faifan was probably right; the old Arab was happier where he was than if we had sought to drag him to some more crowded environment, where he would die anyway.

As we started up the slow ascent, after crossing the flat *ghôr* where the camels walked with swaying motion, we ran into much harder going for our animals. Camels, in descending a trail, have a stiff-legged gait, bracing each step of their spindly legs and jolting the rider unmercifully. On the ascent they move with a succession of jerks that seem about to crack the spine. It is only in the long marches across the flat desert floor that they move rhythmically, and even then their rocking stride makes it necessary to hold the high saddle horn at times to prevent being thrown off sideways. Normally the rider sits with one leg across the horn and the other draped across the ankle, forming a kind of wrestler's half-scissors on the saddle horn. When the going is rough, unlike the romantic cowboys of the American West, he grabs for leather.

I found the approach to Wádi Rumm from the east quite different from the road from Aqaba and Guweira. Lawrence, in recollections of his first ride into this awesome land, describes it in colorful language:

We were riding from Rumm, the northern water of the Beni Atiyeh: a place which stirred my thought, as even the unsentimental Howeitat had told me it was lovely. . . . Day was still young as we rode between two great pikes of sandstone to the foot of a long, soft slope poured down from the domed hills in front of us. It was tamarisk-covered: the beginning of the Valley of Rumm, they said. We looked up on the left to a long wall of rock, sheering in like a thousand-foot wave towards the middle of the valley; whose other arc, to the right, was an opposing line of steep, red broken hills. We rode up the slope, crashing our way through the brittle undergrowth.[2]

Later, on subsequent journeys into this area, which was the core of the northern rise of the Arab Revolt, he wrote:

When we were often riding inland, my mind used to turn me from the direct road, to clear my senses by a night in Rumm and by the ride down its dawn-lit valley towards the shining plains, or up its valley in the sunset towards that glowing square which my timid anticipation never let me reach . . . in truth I liked Rumm too much.

As we plodded across the sun-baked flats of Q'a Desa, leading to the small town of that name at the entrance to

177

Wádi Rumm, the vast panorama of the valley was spread before us. Bedouin are not given to lively displays of enthusiasm over nature, probably because they have had to deal with its harshness for centuries, but I observed that even R'Faifan seemed impressed as we rode across the level of hardened mud. He screamed at his camel to get more speed out of the weary beast. From the western edge of the Ra's an Naqb a break in the plateau spills downward toward the tumbled array of mountains to the west, forming the great Wádi Araba—the dividing line between the Holy Land and the deserts of Jordan. Rumm was directly ahead as we entered Desa. North of the flat were a number of Bedouin tents scattered across the dunes; to the south was the tiny town.

The floor of the Rumm desert is about 3,000 feet above sea level, and the *jabal* rise like spires, merging with the red-tinted canyons that converge into the valley, from 2,000 to 2,500 feet higher. Our level at the western end of Q'a Desa was about 1,000 feet above the desert floor.

The reddish soil predominates on the desert and nearby canyon walls, but the colors of the distant mountains vary from crimson to purple and blue. The effect of this panorama, seen from the entrance at Desa, is astonishment and wonder. Far down in the valley, hardly visible from where we were, was the little square fort of Rumm, surrounded by a scattering of Bedouin tents. The scrub brush and salt grass that grow in tufts on the desert floor are not sufficient for long periods of grazing, and few nomads remain in Rumm for any length of time.

Behind the fort rises the imposing peak of Jabal Rumm, where the Bedouin believe the *ghrôl,* monster of the desert, lives his (or her) Cyclopean eye viewing the desolation, ready to leap out and destroy any nomads careless enough to pass that way. This ancient myth obviously has come into disuse since the establishment of the little fort at Rumm, but in Lawrence's time there was no fort and the legend may have been active. In any event, the Arabs regarded Rumm as a sanctuary.

The valley presented a magnificent spectacle. The surrounding walls were topped by spires of striated rock, appearing like giant edifices built in irregular and monstrous fashion by giant architects of old, who seemed to have flung their creation down upon the barren desert. In certain ways Rumm resembled Petra, the ancient stronghold of Nabataean Arabs, where the main structures were hewn out of solid rock, with facades of Greek columns and rounded porticoes. I had been in Petra, and on my first sight of Rumm Valley from the east I could not help sensing this strange kinship of architectural splendor, one created by man and the other by nature.

As we rested our camels after the jolting ride across the mud flats to the rimrock where Desa was located, I also thought of Lawrence's words: "Our little caravan grew self-conscious, and fell dead quiet, afraid and ashamed to flaunt its smallness in the presence of the stupendous hills."

The name Q'a Desa means mud flat, and Desa itself, at the head of the flat, is as typical of the desert as any Western town in the United States: a scattering of tents around a small schoolhouse, the Jordanian government's basic tool of progress, which is to be found in almost every sizable Bedouin town, and the general store. These, with the pump house and watering place, formed the town. Near the water was a field of grain, irrigated from the well and surrounded by a wire fence. From Desa the trail to Guweira ran northwest, and the road to Rumm slanted off slightly to the south, split by the jutting scarp of a *jabal* extending from the canyon wall.

I was dog-tired, and at R'Faifan's suggestion we made our camp just beyond the village, at the entrance to Wádi Rumm. A few miles beyond was the *bait sha'ar* of Sheikh Sudan, whom I knew, but we had traveled hard during the last two marches, and I needed rest. It was the first day of April, and

179

the glow of spring was in the air. We had reached "Lawrence country" approximately on schedule. As I viewed the vast panorama before me, I felt again the unseen presence in this ancient crossroads that seemed to creep out of the canyon walls after the sun had set.

2

We tethered our camels near the old water hole which formerly was the pumping station for Desa. Along the dunes were a number of tents, and a few Bedouin came out to look curiously at us as we pitched camp at the far end of the mud flat. Below, through the rough channel of hills, we could see bright dots of yellow and orange that twinkled in the night. These were the fires burning in the tents at Rumm, where Bedouin families squatted around their coffeepots, and above was the darkening canopy of desert sky.

Our camels munched the salt grass of an old garden, grown into disuse with the removal of the pump house to a higher point above the grain patch. I examined my *nága*'s feet and found them swollen from small cuts, probably from splinters of volcanic rock that seemed to be mixed with the sandstone of the cliffs. I was not enough of a geologist to verify this, or to know the significance of it if I could.

R'Faifan sat in front of the fire, grinning now and then as if to assure me that he felt all right. His cold had abated considerably, and his only problem was weariness.

Late in the evening, before turning in, I walked a little way down the trail leading to Rumm. During the day the magnificence of the painted desert had been overwhelming, but at night it was a place of awe and mystery. The Bedouin believe that *jinns* come out of the craggy walls at night and may even spirit camels away if a traveler is unwary. As I gazed into the huge bowl of earth, sunk below the level of the desert plateau

The fort at Wádi Rumm: R'Faifan standing on ledge looks down at Rumm fort and the great Jabal Rumm; note tents.

Closer view of Rumm fort: the square, rock-walled Desert Patrol outpost under the towering summit of Jabal Rumm.

over which we had ridden, I thought of the millions of years during which this place had undergone a slow erosion, and how short and swift was the span of man's history in this place, even if one were to trace the few thousand years of his travels through it, going up and down the Arabian Peninsula.

We were up early, and R'Faifan was out at the break of dawn, washing his hands with sand before saying his prayers:

> God is most great.
> I testify that there is no God but God.
> I testify that Mohammed is the Prophet of God.
> Come to prayer, come to salvation.
> Prayer is better than sleep.
> There is no God but God. . . .

After prayer, and a breakfast of dry biscuits and tea, we quickly loaded our camels and started down torard the little fort in the broad highway of desert. Above us towered the massive red parapet of Jabal Rumm, rising 2,000 feet from the plain; to our left, partly hidden by the walls of the canyon, was the equally imposing bulk of Jabal Um Ishrin (the mother of Ishrin) facing the little Rumm fort from the east. The small collection of tents, scattered aimlessly around the fort, became insignificant in the presence of these two mighty guardians, and beyond the settlement stretched the dry expanse of Rumm Valley, fading away toward the distant peaks.

The interplay of shafts of sunlight, slanting down from deep crevices that lined the eastern walls of the canyon, created long ripples of light on the flat desert floor. It was a scene of fantastic color and movement. The wind no longer blew fiercely as it had on the journey down to Bat'n al Ghūl, although I have seen the wind whip across the Rumm Ghôr, raising layers of sand that roll across the desert like waves, cutting shrubs and eroding solid banks of sand at the base of the *jabál.*

182

The camels, with the instinctive awareness these desert travelers have of the presence of other camels, seemed to sense that we were nearing an important stopping place in our journey. They lengthened their swaying gait, and we flew across the desert. I found myself spellbound by the sheer majesty of the great amphitheater into which we rode, and at one time R'Faifan turned and shrieked a warning to me when I was almost jolted off the saddle while daydreaming.

I hoped to meet several Bedouin at Rumm: in particular, Sheikh Aid Awad al-Zalbani, an old campaigner in the Arab Revolt who had been in that area for upwards of 60 years; and I also planned to meet Sheikh Sudan, a much younger man than Aid, and a friend whom I knew from other journeys through Rumm. In addition, I expected to meet Dr. Mack, who was on his way from New York and would come down to Rumm from Ammān.

While there is never any certainty as to the exact location of a Bedouin *bait sha'ar,* since they move from place to place to take advantage of weather and grazing, I hoped to locate Sheikh Sudan through the *badia* at the post. As we neared the small settlement, flung out willy-nilly on the desert floor, I felt again the warm anticipation of meeting old friends.

We reached the Rumm fort about noon on April 2, and I began immediately to lay my plans for completing the job I had agreed to do for Dr. Mack. My old friend Sheikh Sudan came over to the fort to greet me.

"We have expected you for days," he said. "What happened?"

I told him of the storm on the desert above Bat'n al Ghūl. He nodded.

"There are other storms, also," he said. "I will tell you about them."

He looked at me very keenly, and I was quite certain he referred to the reports Doug Manson had brought back from Ma'ān and the radio news broadcasts picked up by the old station keeper at Fasu'a. However, I have learned from years of association with Bedouin not to press for any more information than they are ready to divulge. Since my immediate plans for going into Wádi Araba hung on the situation along the western border between Jordan and Israel, I knew I must be certain of the best and most accurate information. So I bided my time.

I told Sheikh Sudan of my desire to meet Sheikh Aid, and since he knew that my purpose in coming to Rumm was to try to locate old Bedouin who had been guerrilla fighters with Lawrence, he promptly assured me that he would arrange the meeting.

"He was with Lawrence," Sheikh Sudan told me. "You will find that he has much information. He is expecting to talk with you."

I was not too sure of this. While I knew Tony Hallec had sent word to Sheikh Sudan of the reasons for my journey to Rumm, I doubted that this word had spread among all the Bedouin in the desert, and I also knew of the deep desire of all Bedouin to satisfy a guest's curiosity, even if it is necessary to fabricate some sort of story to do it.

Nevertheless I thanked him warmly. It was arranged that I would meet Sheikh Aid the following day. R'Faifan meanwhile had found his inevitable old crony from Camel Corps days: the sergeant at the fort, a genial man with massive physique and, as I later discovered, an even more massive appetite. His name was Mohammed abu Brahim, and I might note in passing that R'Faifan, after witnessing the sergeant's feats of trenchermanship, promptly named his castrated camel Mohammed abu Brahim.

I cannot recall R'Faifan's ever using the name in the presence of Sergeant Mohammed, however, and it is quite possible he neglected to tell his old friend of the distinction that had been conferred upon him.

In any event, as a result of this happy reunion we were given the best quarters at the fort. Sheikh Sudan insisted that we have dinner at his *bait sha'ar,* which was a welcome change from the long siege of bully beef and sardines that had been our lot since we left Doug Manson's camp at Shedia.

The *sheikh* was a well-built man with a hawklike face and sharp eyes. He wore the white *thōp* and black-and-white *agâl* of the Howeitat tribesmen, and in these flowing garments he appeared regal as we sat for a while among the piled cushions in his *raba'a* and discussed my plans.

I said I hoped to confirm what I had long believed: that Lawrence was never the leader of the Arab Revolt (Faisal and Zaid were its leaders) but was an astute and trained expert in the kind of hit-and-run warfare practiced by the Arabs. He was a teacher, trusted by the Bedouin leaders and by Faisal, and his value to the British was his ability to heal wounds of warring tribal chiefs as well as to plan guerrilla forays against the Turks.

Sheikh Sudan, puffing on his long-stemmed pipe, nodded at my words.

"That is so," he said. He leaned forward, jabbing the air with a long forefinger. "Why do you not join with us and become a new Lawrence?"

The remark was both surprising and disconcerting. I explained that Lawrence was a British officer and his country had been engaged in war with the Turks, whereas I was an American, and we were not at war with anyone.

"Nevertheless," he said, "you must have new ideas about fighting. We need money and guns. We have enemies, too, and our *malak* [King Hussein] is a friend of your country. We should be fighting together."

Suddenly, as if to erase even this minor blemish in pleasant hospitality, my host changed the subject.

"Sheikh Aid will be here tomorrow," he announced. "We

185

will take you to the watering hole of Ain O'rens." This was the Arabic name for Lawrence's Spring, which I knew was partway up the canyon leading to Jabal Rumm. I had been at the spring and had often thought of Lawrence's vivid description:

> Its rushing noise came from my left, by a jutting bastion of cliff over whose crimson face trailed long falling runners of green leaves. The path skirted it in an undercut ledge. On the rock-bulge above were clear-cut Nabathaean inscriptions, and a sunk panel incised with a monogram or symbol. Around and about were Arab scratches, including tribe-marks, some of which were witnesses of forgotten migrations: but my attention was only for the splashing of water in a crevice under the shadow of the overhanging rock.

I agreed readily. In my previous journeys into Rumm from the west, I had climbed up through the tangled gulley to visit the spring, which gushed out of the side of the mountain, providing water for the Bani-Atiyah from the south and the Howeitat from the north.

I had another reason for being delighted at Sheikh Sudan's suggestion. If Sheikh Aid, as had been reported, was a former follower of the Arab guerrillas and had ridden on raids with Lawrence, he could provide me with information I needed: the nature and character of the fabled Englishman, which even his books do not fully disclose.

As I passed through the ragged line of tents, returning to the *badia* post, I glanced at fire pits that glowed behind the heavy goat-hair tent cloth. The dark valley seemed alive with mysterious portents. Within these rocky walls much of the history of Arabia had been written. Many generations of nomads had ridden their soft-footed camels over this blood-red ground, and from the craggy parapets that surrounded the valley 40 centuries of living history looked down upon the people who had passed this way.

186

It was possible that the old *sheikh*—if he had ridden with Lawrence—might provide some information to fill in one of the later gaps of history, but even this fulfillment would be only a tiny drop of water on the vast desert of silence that surrounded us. My thoughts about Lawrence, which had been active almost to the point of excitement up to this time, were engulfed in the sudden realization that the span of 50 years since Lawrence and the Arab raiders had ridden through this place was only the infinitesimal ticking of a second or two of time in the periods in which the Bedouin had traveled over the sun-baked *ghôr* of Wádi Rumm.

3

The following morning I made my way over to Sheikh Sudan's *bait sha'ar,* an imposing spread of two large tents—one for animals—that lay snugly against a small bluff facing the north west, where it was protected from the sweep of the wind across the valley. A number of camels and a large herd of goats browsed nearby. I had been advised by Sergeant Mohammed that the *sheikh* was regarded as one of the significant citizens virtually the "mayor" of Rumm.

"Sheikh Aid will meet you this morning," Sheikh Sudan told me on my arrival. "He has much to tell you." He then leaned over and whispered, as if not to be overheard, although there was no one around.

"He is old and does not remember things very well. Also, he does not hear very well, and he cannot see much, either."

This sudden disclosure startled me. I stared at Sheikh Sudan and said: "You mean he can't see or hear—and he doesn't remember anything?"

Sheikh Sudan shrugged. I had to make the best of his cryptic answer, because the subject of his analysis came whipping up to the tent in—of all things—a motorcar. In spite of

Sheikh Sudan's comments on the old man's condition, he jumped out of the car while it was still moving.

He came in an antiquated car, driven by a member of his household—a convenience I had not expected in the wilderness of Wádi Rumm. He was well into his seventies, and his rheumy eyes and almost tottering gait seemed to bear out at least some of Sheikh Sudan's appraisal of him. But he certainly did not lack agility. To my surprise, he ignored the "mayor" of Rumm, sliding briskly past him to greet me. He spoke in a quavering voice, and although my knowledge of Arabic was limited, I understood that he was inviting me to join him immediately on a trip up to Lawrence's Spring.

I wanted to visit the spring again, and this seemed to be a good chance for me to ask questions about Sheikh Aid's experiences with Lawrence. Since I had expected to rely on Sheikh Sudan to do the interrogating in Arabic, I was disappointed to find that he was not even asked to join us. Sheikh Aid merely waved me into the car, still ignoring Sheikh Sudan completely, and whisked me off over a couple of miles of desert trail to the foot of Jabal Rumm, from which we climbed up to the overhanging cliffs under which the spring gushed forth with its perpetual supply of water for thirsty herders.

There is heady stimulation for any traveler who visits Lawrence's Spring. It is an isolated oasis in the rock, halfway up the mountain, and seems to be a place for meditation. The refreshing coolness of its waters contributes to a curious elation that comes over the visitor. Lawrence wrote of his first visit to this place:

In front of us a path, pale with use, zig-zagged up the cliff to the point from which the main face rose, and there it turned precariously southward along a shallow ledge outlined by occasional leafy trees. From between these trees, in hidden crannies of the rock, issued strange cries; the echoes, turned into music, of the voices of Arabs

188

At Lawrence's Spring: R ʾFaifan points to sunken panel with Nabataean inscription near watering place at Rumm.

Bedouin wasm: R ʾFaifan indicates brands of Bedouin travelers near Lawrence's Spring in Wádi Rumm.

watering camels at the springs which there flowed out three hundred feet above ground.

There were no camels or Arabs around at this time, since the pumps in the desert below, at the *badia* fort, provided all the water necessary; but the scene was the same, and I found myself again examining the area, the trail, and the overhanging rock with ancient Nabataean inscriptions on the stone, mingled with *wāsm* of later Arab travelers, chiseled in the walls beside the springs.

I had heard that there was an old aqueduct, probably of Nabataean origin, which once carried water from the spring into the valley below, and I found remnants of this and traced it along the side of the hill. Sheikh Aid followed me, with his sidling gait, gathering his robe around his knees in a mincing fashion and chattering away interminably in Arabic as we clambered down.

I learned from the old man, who could see quite well and talk even better—regardless of how faulty his memory may have been—that he actually had been on raids with Lawrence. He also mentioned other Arab tribesmen, whose names I knew from Lawrence's books, such as Motleg and Zaal and the *sharif* of Harithi.

When we arrived again at the settlement of tents in the valley below, Sheikh Sudan, apparently unperturbed by the rebuff he seemed to have suffered at the hands of the old man, invited me to remain for lunch, and although he also appeared to have invited Sheikh Aid, the latter paid almost no attention to this courtesy, climbing into his venerable car and heading off for home without speaking to Sheikh Sudan. As he left he assured me, in his squeaky voice, that he would assemble from his presumably fading memory all manner of anecdotes and impart them to me when I should have time to visit him. I had the feeling he meant "without Sudan."

Sheik Sudan waved genially to the old man, and I was aware that this display of rudeness on the part of Sheikh Aid was a customary performance. Later I was informed by Sergeant Mohammed that the old *sheikh* regarded Sudan, who was 40 years his junior, as an upstart and virtually a "newcomer" to Rumm, although Sheikh Sudan had lived in this area for more than 30 years.

I expected to spend at least a couple of weeks in the Rumm area gathering material for Dr. Mack, and I was determined not to become a party to the local political or social entanglements. This had a few disadvantages, because I found myself the target of a fairly continuous run of conflicting invitations, each of the *sheikhs* seeking to outdo the other in the way of entertainment. I recalled the gastronomical distress I had experienced at Al Jafr during the feast of Id-al-Adha, when I was required by courtesy to attend four *mansefs* in one day!

Since Sheikh Sudan was my personal friend, I felt obligated to give first consideration to his invitation; and, as a point of personal privilege, I doubt if he would have spoken to me again if I had refused. I had seen Arabs at the United Nations gather their skirts about them and walk out of a state dinner because the most exalted of their number had not been given first preference at the table. They take matters of protocol quite seriously, and this attitude is no less a social factor among the nomads of the desert.

When I received a messenger from Sheikh Sudan at the *badia* fort early the following day inviting both R'Faifan and me to a big *mansef* to be in our honor at Sheikh Sudan's *bait sha' ar* the next day, I accepted without hesitation. Within an hour I had a similar invitation from Sheikh Aid. Since it was quite clear there would be no one to arbitrate my social dilemma, I decided to ride over to Sheikh Aid's tent and try to work my way out in personal discourse.

Apparently it was only a *pro forma* sort of invitation. He

did not even mention it on my arrival, and when I tried to explain, in my halting Arabic, that I would be engaged in important work for the next two days, he waved his hand graciously and said the Arabic equivalent of "Any time!"

The old man seemed far more interested in providing me with information about his exploits in the past, not only fighting alongside Lawrence but in various tribal feuds and skirmishes, and these tales provided a strange mixture of unrepressed savagery and compassion for a broken and defeated enemy.

On the first raid on Mudawwara Station, for example—which Lawrence described in detail, although somewhat differently from Sheikh Aid—a small band of Nuwasra tribesmen, kin of Auda abu Tayi of the Howeitat tribes, had gathered on a ridge north of Mudawwara, primarily in the hope of looting the trains if they should be derailed by explosives. Sheikh Aid was among these.

"We saw more than three hundred Turks, marching slowly along the tracks," Sheikh Aid told me, in staccato Arabic of which I caught only a smattering. "We could have killed them easily. They had been roused from their noonday sleep by the officers and were forced to patrol the tracks. They would have been too sleepy to have fought back."

There was a vague discrepancy between Sheikh Aid's story and the description of that raid that I had read in Lawrence's book. According to Aid, the band of raiding guerrillas retired to the hills several miles north of the station, and before the train pulled out they set explosives in the tracks some distance from the station. When the engine passed over the rails where the charge of explosive gelatin had been buried, the charge was electrically ignited and blew the engine off the tracks. His description of the event was quite realistic. "There were bodies all over the place," he said, "but we did not bother to look at them because they were Turks, and there was much material to be gathered."

Sheikh Aid's account seemed to conform with the general nature of the Bedouin, who have traditionally been desert raiders. He told me how the Arabs gathered their "material" and fled while the Turkish troops on the train were busy regrouping and deciding whether or not it would be advisable to charge out into the desert against a concealed enemy of unknown strength.

Lawrence's version of this incident is quite interesting by comparison:

Through my powerful glasses we [sic] saw a hundred Turkish soldiers issue from Mudowwara Station and make straight across the sandy plain towards our place. They were coming very slowly, and no doubt unwillingly, for sorrow at losing their beloved midday sleep. . . . We began to pack up, preparatory to moving off, having decided to leave the mine and its leads in place. . . .

The watchman cried out that smoke in clouds was rising from Hallat Ammar. Zaal and I rushed uphill and saw by its shape and volume that indeed there must be a train waiting in that station. As we were trying to see it over the hill, suddenly it moved out in our direction. We yelled to the Arabs to get into position as quickly as possible. . . . An Arab stood up on high behind the guns and shouted to us what the train was doing—a necessary precaution, for if it carried troops and detrained them behind our ridge we should have to face about like a flash and retire fighting up the valley for our lives. . . .

Lawrence in his account continues to describe a classic guerrilla raid. Arabs with rifles deployed along the ridges flanking the tracks, after having laid a land mine under a small bridge. Lawrence waited on the far side, concealed by a ridge, and at a signal from him, an Arab guerrilla pressed the charger detonating the explosion.

There is no way of determining which account was correct, except that Sheikh Aid described it as a simple raid on a wrecked troop transport, with the Arabs racing down to the tracks to gather up what spoils there were, and I was convinced he recalled the incident as best he could. In Lawrence's story of this raid on Mudawwara, he wrote in detail about the deployment of the Arab raiders as the train pulled out of the station, the two-engine train running across the bridge over a small *wádi*, 3 or 4 miles north, and his split-second decision to detonate the charges while the second engine was on the bridge, so that if it were derailed it would make it impossible for the first engine to link up with the trailing troop cars and drag them away. This all makes for romantic fiction, but in my own mind the difference between Lawrence's complex account and the simple description of the raid given by Sheikh Aid—a typical Bedouin foray upon a destroyed caravan to gather up the spoils—was further indication that Lawrence had not played the leader's role he had built up for himself in *Seven Pillars of Wisdom.*

It also buttressed my growing belief—augmented later by stories of other old Bedouin with whom I talked—that the legend of Lawrence of Arabia as leader of the Arab Revolt was partly fiction, largely created by Lawrence himself and by certain journalists who knew Lawrence and were impressed by his account of the Revolt of the Desert. It seemed far more likely that Lawrence was simply a British intelligence officer, injected into the Arab Revolt to consolidate and train the Bedouin guerrillas, and that Faisal and Zaid were the real leaders of the revolt.

This offered only a small sidelight in the problem of tracing Lawrence's personal traits and psychological characteristics, which was the task Dr. Mack had set for himself, but it seemed to me a significant aspect of the posthumous effort to "psycho-analyze" a dead man.

When I asked Sheikh Aid why they did not fall upon the Turks, disorganized by the blowing up of the train, and destroy them, he simply said: "They were not our enemies. They did only as their officers ordered them."

194

I decided it would be worth investigating in the Mudawwara area to see whether there were any traces of the raid near the station. If Aid's story were true, it would conform fairly logically with my own concept of a raid by a desert band, but it hardly fitted with Lawrence's plan for destroying the Turkish railroad. This was a point I proposed to look into on our journey to Mudawwara, which would be the next leg of our expedition.

4

During our stay at the Rumm fort, R'Faifan had remained for the most part with Mohammed abu Brahim—the sergeant of the Desert Patrol, not the camel—and struck up a fast friendship. As usual I never understood whether the friendship was born in the heyday of his career with the Camel Corps or began at the moment of our arrival. However, I had no reason to question the origin of R'Faifan's comradeships, as long as they assured us the full cooperation of the *badia* and the comparative luxury of the guest quarters at the Desert Patrol forts. When I made a small effort to inquire into his relationships, R'Faifan merely grinned and with a wave of his hand said: "He who is a friend of one is a friend of all!"

This cryptic reply, of course, offered no explanation, but I concluded that I did not need one. The sergeant treated me as if I were a visiting *emir;* and that night he produced the most lavish repast the *badia* kitchen force could provide: an immense plate of sheep liver, bread, eggs, tea—and even fresh apples! Since the sergeant, a man of tremendous physical proportions, consumed at least half the edibles on the table, I decided this was simply his way of furnishing himself with all the nourishment he wanted without personal embarrassment.

The *mansef* at Sheikh Sudan's *bait sha'ar* was even more lavish and, in fact, was a challenge to the sergeant's enormous capacity. We had been at Rumm nearly a week; while the *sheikh*'s invitation originally seemed to be scheduled for the second day after our arrival, I had learned that time has no real significance for the Bedouin, and I simply waited until I was advised by his messenger of the exact time we were to be guests.

We arrived at what I thought was an early hour—nine o'clock in the morning—but things were already under way. I had hoped to have some time to talk with Sheikh Sudan about many things, and particularly learn his undiluted opinion of Sheikh Aid's tales. The old man had given me much food for thought, and if the things he told me about Lawrence were true, they would be quite important to Dr. Mack.

Both R'Faifan and Sergeant Mohammed had been invited, and in fact almost the entire settlement was there—with the exception of Sheikh Aid. I asked Sheikh Sudan if he would arrive and quickly realized from the sorrowful expression of my host that I had committed at least a minor *faux pas.*

"He will be here," Sheikh Sudan said, "as soon as he has assured himself that his delayed arrival will provide ample proof that he does not need my invitation. However, he will be here. He is a proud man, but he enjoys my food." He leaned over again and whispered with what seemed wholly unncessary secrecy: "The old man remembers very little."

I began to think Sheikh Sudan was pulling my leg.

Meanwhile, all the troops from the *badia* post had been invited to the feast, and they trooped in, led by the burly Sergeant Mohammed. As the huge platters of rice upon which the carcasses of two goats were balanced were brought in from the cooking pit, everyone gathered in a circle and watched the rivulets of boiling butter and fat cascade down the sides of the mounds of meat and rice. There were few sheep in the Rumm area, and it was customary at *mansefs* to serve goat meat in the absence of lamb.

196

Quite as Sheikh Sudan had predicted, Sheikh Aid came hobbling in with his crablike shuffle, walking almost sideways as he passed Sheikh Sudan and greeted the other guests, ignoring his host. Sudan seemed utterly unperturbed by this discourtesy, waving jovially to the old man as he squatted in the circle and tucked his long *thōp* under his skinny legs.

A feast on the desert differs in many ways from those close to larger towns—such as the *mansef* Sheikh Sami had prepared for us on our departure from Jiza—chiefly in the matter of availability of food. The customs are much the same: the host and members of his household do not eat until the guests have been served. But the entire atmosphere is more open and informal on the desert.

The entire eastern end of the tent was taken up by the spread of the feast, with two large *safra,* circular mats upon which the trays were placed. The usual tray is a copper plate called a *sinyah,* upon which is piled the boiled rice and meat, but in Sheikh Sudan's case, since he was a man of considerable means and distinction, he used the more imposing *sinyah abu kursi,* which consists of a tray on a pedestal. The name literally means father of the table. Two of these had been set up near the edge of the *raba'a,* and the guests clustered in a large circle about both trays.

Sheikh Sudan had signaled the beginning of the feast with a jovial *"'Alaikum al afiyah!"*—May you be healthy!—and they all went at it. He had guided me to the place of honor, but I persuaded him that I would like to take pictures of the affair, and he immediately consented.

I noticed that he also ordered one of his servants to see that several tasty tidbits—the meat along the spine, parts of the kidneys, strips of leg muscle, and tidbits of head meat—were laid aside so that I would have the best of the food.

While I circled taking pictures of the group of hungry men that had formed around the two *mansef* trays, all squatting

197

comfortably and reaching out to paw at the food, I watched Sheikh Sudan. Each guest was made to feel comfortable and at ease. I watched him covertly, observing his lean, hawkish face reflecting different angles of light from the fire pit as he looked around the circle, from face to face, to be sure everyone was eating his fill. Sheikh Sudan took no food for himself until he was sure the others had all they wanted, and since I had begged permission to take pictures of the feast before eating, he followed me around to be sure that I finally joined the feast. He actually would not touch the food until I had eaten.

The feast was a tremendous success. One after another the guests literally rolled away from the festive board, some moving to far corners of the *raba'a* to lie and belch in contentment while others wandered off on various missions. The piles of food quickly melted down as the guests plunged their right hands into the greasy mess to pull out choice morsels of meat and handfuls of fat-soaked rice. The Bedouin employ few tools in eating, using only the right hand in accordance with Moslem custom. At the *mansef* board they scoop up rice and meat with their bare hand and eat in the style that nature intended. This might create a shudder among persons of fastidious taste, but to those who sat around Shaikh Sudan's feast it was natural and normal.

Sheikh Aid had followed me around, establishing himself in places where I was about to take pictures of the feast, so that he was on almost every film. When I had finished, he tried to draw me aside, presumably to ply me with additional anecdotes of his early career, which grew more heroic with each revelation. Sheikh Sudan, with superb mastery of the techniques of a host, managed to disengage me from the old man's attention and steer me to the mound of fast-disappearing goat meat and rice, which by this time was reduced to a shambles.

I saw Sheikh Aid stalk off and thought at first he was offended, but he merely circled to the other side, selecting another point of attack, like an Arab raider; and as he dove again into the *mansef* with his thin, clawlike hand, he grinned across the *sinyah* as if he had somehow outwitted his host.

I doubt if I will ever forget that old man. He had grown on me, in a sense, until I felt a fondness for him. I decided it made little difference whether he was lying or telling the truth about his exploits with Lawrence: he was still one of the most fascinating characters I had met, and an interesting page out of the past.

A day or so after Sheikh Sudan's great feast, a major of the Jordanian Security Police came through Rumm on a trip southward from Ammān, either on an inspection trip or merely to visit the *badia* post. He talked with me briefly, and although I did not believe he had been specially directed to contact me, I realized his information was of considerable importance. It was quite possible Colonel Nayef had instructed him to speak to me, if I should be found in Rumm.

"There has been a report of a *coup d'état* in Syria," he told me. "No one is certain how serious the matter may be, but it is well to be prepared for any eventuality."

I asked him if the road into Wâdi Arab was open, and he shook his head.

"We suggest that all those who do not have an official mission remain away from the border," he said.

The rumor of the Syrian coup—which later proved to be wrong—had been followed by a definite report of a pitched battle between Syrian and Israeli border patrols. Pictures had been released from Damascus indicating the Syrians had thrown the Israelis back across the Jordan River line, apparently north of Dera.

"Is the border fighting becoming serious?" I asked the major. He shrugged.

"Who can say? It is always serious when they shoot across the border at us. But we also know how to shoot back!"

We discussed the political orientation of Jordan for some time, and the major remarked quite unofficially that it was his belief that Jordan would always remain aligned with the Western bloc.

The possibility of Syria's falling completely under Soviet domination was always a factor, he said, but he added almost vehemently that Jordan would never follow the lead of Syria or Nasser in Egypt. I felt this was true; there was a basic difference between the Jordanians and the other Arab peoples of the Middle East. Much of this difference was a result of Bedouin influence. The self-reliant nomads formed a political as well as an ethnic ingredient that gave the Jordanians greater resistance to alien control than any other national grouping in the Arab world except the Saudi Arabians.

It may seem an oversimplification, and even a paradox, but to anyone who has traveled among the Bedouin and lived with them, this underlying changlessness and the indestructible core of tradition, going back not only for centuries but for millennia, is at the heart of the Arab spirit of independence. Ruled successively by the caliphs of Damascus and Baghdad, and finally by the Ottoman Turks, the Bedouin have survived the domination of all these political overlords, and probably will never succumb to the force or blandishments of an alien political philosophy. Oddly enough, the democratic creed of Western peoples—and particularly the United States—comes closest to matching the Bedouin's own thirst for freedom, which may account in part for the attitude of Jordan toward the Western block, a stance friendly but not subservient.

VII. *At the Feet of the Prophet*

1

I intended to remain in Rumm for about two weeks awaiting the arrival of Dr. Mack, who planned to spend several weeks in the area, working with me in the task of recording some of the tales of the Bedouin who had known Lawrence and perhaps fought alongside him with the Arab raiders in the Revolt in the Desert. Since a great deal of the activity in the early stages of the Arab Revolt revolved around Mudawwara, I had planned to strike southeastward toward the border between Saudi Arabia and Jordan, where the old Turkish railroad crossed the present border, heading southward across the steppelands toward Medina.

My original plan had been to travel into Saudi Arabia and circle back along the route I believed the ancient caravan trail had traversed, and also to go into Wádi Araba, a wild, mountainous country west of Rumm and Guweira. Dr. Mack, who was to accompany me at least in the latter trip, arrived by car from Ammān, and we immediately laid our plans to head southward in the next two or three days. Our camels were well grazed after two months of hard travel, and there was plenty of grain for them at Rumm.

Meanwhile I had observed a kind of "palace revolution" going on in my own ranks. R'Faifan had expressed in various ways his lack of enthusiasm about leaving Rumm in the beginning of the hot summer. I found that he had struck up a fast friendship with Mohammed abu Brahim (the sergeant), who appeared to want us to stay all summer. The heavyset *badia* commandant had even applied the pressure of his personality directly to me. He insisted on leading me up trails to locations of ancient ruins, often at considerable inconvenience to himself, since he had to force his ponderous body up the steep slopes. He showed me inscriptions of Nabataeans, carved in the stone walls of the ruins, apparently in the hope of luring me into remaining in Rumm, but I was not an archaeologist, and much of what he said was lost on me. On one occasion he showed me with great pride, as if it was his own handiwork, an inscription which he said was "from before the time of the Prophet."

Actually, this was quite a concession for a Bedouin, since time for these people is usually measured from the year of Mohammed's birth, about A.D. 570, and anything earlier than that is regarded as prehistoric. Later I was told by Sheikh Sudan that a German archaeologist had excavated the place years earlier and believed the ruins were of Nabataean origin, perhaps dating from the fifth century B.C. I took several pictures of the broken walls but had neither the knowledge nor the equipment to follow up on my discoveries.

After the arrival of Dr. Mack, however, Sergeant Mohammed seemed to sense that our plans were not subject to as many variations as he supposed. He still persisted from time to time in offering suggestions that would dealy our departure, with that tangential kind of reference that is so characteristic of Arabs—never quite making his point directly but always suggesting it by inference—so that I began to suspect that he and

R'Faifan were in active collusion in an effort to keep us in Rumm all summer.

However, my own plans for early departure were interrupted by an unexpected message from Sheikh Faisal ibn Jazi, whom I had last seen in Ammān. A note, delivered by a *badia* courier, said he planned to return to his home in the desert near Hasa earlier than he had expected, and he felt that if I could interrupt my own journey briefly to visit him, it would afford me an opportunity to enjoy an unusual event. He was giving a great feast for Emir Hassan, the brother of King Hussein!

Dr. Mack was asked to come with me, and R'Faifan was also invited, a matter which unloosed the most emotional Arab rhetoric I had ever heard from R'Faifan's lips. He literally praised Allah for his presumed intervention in an otherwise drab and dreary routine on the desert.

I worried a bit about the camels, but this need not have given me any concern. On the day before the feast, a powerful Land Rover was waiting for us at the fort, ready to take us to Sheikh Faisal's desert home. The feast apparently was part of a general celebration on April 11, or "one Moharam," the 1,397th anniversary of the "beginning of time," which for Moslem purposes was the birth of the Prophet.

R'Faifan, Dr. Mack, and I piled into the Land Rover, driven by a grinning Bedouin dressed in the uniform of the *badias:* olive-drab blouse, with a Sam Browne belt across his chest and a cross-buckler studded with shells, his dark face encased in a tightly wrapped *kaffiyah* of red-checked cloth wrapped around his neck, surmounted by an *agál* worn at a rakish angle. Even the inevitable silver dagger, the pride of the *badia,* was thrust into the studded belt.

We took off at breakneck speed, leaving a cloud of dust behind as we headed up the valley and out through the Desa pass, turning northwest as we passed Q'a Desa, where R'Faifan and I had arrived two weeks before. Within a few

203

minutes we were out on the flat plateau of the Ra's an Naqb, heading toward the King's Highway. It was a journey I never will forget, and one I am not anxious to repeat.

Barney Oldfield in his heyday would have seemed like a Sunday driver alongside this desert chauffeur. We crossed the blazing plain, scorning such conveniences as the established road from Rumm to Guweira, and were soon making our own trail across the flat sand. This part of the desert was known as Q'a abu Ajram, which more or less literally means the place that is the father of the salt grass. This tufted weed is a life-saver for camels, having a salty taste that refreshes them when they have traveled long distances without water.

In the distance I saw the thin purple line of the King's Highway, but our driver spurned this modern mode of travel. As we neared the highway, he wrenched the wheel of the car around so that we tore off northward across the bald desert, actually parallel to the paved road. Dr Mack, R'Faifan, and I hung on for our lives while the driver grinned with un-inhibited delight each time we caromed off a rocky ledge that threatened to spill us into the desert.

We roared past Ma'ān, which lay several miles to our right, and to the left I could glimpse a smudge of what I thought was Wádi Mūsa, the rocky entrance to the Petra gorges some 10 or 15 kilometers to the west. I began to feel as if all my bones were becoming dislodged from their joints.

There are no drivers in the world that can compare with the Arabs, particularly on the open desert, which is simply an endless speedway without grading or leveling of natural bumps. Arabs enter completely and joyfully into the spirit of the race. In this case, our driver was not racing against anything, not even time, since we had no appointed hour for arrival, but he put his heart and soul into getting where he was going in the shortest possible time and by the most direct route. This took us straight across the desert, over gravel ridges, careening down slopes of naked rock and bouncing off ledges.

We must have traveled for about three hours, although it seemed to me like three years, when we suddenly veered over to the highway, bumped across it, and circled east past the 1,300-foot peak of Jabal Quirana. In the distance were the brown blotches of Sheik Faisal's *bait sha'ar* shining against the hillside. We drove through a wooden archway, decorated with green bushes indicating "the *emir* is home." The flags of many tribes were streaming from poles around the main tent, which was as long as half a dozen ordinary *buyút sha'ar,* and more than 100 camels were munching salt grass in nearby pens.

Within the huge tent, as we approached, were gaily dressed figures of at least 200 *sheikhs,* reclining on cushions or lying on the heavily piled rugs; gathered around the tent were clusters of uniformed "security guards"—a branch of the Security Police —to protect the person of the *emir.*

Two *sheikhs* I had met in Ammān—Sheikh Mitub' and Sheikh Jidoor—met us and escorted us into the tent. R'Faifan was quite shy and tried to hold back until I insisted he come along with me. At the far end was a huge coffee urn, half the size of a man, and one of the servants quickly brought us cups of coffee.

It might be noted that Bedouin of the north do not often drink the true "Arabian" coffee. Most of the coffee brewed in cities, such as Ammān, is "Syrian" or "Turkish" coffee. It is boiled to a thick, almost creamy consistency, and has a sweetish scum on the surface after it is poured, and it is served in American-made cups rather than the small bowls used in the Hijaz and other parts of southern Arabia. Coffee served in the *bait sha'ar* on the desert is usually thin and bitter-tasting, however. Customs also differ between the northern and southern parts of Arabia. In the north a guest will continue to be served until he shakes his cup from side to side, indicating he has had enough. In the south, only three cups are usually served to each guest, unless he asks for more.

The ritual of coffeemaking is one of the most respected traditions of Bedouin hospitality. The coffee is first pounded into a kind of flour in a brass mortar, and the ground coffee is then put into a brass coffeepot filled with cold water. This is placed on the fire pit and allowed to boil before it is served. The host, or servant preparing the coffee, lifts the pot from the fire with a ceremonial flourish and strikes the pot three or four times. This seems to bring it to a froth, and he puts it back on the fire again. This is repeated two or three times, until the froth is thick and begins to boil over.

At a feast such as Sheikh Faisal's, the making of coffee is assigned to one of the most experienced and trusted servants, and sometimes to the host's son. Failure to produce good coffee may cause the server to be banished from the presence of his master for weeks.

R'Faifan, Dr. Mack, and I sat back among the cushions, sipping our coffee—holding the cup between thumb and fore-finger, according to the Bedouin custom—waiting for the *emir* to arrive. He finally drove up in a car with Sheikh Faisal, and the entire entourage poured out of the tent and formed two lines beside a red Persian carpet which had been laid out to the *emir*'s car. Someone fired a pistol, and for an instant I thought an assassination was taking place, but I quickly found out that this is the customary salute announcing the *emir*'s arrival.

A loud wailing suddenly broke out, coming from the *muharram,* which in this case was a considerable distance from where we sat, since the *raba'* a of Sheikh Faisal was several times the size of an ordinary Bedouin tent. This was from the women

Arrival of the *emir*: Prince Hassan, brother of King Hussein of Jordan, is escorted under an arch of flags to tent.

Relaxing after the feast: Sheikh Mohammed (left) and Sheikh Jidoor reclining in luxury; note Persian rugs.

of the *háram,* who began a strange la-la-la-la sort of sing-song as the young *emir* walked up the red carpet. He came into the tent near the center and took his place on a large yellow chair, or throne, at one of the recesses of the *raba' a.*

I was startled to observe that instead of the familiar Bedouin *thōp,* he wore *mufti*—ordinary civilian clothes and a necktie! He was a young man, about twenty, and I learned he had just returned from attending school at Christ Church College of Oxford University in England. He greeted those around him warmly, then stood up and delivered a short speech. The audience shouted in Arabic, which I could not understand, and clapped their hands; now and then some sally of Arabic wit brought peals of laughter from the *sheikhs.*

Sheikh Faisal then read a brief speech of welcome, and the *emir* was shown plans of a public project—a village and school plan that had been under development in the area of Hasa. Suddenly many of the guest converged around him. Whenever an *emir* appears in a public gathering, it is an opportunity for anyone to present petitions of various sorts. Any subject, rich or poor, may importune the prince for a hearing on his plea or complaint, and in many cases the pleas are requests for a pardon for some offense.

The rules of royalty in Jordan are far less stringent than in the south, where the king can—and often does—mete our summary justice, such as cutting off the hand of a man who steals or the tongue of a talebearer who lies about his neighbor. In one instance, which I could vaguely follow with my limited command of Arabic, a woman was brought in to plead for the freedom of her son, who was in prison; and from my understanding of what she said, I gathered that her plea was granted, chiefly on the grounds that she needed her son to help her while the father was away herding camels!

My own social cup was filled to the brim when I managed

to get a personal introduction to the young *emir*. A Jordanian general, sitting beside me on the cushions, apparently recognized that I was an American from my remarks to R'Faifan, and he leaned over and engaged me in conversation.

I explained briefly that I was traveling by camel through eastern Jordan trying to trace stories that might cast new light on the personality of Lawrence of Arabia. He nodded as I talked. Finally he rose and walked over to where the *emir* was sitting and spoke, moving his hands in a curiously agitated manner that is characteristic of Arabic people. Prince Hassan nodded in turn, and a short time later the general came back and asked Dr. Mack and me to join him.

R'Faifan immediately drew farther away, and I had to urge him to accompany me. The Jordanians are essentially a democratic people, and I was certain there would be no violation of protocol if I took R'Faifan with me into the presence of the *emir*.

He came along, still reluctantly, and when he reached the chair where the young prince was sitting, he lunged forward so quickly I thought he was going to sprawl on the ground. He grabbed the prince's hand and kissed it. Hassan smiled and made a gesture of understanding.

He turned to me and in Oxford English expressed his delight that Dr. Mack and I had come from the United States to travel in Jordan.

"We should know more about each other," he said. "It is only in this way that people of the world will come to understand each other."

He then told me he had noticed me in the group and had thought I was a Circassian because of my blue eyes—an indirect tribute to the burned complexion I had acquired in the weeks I had spent out on the desert under the broiling sun. My face had become as dark as any Bedouin's, and the mustache I had grown—while American in contour—was also dark, so my features probably resembled those of a desert nomad.

Sheikh Faisal had observed me talking with the *emir,* and he came over and shook hands.

"You made good time from Rumm, I see," he remarked. His expression was grave, but his eyes seemed to twinkle, and I had the odd thought that perhaps the driver who brought us from Rumm might have been under instructions to see to it that I understood the difference between the ancient mode of travel by camel and the more modern method employing high-powered motorcars.

Sheikh Faisal's face had the brooding expression characteristic of many Arabs; it seemed to combine the wisdom of the ancient lands and disenchantment with political and social trends swirling about the Arab peoples today in the turmoil of international affairs.

I knew he was one of the most powerful men in the country, as a titular head of the Jazi clan of the Howeitat and a friend of King Hussein, also a Bedouin. The possibility that he might have ordered his driver to give me that roaring ride from Rumm was merely another facet of these strange nomadic people, whose sense of humor is often as subtle as their character. I also appreciated the fact that he had been sufficiently interested in my rather small efforts, as I outlined my plans to him at Jiza, to send an invitation to me at Rumm to join the feast for Emir Hassan. In spite of my jolted joints, I nodded politely and agreed that we had had an interesting ride.

We headed back to Rumm late in the afternoon, arriving after dark at the gap in the canyon walls above the fort. The return ride, chiefly over the paved King's Highway, was uneventful, and I was more than ever convinced that my suspicion that Sheikh Faisal possessed a subtle sense of humor was well grounded.

2

One interesting outcome of the trip to Sheikh Faisal's desert home was an incident that apparently bound R'Faifan more closely to me than before, if that were possible. It was a matter with which I actually had no direct concern, but it illustrated the queer workings of Bedouin "law" governing marriage and divorce, which in reality is more tradition than legal enactment.

It appeared that R'Faifan's older son, Jizar, had been married, and his wife had gone back to her family. The father then demanded alimony of Jizar! After our brief talk with the *emir,* R'Faifan had drawn me aside and quickly explained this matter, suggesting that in view of the fine relations that now existed between Hassan and myself, I might interceded in his son's behalf.

I was not sufficiently familiar with Bedouin customs or Jordanian law relating to marriage and divorce to know the strength of the young man's case, but I certainly was familiar enough with human psychology to know when to keep my nose out of internal domestic problems such as this. However, R'Faifan begged me to speak to the *emir,* and finally I went to the Jordanian general, who turned out to be commander of the eastern army, and explained R'Faifan's problem.

He readily agreed to speak to the *emir,* and before we left— to my considerable surprise—he informed me that Hassan understood the situation and would personally look into the matter. R'Faifan gave me all the credit for the intercession and was so overjoyed that when we reached the fort at Rumm he assured me he would have the camels ready to leave at the crack of dawn if I so desired.

That night, as I turned in at the little fort, I could hear R'Faifan in the next room, singing out praises to Allah for the great things that had been accomplished in his behalf that day, and from my meager knowledge of Arabic, I understood that he was also putting in a good word for me.

Early the following morning, true to his promise, R'Faifan had our two camels assembled, with grain loaded on the bull, who carried twice the load of the female. As we rode out of the little compound, Sergeant Mohammed abu Brahim waved at us with such sweeping gestures that I was not at all sure he had not included his namesake, the castrated bull, in his emotional adieu.

We had an additional member in our entourage, besides Dr. Mack, R'Faifan, and me. This was a Bedouin named Sab'ah Ji-Ji, who had been a comrade of R'Faifan in his Camel Corps days and who lived at times in Rumm and at times on the trail to Mudawwara. His father, according to R'Faifan, had been a raider with Lawrence, and he knew the territory around Rumm and Mudawwara very well. Much of this knowledge seemed to have been passed down to Sab'ah. I was glad to have him accompany us and provide some firsthand information about the raid at Mudawwara, which Sheikh Aid had related in a somewhat different fashion from the story told by Lawrence.

Sab'ah was a strong, wiry man in his early forties. He was given to sudden expressions of his thoughts and feelings as we rode along and seemed to be a kind of desert philosopher. At one point, half a dozen miles along the old trail used by Lawrence to ride from Aqaba to Rumm, which turned off sharply to the east, he suddenly leaned toward me and screamed: "This is the secret trail of Lawrence!" He reached over and tugged at the sleeve of my *thōp* and pointed ahead toward a huge column of rock, rising some 1,500 feet sheer from

212

the desert floor. "That is Jabal Mahraj. It is also known as the Prophet and the Horse!"

I was not quite certain of the logical connecton between the two remarks, but as I looked ahead at the spire of rock, I observed that it actually looked like a red-robed figure standing beside an animal. It seemed quite remarkable that this desert statue should have been created in this shape by erosion over countless millennia, long before the time of the Prophet. My companion looked keenly at me to determine my reaction, and then went on: "In the words of the Prophet, 'Whoever treats a horse kindly shall sit at the feet of God, and whoever mistreats a horse shall be accursed of God!' "

I nodded appreciatively, although I still failed to follow Sab'ah's logic. Mohammed's fondness for horses was a Moslem tradition, of course. There is even a story that he sponsored the first horse race on Arabian soil, at a place called Kaffiyat, over a distance of 6 miles, and wagered on his own mare. Another Bedouin story tells of a race in the time of the Caliph Omar, whose son rode in a race and invoked the help of Mohammed as he started. The horse, possibly encouraged by this backing, not only won the race but continued until it ran into a nearby mosque!

However apocryphal these stories may be, there is something about the Bedouin and the horse that go together, like salt and pepper. For many centuries, even before the time of Mohammed, the Arabian horse was virtually a sacred animal, as the cow is in India. In some cases horses were believed to possess the "evil eye," a supposition which Mohammed himself denounced as a form of pagan idolatry but which persists to this day among many Bedouin.

The horse is so significant in Arabic literature that in the legendary account of creation it is said that Allah first created man and then a stallion, even before he created woman and

213

a mare. There is an ancient Arabic saying, attributed to Allah: "I will create a being in which happiness will be for the good, and misfortune for the bad: happiness on the forehead, bounty on its back, and joy in the possessor." This obviously refers to a horse, not a man.[1]

This high priority of the horse is somewhat at variance from the injunction of Mohammed that "after woman came the horse, for the enjoyment and happiness of man," but there seems little question that the Prophet, along with most Bedouin, had a respect for the horse above any other animal.

Sab'ah continued his interminable discourse on the importance and habits of horses, hollering at me from time to time as we jolted along, only a few feet apart. I remembered hearing a story that the favorite horse of Mohammed, among his string of a dozen or more, was a mare called Sab'ah, and I wondered if this had some connection with Sab'ah's enthusiasm on the subject.

As we passed the configuration of rock that resembled the Prophet and the horse, he leaned over and yelled: "We ride always at the feet of the Prophet!"

It struck me that this was a singularly appropriate remark, and it was never more true than in the red canyons of Rumm. As we headed away from the faint traces of the old Lawrence trail southward from Rumm to Aqaba, which curved off to the west, we were indeed riding over unmarked desert where only the spirit of Allah prevailed. Jabal er Rakh'a, to our left as we rode eastward, rose some 1,500 feet above the canyon floor and seemed to look down upon us with the indifference of an Olympian god, who had looked upon many other travelers over this lonely road for thousands of years. In a very real sense, Mohammed—the Seal of the Prophets—was the intervening spirit that formed a bond between man and Allah, the creator of all things. As we rode through this im-

214

mense natural temple, one could not be unaware of the fulfilling presence of that spirit that had created a historical entity out of the wandering tribes of camel herders who had been the Bedouin of pre-Mohammedan times.

The very presence of these majestic monuments of rock rising in pure grandeur from the flat *ghôr* contributed to this sensation of riding down through the corridors of time. Jabal Um Ishrim towered behind us, and the long shallow depression of the Wádi Um Ishrim, across which we now rode, lay like a whitish scar on the face of the valley. Beyond, among the purple peaks to the north—which had been south of us on the earlier journey from Bat'n al Ghúl into Rumm—were tiers of solid rock that had been carved out by ancient rivers that may have swirled around these cliffs at the time of the flood. These massive edifices had been cut out of solid stone, just as the Grand Canyon of the Colorado has been shaped by wind and water during aeons of constant erosion.

About 25 kilometers from the point where we had turned eastward from the main trail from Rumm to Aqaba, we saw a couple of miles ahead a broad dry stream bed, sloping down from rounded hills. R'Faifan pointed beyond the end of the valley into which we were riding and called out to me: "Do you remember the old man we saw on the road, Abu Ghaith? It was only a few miles from here!"

He grinned, as if the recollection would arouse my sense of humor, and once again I was acutely aware of the difference in attitudes toward life and nature on the part of those who were bred on the desert and those who have lived in the festering cities. There was something simple and logical, even if it was harsh, in R'Faifan's reaction; yet I could not forget the hopeless misery of an old man, diseased and ready to die, squatting beside a lonely desert trail where the traffic might amount to only half a dozen travelers in a month, holding out

215

his hands to us and crying out that he was ready to die—and then turning to look toward Mecca when we passed by.

My reflections were so vivid that I was almost on the point of suggesting that we shift our course and strike for the trail across the hills, just to see if the old man was still there. However I quickly dismissed this as being a bit senseless, particularly as I would not want to ride past the dying Bedouin again and ignore his pleading the second time.

It would require only a few kilometers of extra riding—perhaps an hour's time—to reach the trail where the old Arab had squatted on the sand dune, but the renewal of the incident in my case would require that I traverse hundreds of years backward in time in order to understand the event. I suppose incidents of this sort happen to everyone, yet I must confess that even today I am not sure whether my own response to the dying mendicant's plea was right or wrong.

As we jogged toward the hills where Sab'ah's tents were pitched, it seemed to me there was a magic city, swimming in the haze above the valley. I realized that this uneven fantasy was simply the effect of an illusion of heat and light, with the sun's rays, glancing off the stone face of the canyon wall, creating a mirror of queer rock structures, yet it all contributed to my feeling of unreality as I rode down that forgotten road.

We had decided before leaving Rumm that we would take a route following a secret trail used by Lawrence and the Arab raiders to Mudawwara. This route, as far as was known, had never been followed by modern travelers other than Lawrence's raiders. It split off from the main road through Rumm a few miles below Jabal Rumm and curved eastward into a chain of dry lake beds—"twenty miles of hard mud," as Lawrence described it—between towering columns of red rock that rose high above the desert, the peaks of Jabal er Rakh'a and Jabal

Mahraj. To the south a series of rising cliffs led upward to the Arabian plateau.

As we rode to the southeast, I thought of Lawrence—often the only Westerner on these guerrilla raids—riding through the night intent upon the destruction of the Hijaz-Medina rail artery between Syria and Arabia. I wondered what his lonely thoughts may have been.

I recalled a strange story Lawrence had told of an "old man of Rumm"—a bearded patriarch of an older day "with a hewn face of great power and weariness"—who had stumbled on him while he was bathing in the pool near Lawrence's Spring. He had peered at the naked man in the pool with old, weary eyes and said: "The love is from God; and of God; and towards God."[2]

This, Lawrence noted in his book, had "overturned" some of his theories of the nature of the Arab, but it seemed to me, in the presence of these magnificent crimson canyons and pinnacles of rock standing high on the desert floor, that nothing could have expressed more profoundly the nature of the nomad who chose to live out on the desert waste, scrounging an existence from the barren soil, his whole life and even his belief in life rooted in the absolute faith that all things come from God and all things are directed to God.

Lawrence's "old man of Rumm" may have been his own fiction, as so many things in his stories seem to be, yet the "revision" of his own theories of the Arab was quite possibly the subconscious reflection of what he knew and understood as a result of living with the Bedouin. The lands around Rumm and along our trail to the southeast were etched deeply in the rock and were somewhat different from the open steppelands of Arabia itself, yet the same force of nature that had persisted in these red canyons had also become engraved on the Bedouin character, a hardness of human life born out of the hardness

217

of the very soil over which he rode, soil which yielded only the scantiest nourishment to his camels, goats, and horses— and to the *bedu* himself.

Sab'ah must have sensed my musings as we rode along the dry mud flats toward his desert home which lay on the far side of the shallow valley. He looked at me from under the rim of his white *kaffiyah,* his beaklike nose protruding from the cloth and his dark eyes glinting with secret humor. Unexpectedly, as if reading my thoughts, he called out: *"'Arab al masta 'áriba!"*

This, according to my limited understanding of the Arabic language, was a salutation to one who has become an Arab as opposed to the *'arab al 'áriba,* one who is already an Arab. It originally denoted those Arabs supposed to have descended from Ishmael, as distinguished from the descendants of Joktan, who came from the line of Shem, and the legendary Yarab, son of Joktan, who founded the kingdom of Yemen and is believed by many to have been the origin of the word Arab.

Sab'ah's remark was an accolade indeed. I smiled back, feeling again the old warmth of comradeship with these desert wanderers whom I had come to know perhaps better than my own people. The Bedouin are among the proudest of races, believing the pure Arab strain is far superior to any other, yet among the most human and generous of any people I have ever known. It is well recognized by all who have traveled and mingled with Bedouin that they regard non-Bedouin with an air of superiority, and sometimes disdain, as belonging to essentially inferior strains of the human race. In spite of this remoteness of manner, however, they possess an ingrained quality of human courtesy and a sense of hospitality toward strangers that, in psychological contrast, is little short of a paradox.

We reached Sab'ah's *bait sha'ar* in midafternoon, and

218

Bedouin and camel: Sergeant Mohammed abu Brahim of Desert
Patrol and R'Faifan's camel, also named Mohammed abu Brahim.

Old man and the pipe: Sheikh Sa'bah is smoking the author's pipe,
which he traded for his own stone pipe.

rather than lose time, since our schedule had tightened as a result of the delays at Rumm, I decided to push on and camp farther along the trail that night. This would enable us to reach Mudawwara the following day in a single march.

Sab'ah, who had spent many years in this part of the desert, where Lawrence's guerrillas had operated in the first phases of the Arab Revolt, had agreed to come with us to supply information about the locale, which he knew intimately. Since I had contingent expeditionary funds for just such purposes, I had readily accepted his offer.

Meanwhile he called in all his neighbors as we rode up. There were six tents in the area, surrounding a well shared by all, forming a kind of desert community. One of the *sheikhs,* whose name also was Sa'bah, an old man with a wasted body and a nose like a parrot's bill, told me he also had ridden with Lawrence and the tribal leaders, such as Sharif Aid and Zaal, and he sat in his tent for more than an hour recounting his adventures. His voice was querulous and his memory thin, and I felt I could put more trust in the accounts of my cantankerous old friend at Rumm, Sheikh Aid. In the end, we traded pipes—my briar for his stone pipe, and we parted on the best of terms.

After a couple of hours we reared ourselves from the comfortable cushions in Sab'ah's tent, made elaborate adieus with much bowing and clasping of hands, and set off on our journey southward. Sa'bah's remarks on the way down from Rumm had made me feel more and more that I was becoming a Bedouin in fact as well as fancy.

3

We camped that night on the open desert on the far side

of an 800-foot mound some 7 or 8 kilometers beyond Sab'ah's tent. Around us on three sides were blackish hills and cliffs, and I believed we were entering the area of limestone and flinty gravel known as Al Alhala. There were several small trees scattered around us, indicating underground streams and it struck me this was probably one of the summer grazing grounds which would be used later in the year. The nomadic herders move in circles around their tribal grazing grounds, in a process not unlike crop rotation, although the crops were only salt grass, *hamdh*.

R'Faifan pointed to the east, where the old trail from Mudawarra to Guweira crossed the Suwwana flats, and said we would reach it early the following day.

We gathered a pile of dried camel dung—known as *jala*—for our fire. This was further proof that the little valley, with its touches of green, was probably a grazing ground that would be used at a later season of the year.

We laid out our map, still glued to the oilcloth, on the ground, and R'Faifan, Sab'ah, Dr. Mack, and I studied it, planning our route to Mudawwara. We had been traveling along a course almost parallel to the old camel trail from Mudawwara to Guweira, but from 8 to 12 kilometers south and hidden from the other route by reddish mountains. This probably was the reason Lawrence chose this "back road" to Mudawwara, and I began to take keen interest in the topography and layout of the land as we progressed southward. Sa'bah told us we would have to cover 50 kilometers the next day to reach the Mudawwara wells, where there was a *badia* post.

Since we had a long day's march ahead, R'Faifan aroused us before dawn and quickly brought in the camels. After washing their hands in the sand, he and Sab'ah sang out their morning prayer:

Allah is most great!
I testify there is no God but Allah!
I testify that Mohammed is the Prophet of Allah. . . .

On each occasion when we camped alone on the desert, outside the *badia* posts or the hospitable *bait sha' ar* of a Bedouin family, R'Faifan had strewn the line of stones that formed his *masjid* with a loop pointed in the direction of Mecca. The prayers were always simple, direct, and quickly accomplished. According to Moslem requirements, the morning prayer must be just at dawn, "when a single hair, held before the eyes, can be seen by the one who is praying." The noon prayer is the second of the day; after that there is the afternoon prayer, three or four hours later. At sunset the *maghrab* prayer fixes the time of day, and finally the evening prayer, following dinner, ends the Moslem day.

As the four of us rode out toward the brown hills and down into the Kuweirat flat, I began to recognize the area over which we had come from Bat'n al Ghūl. The desert trail was marked only faintly. The main pilgrims' highway ran northward from Mudawwara through Bat'n al Ghūl and along the track of the old railroad to Fasu'a and Ma'ān; but I was certain Lawrence would have stayed well to the west of this route which in his day was patrolled by Turkish soldiers, to avoid being seen.

In *Seven Pillars of Wisdom* this backdoor route from Rumm to Mudawwara is described in detail, Lawrence pointing out that it was "important to our armored cars because its twenty miles of hard mud might enable them to reach Mudowwara easily." He indicated that the unused trail from the south end of Rumm canyon, over which we were now traveling, would be like a shuttle service and they would be "able to hold up the circulation of trains when we pleased."[3]

222

This would appear to be a bit fantastic to anyone traveling the route. The distance is a good 80 kilometers from the lower end of Rumm Valley, where we turned east from the main track into Aqaba, and the terrain is not all mud flats. Much of the going was over steep hills, flanked by sharp ridges of rock, and it obviously was not a trail frequented by travelers for any except clandestine purposes. This again was one of the chinks in Lawrence's armor of fact which would pass unnoticed except to one who had covered the same ground.

Sa'bah jogged his camel over so that he was riding alongside mine. He resumed his rambling discourse, in which he seemed to mix nonessentials with matters of importance, and at times with words filled with wisdom.

"This is a land where many men have died," he said, adding sententiously: "This must always be when men fight for their freedom."

I could have readily agreed, except that there was little killing on the road from Rumm to Mudawwara; the most compelling motive the Arab raiders seemed to have had in their early attacks on the Turkish railroad was to make off with booty rather than destroy the train. However, I nodded agreement with Sab'ah's basic contention that men must fight for freedom.

The Bedouin had maintained their freedom under oppressive circumstances for many centuries, unaffected in small matters of personal independence, and they retained their customary living habits, whether the yoke of oppression was of their own caliphs, the Persians, or the Ottoman Turks. Oddly enough, the Arabs also had a reciprocal regard for the independence of others. The Moslem creed never required non-Moslems to join the faith; Moslems merely imposed heavy taxes on infidels, thus offering an excellent economic remedy for nonparticipation in the faith. The Jews, for example, were not required to

223

disclaim their own religious faith under Arab conquerors; they merely had to pay a heavier burden of taxation.

This simple and direct formula for coordinating discordant religious beliefs is somewhat in contrast to the bigotry of many Christian religious organizations, which managed not only to collect tithes but also imposed heavy penalties, such as death on the rack or by burning, for religious dissent.

In any event, I had become conscious of the new stirrings of thirst for freedom among the Bedouin of Jordan. It seemed that each new encroachment had destroyed some part of their freedom, but never the intensity of their desire for it; and yet each break in their independence made them more vulnerable to new attacks. I thought of the rumors I had heard, such as the reports of "trouble in the west" that Doug Manson had mentioned and the sudden decision of the Jordanian government to place the Arab region between Jordan and Israel "out of bounds." The rumbling sounds of trucks I had seen at Ammān and at Jiza, the jet planes over the desert at Bāyir . . . all contributed to the feeling that a new menace hung over these nomads of the Arabian Steppe with their ancient traditions and habits of life.

We turned southward along the old trail to Mudawwara, crossing a flat, arid stretch of *ghôr* with tall spires of rock shimmering in the distance, I thought of the cruelty that had ruled this land for so many centuries—on the part of both the oppressors and the Bedouin themselves. They are not given to niceties of human compassion; the old law of "an eye for an eye and a tooth for a tooth" still is a basic formula of Bedouin life. The right of the *malak,* or king, to have the hand of a thief struck off, merely on his own judgment, is a kind of harshness to which Westerners are not accustomed, and which they would regard as barbaric, yet the same ruler might dismiss a more serious charge out of kindness and human sym-

The well at Mudawwara: the three palms surrounding the watering place with camels kneeling beside the well.

pathy to prevent a mother's loss of the needed services of her son!

The road over the desert crossed one of the most desolate stretches of land I have ever seen. There was hardly a blade of scrub grass to be seen, and except for an occasional ridge, rising like a gaunt rib from the flat surface, the plain was unrelieved by hills or deep gulleys. The sun beat down until it was as if a baking oven surrounded us, with the mountains in the distance suspended on shimmering waves of light and heat. We rocked along in the saddle for nearly twelve hours, except for a short stop for the noonday lunch of warm tea and sardines, and the brief period of prayer, and by the end of the day we could see the outline of a small cluster of mud-walled huts, topped by a dark bulk that I assumed was the old Turkish fort at Mudawwara.

We urged our tired camels to the top of a long ridge and sat there several minutes in our saddles, silently staring at the rolling land below us. This was the historic ground over which Lawrence and his Arab companions had crawled across the gulleys on the moon-filled night when they made the first guerrilla raid on the railroad north of Mudawwara Station, and I tried to picture the scene as Lawrence must have observed it.

The hill on which we sat was probably the covering ridge behind which the silent Arabs had approached the place, and I could see in the distance, under the darkening shadows, what seemed to be a line of tiny broken hills that may have been the bed of the old Hijaz-Medina railroad. I had read Lawrence's description minutely and was interested in comparing it with what Sheikh Aid told me and what I saw. Lawrence's accuracy in describing the area would be to some extent a measure of his faithfulness in recording other elements of history. Under normal circumstances, such things could be checked against contemporary records, but in the case of

226

Lawrence, there were no actual records except his own, and the various Bedouin stories are so apocryphal, having passed through several hands, that they offer no real substantiation, one way or another.

While Dr. Mack's primary interest was in the character and personality of Lawrence, it followed that what he did and what he said about his doings were basic elements in the posthumous psychoanalysis, and I wanted to provide all the material possible. We had taken a number of tape recordings from old Bedouin who claimed to have had some contact with him, and their accounts, together with the physical setting I now witnessed, might be patched together into a reasonably complete report for the psychological study.

From our vantage point above Mudawwara, we were able to survey the area. It was late in the day, and I was tired; but I felt that I would not again be able to capture in my own mind the impression of the spectacle before me as it was at this moment of my first observation. The station at Mudawwara could be seen about 4 miles away, as Lawrence described it, a yellowish building against a background of dun-colored desert. The old Turkish fort loomed in the foreground, with a cluster of three date palms near it, apparently around the well. The town itself lay at the edge of a *wâdi* that extended southward into a sea of sand; somewhere in the arid expanse was the border between Jordan and Saudi Arabia.

As I have previously noted, borders are not as accurately traced in Arabic lands as in many other parts of the world, where sharp political or national cleavages divide countries with precise boundaries. The nomads seldom marked out boundaries for anything, even in their tribal domains, and for all practical purposes the station at Mudawwara was the entry point between Jordan and Saudi Arabia. Much of the borderland east of this place had been shifted back and forth with

227

tracts the size of a small state such as Rhode Island exchanged for some equally barren waste farther along the border, in order to fit the convenience of some tribal chief. The so-called family line between the United States and Canada would seem like a bristling barricade compared with the flexible frontiers that constitute the lines of political demarcation between Arab countries.

R'Faifan, Dr. Mack, Sab'ah, and I had pushed hard to reach Mudawwara that day, in order to be able to explore the surrounding hills the following day and if possible trace the guerrilla raid on the railroad some 50 years before. However, I wanted to savor the first sight of the place, which for me had considerable historic significance. I tried to picture the deployment of the Arab forces of about 100 men, as Lawrence had described it: the ledges behind which they lay in wait for the Turkish troop train; the *widyân* over which the small trestles were built; the troop train belching smoke as it steamed out of the station. However, we were so dog-tired I quickly decided to push on to the little *badia* fort which was clearly visible, with its flag flying from the tower, at the outskirts of the town.

We rode our weary camels down through the winding valley. R'Faifan dismounted for the last few yards, apparently as a concession to his bull camel, which had borne a much heavier load than my *nága*. We must have looked like pilgrims from nowhere as we plodded through the gate, where we were greeted by the sentry and later by the corporal in charge, who —by some curious coincidence—happened to have been an old buddy of R'Faifan in his Camel Corps days!

We were given quarters at the *badia* post, but the exhilaration of having arrived at this place which rekindled my thoughts about the Lawrence legends made it impossible to turn in early. There were several members of the Desert Patrol and others at the little store near the old railroad station, and since it was still only dusk we walked over for a few purchases and exchange of small talk with the troopers who were there.

VIII. *The Raid at Mudawwara*

1

Mudawwara, one of the landmarks of the Arab Revolt, is little more than a way station today for pilgrims on their journeys southward to Mecca and on their return over the old road into Jordan, Syria, and Iraq. The series of desert trails from the south converge at the station, long since abandoned as a railroad stopping point. Most of the traffic now stops at the combined general store and café. Aside from the station, the store, the *badia* post, and the old Turkish fort, there was little in the town except for the well, a few abandoned mud huts, and a sparse scattering of tents on the hills around the town.

An English construction engineer working on the rebuilding of the old railroad came through the station late that night in a truck on his way from Tobuk, in Saudi Arabia, and after we had exchanged a few bits of information, I outlined my plan for probing the eastern side of the desert. He quickly offered to transport me to Tobuk if I could arrange a Saudi Arabian visa. I assured him that my purpose was to travel as the Bedouin traveled for centuries past, and while I thanked him for his offer, I had no particular desire to take a truck ride across the Arabian plateau!

Later in the evening a strange-looking man rode into the station on a scraggly camel. I discovered, in talking with him, with the help of Sab'ah and R'Faifan, that he was a pilgrim from Afghanistan who had been to the Hijaz and now had covered some 700 miles of the return journey, riding alone. He had only another 1,000 miles to go to reach his home on the Iranian plateau. Here was a man who rode without company for almost 4,000 miles to fulfill his religious faith by visiting the holy city of Mecca!

I thought of a quotation from Chapter 76 of the Koran: "Allah will make his faith a light unto man: for man was created weak."

It struck me that willingness to ride farther than the distance from New York to San Francisco over the bleak desert in order to fulfill the fifth command in Mohammed's Five Pillars of Islam: "Go ye to Mecca at least once!" was hardly to be regarded as an act of weakness. I remembered a story I once heard of a crew of Moslem lascars on a voyage into the Arctic during the month of Ramadan when the faithful fast from dawn to dusk. The Moslems refused to break their sacred fast until the end of daylight, and since there is six months of continuous daylight in the Arctic, they starved to death!

I had planned to make the decision at Mudawwara whether or not to strike out eastward in the hope of intercepting the line of old wells somewhere in the area of the Wádi al Ghadah, about 160 kilometers east of Mudawwara near the southeastern corner of the Hashemite Kingdom of the Jordan. This territory is still only vaguely defined in maps. Although most maps show the border between Jordan and Saudi Arabia running due east along latitude 29° 20' north for perhaps 200 kilometers, then turning northward to form the jutting northeast shoulder of Saudi Arabia, there is some question as to which country owns the territory along this line.

On my map I had marked Q-7 as the location of the seventh of the line of old wells, and I thought if I could discover this abandoned watering place in the unmapped area in which the Wádi al Ghadah lay, I might follow the trail northward, tracing the wells along the edge of eastern Jordan through the Wádi Sirhan, without crossing into Saudi Arabia territory until I reached Q-4, due east of Bāyir. There was known to be a complex of camel trails where Bani-Atiyah and Howeitat tribesmen ranged in two fairly well watered valleys north of Wádi al Ghadah. If we were lucky enough to locate these ranges we would undoubtedly be able to refresh our camels and continue northward. The two valleys extended for perhaps 30 or 40 kilometers and were known as the lands of the Banni Murrah and the Kuwakahbah tribes.

Beyond these places there was an established watering hole called Bi'r an Naam, about 120 kilometers due east of Jafr. Surrounding this oasis, however, was one of the wildest and least traveled sections of the Eastern Desert, without a single camel track marked on any map I could find. Between the two *widyán* and the Jordan-Saudi Arabia border lay 10,000 square miles of dry desert. The total distance from Mudawwara to Bi'r an Naam was about 250 kilometers, a minimum of ten days' travel without water. While strong camels from the south can cover far greater distances and travel for longer periods if they are finely bred and in good condition, our *jamál* from north Jordan were of an inferior breed, and three or four days without water would be their limit.

In order to grasp the geography of this region it is necessary to mark out—either mentally or on a map—a great block of territory roughly from Mudawwara due eastward for about 200 kilometers, and then northward along the Saudi Arabian border to Bi'r an Naam. This area covers the southeast corner of Jordan, approximately 26,000 square kilometers, a third larger than the state of New Jersey.

Somewhere within this vast region were the ranges of the two tribes of Bedouin nomads who roamed over well-watered *widyân*. The rest of the area consisted of black gravel sand, dry steam beds, and barren ridges: almost as perilous to the traveler as the white sands of the dread Rab' el Kháli, 1,000 miles to the south. The danger of missing the intervening watering areas and possibly perishing on the desert, compounded by the risk of wandering illegally across the border into Saudi Arabia, decided us against this route. There was also the problem of Sa'bah; he had agreed only to accompany us to Mudawwara to help unearth information about Lawrence and would not want to accompany us into the Eastern Desert.

The alternative course was to head north to Bat'n al Ghūl as far as Fasu'a, the abandoned railroad station where we had taken refuge during the storm, and then to swing back into western Jordan where there were *buyút sha'ar* of many *shiekhs* I knew, including Sheikh Faisal ibn Jazi. After poring over the maps, we agreed that the journey to the east would offer risks that we could not afford to take, so we decided on the alternative course.

Meanwhile, we had certain final investigations to make, based largely on what Sab'ah had told us and the material we had gathered in taped interviews with Sheikh Aid and other old Bedouin at Rumm.

After talking the situation over, Dr. Mack, R'Faifan, Sab'ah, and I decided to ride over the area north and west of Mudawwara, described by Lawrence in *Seven Pillars of Wisdom,* and examine the terrain for the purpose of comparing it with the passages in his account of the raids on the old railroad. It seemed fairly important to corroborate his version, or to determine in which respects it was at variance with what we found, since this would offer the only tangible clues to the validity of his story.

Sab'ah's attitude in this matter was quite surprising, and for a time it puzzled me until I realized that it was merely the age-old pride of the Bedouin, who were unwilling to concede that anyone—even Lawrence—could have been superior to the Arab guerrillas themselves. In his disconnected discourse he hinted that Lawrence was not, in his opinion, the real leader of the Arab Revolt, but was in a sense a follower of Emir Faisal and his brother, Zaid.

In his eagerness to make this point clear, Sab'ah entered energetically into seeking by suggestion and innuendo to discredit Lawrence's accuracy in reporting the raids. When we set out the following morning on our general examination of the terrain, he took me over the route which according to the tradition of the Arabs had been the course followed by the raiders. Now and then he would halt his camel and point to certain ridges and gulleys where the raiding band had found concealment.

I will confess I was quite surprised at the number of variations between what I had gleaned from a rather careful study of Lawrence's account of the famous raids and the actual configurations of the country over which we rode, particularly with respect to the possibility of concealment from the Turks at Mudawwara Station; I was hardly prepared, however, for Sab'ah's denouncement, which seemed to be that there had never been a raid such as Lawrence described!

2

It was not my intention to make a searching inquiry into the authenticity of Lawrence's account of various raids and other activities in which he was engaged during the time of the Arab Revolt. We were interested only in tracking down such information as might be available on Lawrence's personal character, to provide material for the psychological study my friend was preparing.

However, the question of whether the Arab raiders who rode with Lawrence were politically motivated guerrillas carrying out a quasi-military operation or simply desert marauders whose sole purpose was to wreck a railroad train and gather in the loot stirred my curiosity. In order to understand what Sab'ah was driving at, it may be helpful to review Lawrence's story of the raid at Mudawwara in *Seven Pillars of Wisdom* for purposes of comparison.[1]

Lawrence himself was not quite clear on the question of Arab motivation, and his wordy fluctuations between admiration and disdain for certain Arab tribesmen make it difficult to follow his own thinking. He undoubtedly regarded the area east of the Dead Sea as being strategically important in a grand plan to support the English by harassing and obstructing the Turks from the rear—his supposed contribution to the history of guerrilla warfare.

There was some reason to believe, from comments I had heard from the Bedouin themselves, that the Arab raiders were prompted more by a desire to loot Turkish trains in retaliation for centuries of oppression, heavy taxation, and disregard for the sentiments of the Arabs as a racial group than they were by any wish to help the English. They had been too long under the rule of alien peoples, beginning with the influx of Persians under the Abbasid caliphs in the eighth century and ending with the Ottoman Turks in the nineteenth, not to relish the notion of simply despoiling their tormentors, regardless of the military importance of their activities.

Furthermore, the Bedouin is historically and habitually a tribal creature. During the days of the Prophet, tribal allegiances were the core of the Meccan insurgence, the Medina revolt, and the rise of Mohammed's power; and before and since there has been nothing in the character or conduct of the true Arab— the nomads of the Steppe—that would indicate any real change in this attitude. The fact that Islamic religious forces unified the tribes under a common faith did not in any way reshape the character or habits of the Bedouin; they remained families of nomads, whose chief occupation for several thousand years had been raising camels and sheep and raiding caravans.

In trying to shift out fact from fiction in Lawrence's own record of his activities, it was obviously necessary to recognize the kind of people he was dealing with—not a friendly military force, as he well knew, but a conglomeration of desert fighters who for centuries had followed their own mores and were not likely to change their habits for the sake of the British.

The historic raid at Mudawwara Station was the first case in point in which a conflict of interests would have been evident. If the Arabs had shifted from the role of raiders to that of planned military strategists, assigned to create dislocation of Turkish forces by an attack from the rear, the raid on Mudawwara would have been carefully calculated to achieve this purpose. This was undoubtedly the British intention, and Lawrence was the British agent. But was it actually what the Arabs sought to do?

In order to evaluate Lawrence's character, even at this late date, it seemed quite important to decide what his actual part was in the Arab Revolt. In the preliminary phases of the British efforts to establish common cause with the Arabs of the Hijaz, Lawrence had played a role somewhere between a messenger and an undercover agent. In *Seven Pillars of Wisdom* he gives an unexpected hint of this:

Suddenly Feisal asked me if I would wear Arab clothes like his own while in camp. I should find it better for my own part, since it was a comfortable dress in which to live Arab-fashion as we must

237

do. Besides, the tribesmen would then understand how to take me. . . . If I wore Meccan clothes, they would behave to me as though I were *really one of their leaders* [italics mine]; and I might slip in and out of Feisal's tent without making a sensation which he had to explain away each time to strangers.[2]

The significance of this comment becomes apparent in some of Lawrence's later remarks about his own position among the Arabs, which at one point he refers to as "something like a general," and speaks of the Arab irregulars assigned to him as being "very proud of being my bodyguard." He even notes that General Bols, one of the British commanders, had dealt directly with Bani-Sakhr tribal chiefs and thus made an "inroad into my province."[3]

One of the critical points in this retrospective analysis of the story of Lawrence of Arabia obviously would be the actual status he held among the Arabs. Sheikh Aid had already told me that Lawrence was generally believed by the Bedouin to have been a servant of Emir Faisal, one of the four sons of Hussein of Hijaz, the *sharif* of Mecca. I learned from other Bedouin that Lawrence was not even considered by some Arabs to have been an Englishman, but was regarded as a mercenary of some sort, of uncertain national origin, who called himself an Englishman and hired out as a technician in guerrilla warfare.

Lawrence's own account would indicate that he had been assigned by the English general, Lord Allenby, commander of British forces in Egypt and Palestine, to go into Arabia and assess the worth of the *sharif* of Mecca or his sons as Arab leaders. He traveled to Medina for this purpose in 1916 and, after exploring the possibilities, came to the conclusion that Sharif Hussein himself was too old for consideration, and probably was more friendly with the Turks than with the British. He then investigated Hussein's four sons—Abdullah, who later became head of the royal family of Jordan; Ali, who became king of Hijaz; Faisal, and Zaid. These were the natural leaders of the Arab Revolt. However, Lawrence found Abdullah "too clever," Ali "too clean," and Zaid "too cool." So he settled upon Faisal as the best of the leaders, and the man who would be most likely to stir the Arabs into action.[4]

Lawrence admitted that in forays along the Hijaz-Medina railroad he was carrying out plans agreed upon with Faisal, but whether he directed the attack, as he hints in his account, or merely accompanied the raiders as a technical adviser is still pretty much of a mystery. I hoped my investigations around Mudawwara, as well as things I had learned from the old *sheikhs* at Rumm, might shed some light on this question.

Sab'ah assured me before we rode out of the little *badia* fort that morning that it would.

"You will see," he had told me the night before, as we looked over the maps in the light of a kerosene lamp, "that the wrecking of the trains was quite a different thing from the way it was reported. The big thing was to gain materials."

I was not quite clear as to how our examination of the terrain some 50 years after the raids occurred would furnish any evidence, one way or another, on this point, but Sab'ah was so enthusiastic that I decided to let him guide me across the hills where the attack on the railroad supposedly took place.

It should be understood that the town of Mudawwara—if it can be called a town—is not much different today from what it was in Lawrence's time. It is not a compact village but rather a scattering of a few buildings, mostly government installations, along a stretch of about 4 miles parallel to the border. Our approach the evening before had been from the northwest, following the long dry valley which Lawrence described; it undoubtedly was the same route the Arab guerrillas had taken from the lower end of Rumm Valley. The last 50 kilometers, which we covered in a single day, crossed a sandy desert between rows of rocky hills, and as we topped the ridge above

Mudawwara the previous evening, we probably saw the layout of the town about as Lawrence saw it.

There were a few notable exceptions. He had written of riding "downhill in a narrow valley between moderate sandstone walls: till before sunset we were out on another flat of laid yellow mud."[5] This was the *ghôr* over which we had ridden before topping the rise where the town came into view. But he did not mention the old Turkish fort, a square, two-story structure with the rows of slits in the stone walls from which guns could be fired, which was still standing near the northwestern corner of Mudawwara. It had long since been abandoned by the *badia* for a more modern fort and stockade across the main road from the combined café and store. The latter must have been built since Lawrence's day, and a quarantine station near the border also was new.

Lawrence's account indicated the Arab raiders first reached the well, which he described as "an open pool, a few yards square, in a hollow valley of large stone slabs and flint and sand." The Turks had thrown camels into this well to pollute it, and Lawrence refers vividly to "the green mantle of slime, from which swelled curious bladder-islands of floating fatty pink"—the carcasses of the dead camels. However, he does not mention the Turkish fort, which he could hardly have missed since it stands gray and alone on a sandy hill only a short distance west of the well, surrounded by three date palms.

It is exactly 5 kilometers from the well, at the western end of the town, to the old railroad station at the eastern end, and it is difficult to understand how Lawrence and his raiding party, hidden behind the ridge, were able to observe the station from this point without also seeing the Turkish fort. It may have been the place referred to by Lawrence as Hallat Ammar (see page 193) from which smoke was seen; but this more than likely referred to the station itself.[6] If the Turks had come out of the fort, they would have been *behind* the raiders, not in front of them, and this would have constituted a serious peril in any guerrilla maneuver.

The ridge where the Arab raiders were concealed flanks the railroad line from the west, and as we rode across this area we could see the roadbed of the old line, from which most of the rails had long since disappeared. We also saw a large stack of rusted rails and junked railroad equipment piled beside the abandoned station. From our point of observation, riding our camels across the ridge, it was hard to understand how the raiders could have descended upon the train after the blast of gelatin, as Lawrence called it, had wrecked the engines, without being seen from the station.

In Lawrence's account, he tells how he and one of the Arab raiders, on a reconnaisance of the station on the night of their arrival, "crawled across the last flat, till we could count the unlighted tents and hear the men talking."[7] This would have placed them behind sand dunes, above the location of the new *badia* fort, but the station itself would have been at least a mile away.

It was at this point, apparently, that the raiders decided not to attack the station directly but to return to the hills and lay the charges that would blow up the train. In order to check on this part of the story, Dr. Mack, R'Faifan and I rode back across the sandy hills to a point some distance from the station and made an effort to reconnoiter the layout, so to speak, putting ourselves in the position of Lawrence and his guerrilla band.

In Lawrence's book this location is indicated as a sandy ridge only a short distance from the railroad line but a good 4 miles from the station, from which they crawled to the roadbed and sought a good spot under a bridge crossing one of the gulleys where they could bury the charge of dynamite. We studied the entire layout, while Sab'ah followed us, and now and then I observed on his hawklike visage what seemed to be an expression of cynical amusement.

The rails that remained on the roadbed were rusty and broken, and the roadbed itself had suffered from many seasons of storms and rains. The line of the old tracks curved around the low, sandy hills north of the town, crossing several small, dry creek beds. We rode our camels along the line of tracks but found nothing to indicate that there had been any wreck in the area.

Sab'ah watched me with keen eyes, his head bobbing up and down now and then in its wrapping of white *kaffiyah,* as if to affirm my failure; I almost detected a glint of satisfaction in his sharp glance as he observed the lack of any significant discoveries on my part. It seemed to me he derived personal enjoyment from my frustration, but this may have been my imagination. There are many things about the psychology of desert people I find it hard to understand.

As the four of us rode across the ridges and depressions, I became engrossed in determining how closely the terrain conformed with the description given by Lawrence. The accuracy of his account is not important in itself; he may have trusted to memory in many of the details. What would be significant, however, would be evidence of a deliberate effort to create a situation that lent itself to a classic military concept of a guerrilla raid. If such were the case, there would have to be tactical objectives and a reason for blowing up the train within sight of the station. On the other hand, if the Arabs had merely intended to wreck the train and collect loot from the disorganized Turks, as Sab'ah had suggested, they would have tried it some distance away.

Lawrence's own account in *Seven Pillars of Wisdom* throws some light on this question:

242

Next morning we returned . . . and then marched south across the sandy flat; seeing tracks of gazelle, oryx and ostrich; with, in one spot, stale padmarks of leopard. We were making for the low hills bounding the far side, intending to blow up a train. . . .

So we turned east in the southern ridges till within half a mile of the line. There the party halted in a thirty-foot valley, while a few of us walked down to the line, which bent a little eastward to avoid the point of higher ground under our feet. The point ended in a flat table fifty feet above the track, facing north across the valley.

The metals crossed the hollow on a high bank, pierced by a two-arched bridge for the passage of rain-water. This seemed an ideal spot to lay the charge.[8]

Dr. Mack, R'Faifan, and I rode across the level of sand, observing whether or not we were out of sight of the railroad station about 3 miles to the southeast. We were able to see the station from the top of a ridge, and I concluded we had followed the course described by Lawrence. The distance from the small bridge to the point of concealment on the far side of the ridge from which the charge apparently was detonated was about 200 yards, which seemed reasonable, using—as Lawrence described it—"two-wave electric wires." However, there was no sign of wreckage or a dismemberment of the rails.

Sab'ah, who had been cruising around the place on his camel, rode up while we were drawing retrospective conclusions about the affair. He smiled sadly.

"Of what use would it be to blow up a train at this point for military purposes?" he asked. "Nothing could be accomplished except perhaps to stop one train. The troops guarding the station would be out chasing the men who blew up the train, and there would be no time to gather things from the wreckage."

I recalled Lawrence's vivid description of the "gathering of

243

materials" following that raid on the Mudawwara station, and it struck me that Sab'ah had made a point, probably speaking from an intimate familiarity with Arab motives, which have usually been for booty rather than political or military objectives.

Sab'ah pointed northward.

"On our way," he said, "I will show you where the wrecking of the train happened. It is some fifteen kilometers north of this place."

We examined the area more extensively and found no sign of a wreck or even a demolished bridge. Finally we brought our little caravan together and started northward along the trail toward Bat'n al Ghūl, following closely the line of the old railroad. The rails for the most part had been scattered, apparently carried off by Bedouin who had some use for the metal, but the roadbed was still intact, with a few washouts that interrupted its course.

After about four hours of riding we sighted the ruins of an abandoned station at a place called Tulul es Shahm. Just beyond the station were remains of wreckage, with three overturned railroad carriage wheels lying in the sand. I took pictures of the relics, merely to record their existence. They showed signs of having been dynamited from the tracks, one of the carriages having been blown into an S shape.

There was little doubt in my mind that the Arab raiders could have swooped down at this point well out of sight of the Mudawwara garrison. In fact, Lawrence's account of the affair offers a lively description of looting. "Our greatest object was to destroy locomotives," he wrote in *Seven Pillars of Wisdom*. "Yet they would not finish their looting before the Turks came."

He continues:

The valley was a weird sight. The Arabs, gone raving mad, were rushing about at top speed bareheaded and half-naked, screaming, shooting into the air, clawing one another nail and fist, while they burst open trucks and staggered back and forward with immense bales, which they ripped by the rail-side, and tossed through, smashing what they did not want. . . .

There were scores of carpets spread about; dozens of mattresses and flowered quilts; blankets in heaps, clothes for men and women in full variety; clocks, cooking-pots, food, ornaments and weapons. To one side stood thirty or forty hysterical women, unveiled, tearing their clothes and hair; shrieking themselves distracted. The Arabs without regard to them went on wrecking the household goods; looting their absolute fill. . . . [9]

Lawrence's report of the conduct of the Arabs involved in the raid—whether it occurred 4 miles from Mudawwara or 15—offers an interesting clue to the whole affair, since it presents a typical portrait of a Bedouin attack on a caravan, one of their principal practices over 40 centuries of history, and it seemed to have had little to do with a military operation such as Lawrence had described.

Whatever the importance of these matters may have had for Dr. Mack, they tended to strengthen in my mind the belief that there were some missing parts in Lawrence's account of his adventures in the Arab Revolt. Perhaps the most significant element of our reappraisal of the story of the raid on Mudawwara Station was the partial confirmation of Sab'ah's contention that it was actually only a raid, a normal activity for the Bedouin of that day, or any other day.

Having more or less exhausted the Lawrence legend, we continued northward for several miles to a small, protected wádi through which the trail dipped, and at evening we made our camp in the lee of a bluff where there was sufficient salt grass for the camels and cover from the chill wind, which was rising again from the west.

I had about concluded that the credibility of much of the Lawrence story depended upon the unfamiliarity of the reader with the area in which Lawrence operated. While the importance of his intelligence mission would not necessarily be diminished by disclosure of the fictional nature of what he wrote, it tended to dilute his personal views, particularly those relating to his own importance in the Arab Revolt.

There was a further aspect of this development that impressed me as I pondered over the results of our inspection of the Mudawwara area. The history of the Arabs since the surge of Islamic conquest in the seventh and eighth centuries has established a certain character of Moslem rule over territories the Arabs had possessed. There has been an absence of any directed plan for political expansion. As has been noted (Ch. II) this expansion was largely accidental, a pushing forward into new territories primarily to collect tribute. The Arabs generally sought rewards in taxes rather than additional lands. They were satisfied if their new vassal states paid higher levies, without requiring that they conform to the Moslem religion or even Islamic administration.

This practical attitude was expressed by Joseph Carmichael in *The Shaping of the Arabs:*

The Arabs, either through insight or common-sense acceptance of the state of things as they were, had never made the slightest attempt to get rid of the administrative apparatus of the countries they conquered so quickly. . . . Illiterate and unused to any sedentary occupation at all, they would surely have found the chores of administration beyond them. In any case, they never attempted it. Their basic attitude was, after all, a desire simply to sit on top of an existing society, benefitting economically by all of its activities. . . . The Arabs' main concern was simply the securing of the annual tribute, and they were perfectly satisfied as long as the local authorities, with their knowledge of local conditions, kept on transmitting it to them.[10]

246

3

As we jogged along the snakelike canyon leading through irregularly spaced spires of reddish rock that rose like weird stone guardsmen from the desert floor, I began to shake together some of the random thoughts that had beset me on this latest leg of my journey. It seemed to me my task with respect to Lawrence was about completed. Aside from a few chance bits of information I might pick up circling back across the central desert toward Bāyir, there seemed little more to learn.

I had begun to assess the results of my inquires up to this point on the role Lawrence had played in the Arab Revolt. The tape recordings I had collected in my visits with the various *sheikhs* who claimed to have known him offered some interesting sidelights on the personality of the strange English intelligence officer who is credited with modern initiation of guerrilla warfare, and I hoped they would assist Dr. Mack in his effort to psychoanalyze Lawrence a quarter of a century after his death.

However, there seemed to be nothing definitive about all this. I knew Lawrence had retreated into obscurity after the war, refusing many public honors, including knighthood, and that he finally enlisted in the Royal Air Force and was killed when he was still a comparatively young man, at the age of forty-seven. The curious combination of recessiveness and blurting out his innermost thoughts in *Seven Pillars of Wisdom* was a psychological complex that was beyond my understanding, but I assumed Dr. Mack would make something of it.

What had begun to intrigue me as a result of my inquiries about Lawrence was not so much the personality of Lawrence himself, as the reflection of the Bedouin character mirrored in his writings and in the outcome of my own investigation. It seemed to me that this was beginning to be linked vaguely with the larger purpose of my expedition, which was to trace the origins of the Bedouin themselves through a study of their habits and traditional customs.

Our cursory examination of the terrain around Mudawwara actually had brought to light nothing of real significance, beyond exposing the possibility that some of the details of Lawrence's story had been the result of either faulty memory or a lively imagination. He made no secret of his disgust with the Bedouin love of booty and referred at times to the sordid bickering of tribal leaders over the funds allocated by Lord Allenby for the support of his spring offensive in 1918— funds which in some cases had been dissipated in pay-offs to tribal leaders.

During the brief period we had stopped at the ruined station at Shahm, where I took pictures of Sab'ah and R'Faifan posing over the rusted wreckage of the demolished railroad car carriages. I had observed the expression of satisfaction on Sab'ah's face, and I concluded he was happier over the apparent proof that there was no raid on Mudawwara Station or its immediate environs than he would have been if we had uncovered evidence of a heroic charge of the Arabs in the teeth of Turkish guns. When I asked him what he thought of the evidence of the raid—or the lack of it—he merely grinned and shrugged.

"They know where to attack," he said. "It would not be under the eyes of the Turkish guards, the *badu* is not a tool!"

It occurred to me that this point of view had some significance. Throughout their long history the Arabs were put constantly to the task of proving their worth. Deep pride is ingrained in the Bedouin character; he believes himself to be superior in moral faith and in manhood to any of his neighbors, and in fact to anyone anywhere. This may account for the

248

current hostility between the Arabs and the Jews: one racial group believes itself superior to all others, and the other regards its members as the chosen people.

Pride among the nomads of the desert consists of emotions very different from those that prevail in Western cities. Individuality and freedom are subject to different interpretations, and the historic glories that may be accepted by the Western mind are not necessarily of any value to the Bedouin.

Sab'ah's reaction to our discoveries at Mudawwara was a case in point. Why had he led me to various small indications of the flaws in Lawrence's story? Instead of glorifying the work of the Arab raiders as an example of selfless and patriotic devotion to the Arab cause, he seemed almost to ridicule this aspect of the affair at Mudawwara Station. By innuendo and finally by direct remarks, he made it clear that in his opinion the raiders with Lawrence were doing nothing more than carrying out a time-honored tradition of the desert, which was to pounce upon a disabled caravan and loot it for all removable goods.

The purpose of this attitude had seemed obscure until I realized that the choice was between admitting that Lawrence led the Arab Revolt and not admitting it. The greater thing, from the standpoint of the Bedouin, was that they were not vassals of anyone: the revolt was their own, and they did what they wanted with it. Lawrence was merely "a servant of Faisal."

I remembered that the namesake of my colleague, the parrot-nosed Sheikh Sab'ah who lived at the watering hole south of Rumm, had hinted at this in some of his rambling stories, which I had recorded on tape for Dr. Mack. The tenor of his tale concerned memories of having ridden with Sharif Aid and Zaal, both mentioned by Lawrence—and not that he had ridden with Lawrence himself. He was at pains to minimize the latter association.

In all this complex of contradictions, one question persisted: What was the motivation of the Arabs in the Revolt in the Desert? The answer might have some historic significance, aside from its reflection on Lawrence's story. There was no doubt that Sab'ah wanted me to believe that the Arabs were more interested in gathering booty from the wrecked train than in striking a military blow at the Turks. But why?

I came to the conclusion, thinking back over some of the remarks and general viewpoints expressed by Sheikh Aid, and to some extent by Sheikh Sudan, at Rumm, that this attitude was probably a combination of two traits of the Bedouin: the desire to please a guest or visitor by telling him what he would like to hear, and an unquenchable individuality and pride. The two traits, although outwardly dissimilar, betray different aspects of the same psychological characteristic: generosity toward strangers and an austere sense of personal individuality.

Gibbon, in *The Decline and Fall of the Roman Empire,* offers an interesting digest of this complex of Bedouin character:

His [the Bedouin] breast is fortified with the austere virtues of courage, patience and sobriety; the love of independence prompts him to exercise the habits of self-command; and the fear of dishonor guards him from the meaner apprehension of pain, of danger, and of death. . . .

In the study of nations and men we may observe the causes that render them hostile and friendly to each other, that tend to narrow or enlarge, to mollify or exasperate, the social character. The separation of the Arabs from the rest of mankind has accustomed him to confound the ideas of stranger and enemy. . . . According to the remark of Pliny, the Arabian tribes are equally addicted to theft and merchandise.[11]

Gibbon's harsh comment, culled from an exhaustive study of the Arabs but probably without familiarity with them as

250

people, provides a clue to the paradox of pride and generosity that are mingled illogically in the Bedouin personality.

It struck me, in my meandering thoughts, that perhaps the only way to understand these people was to do as Dr. Mack and I were doing—ride on camels over the desert trails, enveloped by the same ancient hills and plains, absorbing the same cruel hardness of the unyielding soil.

I wondered idly, as my *nága* clumped along over mile after mile of sun-baked *ghôr* toward the little teahouse at Bat'n al Ghūl, what the future would hold for these nomads of the desert. Far back in the dark ages of pre-Christian times they had emerged from nowhere to become a part of history on the strength of having domesticated the single-hump camel. They continued unchanged for all outward purposes, breeding and herding camels and goats on the barren steppelands for a longer period of time than any other civilization of which there is any record. They had been flung into the zenith of world power on the crest of a wave of Moslem religious and political fervor, and yet in all parts of the world once ruled by the Arabs, the Bedouin himself seemed to be least important.

The races that were overcome by the first avalanche of Islamic power—Persians, Turks, Berbers—outlasted the truly Arab rule from Medina and Damascus, and surged into control of all of Islam, yet the Arabic tongue was still the root of their entire world. Carmichael, in a chapter of *The Shaping of the Arabs* entitled "The Arab Kingdom and the Moslem Empire," mentions this curious acceptance of Arabic language and culture long after the true Arabs had been deposed: "If you were to ask him [the Arab] in his own Arabic language whether he was 'Arab,' it would be an altogether meaningless question, since in Arabic the word would simply have referred to a Bedouin, a member of one of the nomadic tribes, who were all lumped together as the only 'Arabs.' "[9]

When I had been in Ammān, in the populous areas where Bedouin and non-Bedouin mingled, I had realized the great difference between the two. Many alien bloods flow in the veins of the people referred to as Arabs, but the Bedouin are the only true Arabs. Oddly enough, there has always been a queer sort of recognition of this by many of the peoples—such as Persians and Syrians—originally absorbed in the Islamic expansion of the seventh and eighth centuries. The Abbasids, after taking over power from the Omayyads, had displayed contempt for the Bedouin as people, but they continued to use the Arabic language and even fabricated their genealogy with names culled from the Arabian Steppe to cover their own uncertain ancestry.

There was a mixture of tragedy and strength in these people of the desert, and I wondered as we rode over the hard sand of the "ghoul's belly" whether history, or the understanding of other peoples, would ever truly recognize their real character, so full of cruelty and generosity, a combination of hardness and compassion.

Twenty-five centuries ago Herodotus wrote: "The Arabs keep pledges more religiously than almost any other people. . . . The Arabs were never subject as slaves to the Persians, but had close friendship with them. . . ."[13]

This strength of mind and spirit has persisted through the ages, and it may have removed the Bedouin from the understanding of all but themselves. They are among the most religious people on earth; their religion leaves no room for an alien faith, or even dissent from the teachings of the Koran. In Chapter 98 of the Koran it is written:

The unbeliever among the People of the Book [i.e., the Christians and Jews; all others were not even "people"] and the pagans shall burn forever in the fires of Hell. . . . They are the vilest of creatures. But of all creatures, those that embrace the Faith [the Moslem creed] and do good are the noblest.

Even more strikingly inflexible are the first words of the Koran, the Exordium:

Praise be to Allah, Lord of Creation,
The Compassionate, the Merciful,
King of the Last Judgment!
You alone we worship and to You alone we pray for help.
Guide us to the straight path,
The path of those whom You have favored,
Not of those who have incurred Your wrath,
Nor of those who have gone astray.

I watched R'Faifan and Sab'ah, my two Bedouin friends, slumped in their ornate saddles as they jounced along with the unending, swaying rhythm of the camels' ungainly gait, and I thought of this inflexible adherence to words that had been divulged to their people centuries ago. I wondered how deeply the Western mind could ever penetrate their innermost thoughts.

Was Sab'ah's deliberate effort to reduce the heroic stature of Lawrence's raiders to that of desert marauders a sign of strength or weakness? Was it a symbol of pride or merely racial hostility toward anything "alien" to the Arab himself?

The enigma of the Bedouin himself all at once seemed to me to be far more important than the trivial incidents of Lawrence's account of the campaigns in the desert. I felt a renewed desire to get on to Bāyir and ride out over the unmapped lands where part of the secret might still be buried in the sand-covered watering places of the ancient caravan trail from Mesopotamia to Arabia Felix.

IX. *Trouble in the West*

1

By two o'clock the following afternoon we reached the tea-house in the middle of Bat'n al Ghūl. The old man, whose name I found was Nassar, greeted us as if we were steady customers. It probably was one of the few occasions in his lonely tenure at the tiny café in the desert that he had seen the same faces twice within the space of a year, let alone in less than a month. He rose to the occasion, greeting us as if we were a trio of *emirs* trekking northward from luxurious desert homes in the Hijaz.

Nassar's place of business was poorer than any roadside stand one might find in the outlying sections of the western United States. Behind the lean-to a half-dozen gaunt-looking goats, useful only for producing a thin supply of milk, wandered aimlessly in a small pen.

I could not help wondering, as I had a month earlier, what sort of entrapment kept this old man tethered to this place. At the price of about three cents a cup there could hardly be enough trade, except perhaps in the season when pilgrims traveled to and from Mecca, to pay for the upkeep of one of the goats. Yet he seemed quite satisfied with his lot and beamed as he prepared to serve us a meager dinner.

There were a number of stools set out in a porte-cochere arrangement, shaded by palm boughs. A drum in the corner provided lukewarm water. We sat on the stools and ate a dinner of bread and milk—the only fare Nassar had left on his menu after the run of pilgrims during the previous weeks—and chatted about affairs of the world. His radio had been crackling when we arrived, and he quickly informed us that a "great battle" had been fought between troops of Syria and Israel, with the Syrians the victors.

I did not know whether this was the "pitched battle" I had heard about at Rumm, in which the Syrians also were reported victors, or some new skirmish. The constant reiteration of incidents of this sort worried me, because I still hoped R'Faifan and I might detour from our general route and cross into Wádi Araba before heading eastward for Bāyir.

That evening R'Faifan and Sab'ah remained in the small, poorly equipped tent of Nassar, discussing problems of the desert while Dr. Mack and I retired to our own camp to study our maps and decide upon the best course to follow. I planned to push northward as far as the railroad construction camp near Shedia in the hope that I might find Doug Manson and learn from him what was happening in the world beyond the desert. While my own position, although sympathetically on the side of the Arabs, was outwardly neutral—since I was a foreign national—I had no desire to find myself pinned between Jordanian and Israeli forces if there was increased activity along the border.

The Security Corps major at Rumm had informed me that travel was now restricted to military purposes west of Guweira. This area extended along the fringe of the domain of the Nebataean Arabs, one of the most mysterious fragments of the widely scattered nomadic Arabs of pre-Christian eras, who ruled a segment of the Bible lands east of the Dead Sea described in the Bible as the land of Edom.

My interest in this area was personal rather than scholarly. I did not regard myself as an expert on archaeological or historical matters, but I had traveled over Bedouin lands for years and I understood the antiquity of these people, the feeling of depth in their history that is ground into one's bones by the windblown sands of the desert—particularly when one travels by camel.

The region once ruled by the Nabataeans extended as far north as the border of Syria and south to the Gulf of Aqaba, covering most of what is now known as the Eastern Desert of the Hashemite Kingdom of the Jordan. However, nothing much is known of the origin of the Nabataeans themselves. They emerged from the desert, as the Bedouin so often seem to have come into historical perspective out of nowhere, sometime during the first millennium B.C., perhaps as early as 800 B.C., when the Edomites were driven out.

The land of Edom is referred to in the Book of Genesis as having been ruled by kings "before there reigned any king over the children of Israel" (Gen. 36: 31). From the biblical account, they were descendants of Esau, brother of Jacob (Israel) who founded the tribes of Israel: "Now these are the generation of Esau, who is Edom (Gen. 36: 1). Esau left Canaan and "went out into the country from the face of his brother Jacob. . . . the land could not bear them because of their cattle (Gen. 36: 6-7).

The first biblical reference to Edom is partly confirmed by archaeological diggings southeast of the Dead Sea, which have disclosed sites of Bronze Age people who lived in the nineteenth century B.C. along the Zeid River (now the great Wádi Hasa, north of the *bait sha'ar* of Sheikh Faisal ibn Jazi, where I attended the feast in honor of Emir Hassan.) This was about the time of Abraham's journey from Ur of the Chaldees into Egypt and the Promised Land, forming one of the strongest links between the biblical account of early migrations of the Jews and the Arabs

257

and the archaeological researches in the Holy Land.

The early hostility between the people who had settled in the fertile coast of Canaan and those who lived east of the Dead Sea was vividly portrayed in the account of Moses' efforts to lead the Israelites back to the Promised Land in the thirteenth century B.C. Having been rebuffed at the borders of Canaan, he turned westward toward the land of Edom, assuring the Edomites—who were, in a sense, his cousins—that "we will not pass through the fields, or through the vineyards, neither will we drink of the water of the wells: we will go by the king's high way, we will not turn to the right hand nor to the left, until we have passed thy borders (Num. 20: 17).

The reply of the king of the Edomites was: "Thou shalt not pass by me, lest I come against thee with the sword" (Num. 20: 18).

This was probably the first recorded incident in the intermittent hostility between the Arabs and the Jews. There had been a gap of about 500 years between the first mention of Esau and the Edomites and the time of the Exodus, and there is another historical period of equal length between the time of Moses and the disappearance of the Edomites, apparently driven out of their lands by the Nabataeans. There is brief mention of Edom and Mount Seir in the biblical accounts, in connection with the Horites (Num. 22: 21), and Edom is also referred to in the records of the Egyptian Pharaoh Merneptah (about 1234 B.C.), but it was not until the eighth century that actual warfare between the Jews and the Arabs broke out over the borderlands of Wádi Araba. The dispute was over control of the copper and iron mines which formed one of the chief sources of minerals in pre-Roman times in Palestine.

During the reign of David and later of Samuel border bickering was carried on almost continuously (II Sam. 8: 12-14), until the overthrow of the Edomites by the Nabataean Arabs, whose interest seemed to lie in the business of raiding caravans passing along the King's Highway, bearing rich loads of spices and herbs from South Arabia, rather than in mining copper and iron in Wádi Araba.

The rise of Nabataean power, which dominated the Eastern Desert for four centuries prior to the conquest of the Middle East by the Romans, was the direct result of their establishment in the fortified city of Petra, deep in the mountains southeast of the Dead Sea. This place even today remains one of the mysteries of archaeology. Hidden in the craggy mountains of Wádi Araba, it was the seat of power of a race of nomads who came out of nowhere and disappeared into the void of unrecorded history.

Under the benevolent patronage of Egypt, the Nabataeans for a time held what may have been the first legalized "black market" monopoly—the right to "protect" caravans traveling along the King's Highway between Arabia and the rich cities of the north. This protection service, reminiscent of certain activities carried on by bootleg mobs in the United States during and immediately after the Prohibition era, presumably was designed to regularize commerce between the Red Sea ports and Damascus and Philadelphia (Ammān). Originally the Nabataeans had set up a form of open piracy, swooping down on caravans and looting them, but later the more efficient policy of the Egyptians permitted them merely to levy tribute in return for protection.

In the third century B.C. Egyptian Pharaoh Ptolemy II (Philadelphus) broke up the monopoly, and the Nabataeans finally became absorbed in the Roman conquest of the Middle East. They injected themselves into the affairs of the Jews by assisting Hyrcanus in his effort to unseat the Hasmonaean kings of Judah, and gradually disappeared from historical records after Trajan annexed the kingdom of the Nabataeans in the second century after Christ and established the province of Arabia.

The Nabataeans have always held a fascination for me. I had

259

been in Petra and seen the magnificent ruins of edifices carved in solid sandstone; they were of particular interest now, since their motives and *modus operandi* seemed to conform with that of the Bedouin who rode with Lawrence in the Arab Revolt.

2

We headed north at sunrise, immediately after R'Faifan and Sab'ah had completed their morning prayers. Within a short time we reached the ascending trail leading up toward the plateau of Ra's an Nagb, where we had narrowly avoided being blown over the edge in the violent desert storm that struck us near the abandoned station at Fasu'a a month earlier. I was considerably surprised, and to some extent disconcerted, when we seemed to be running into the same kind of weather as we neared the top of the winding path that followed the old railroad up to the rim of the desert.

R'Faifan, who was more sensitive than I to the vicissitudes of the weather, waved us to a halt and with his *kaffiyah* blowing across his face, screamed into my ear: "We must find shelter, Abu Ghaith! It is another storm—perhaps worse than the one before!"

It seemed impossible that this kind of evil luck would overtake us again; but I was not willing to dispute anyone who knew the desert as well as R'Faifan, and we veered off toward the Q'a Fasu'a where Sab'ah said he believed there were ruins of an old Turkish fort that once guarded the railroad. We found the place, in a partly concealed depression about 2 kilometers west of the roadbed. It was filled with camel dung and other debris left by Bedouin travelers who had sought shelter there, so we built a fire and settled ourselves until the storm abated.

Sab'ah immediately began to gather bits of camel dung. He laid them out in neat rows and explained to me how to play the Bedouin game called *see ga* which consists of a complex method

Games in the desert: Sab ʾah (left) is explaining the game of *see ga*, a cross between jacks and checkers, to the author.

Desert minstrel: a Bedouin playing the *rabába*, a single-string, violin-type instrument used for centuries on the desert.

of exchanging camel dung for stones. I had played the game during the evenings at Azraq and later at Bāyir, but I understood it only slightly. I quickly became aware that there was a certain talent for winning which I did not possess, and in fact did not fully comprehend.

When I finally decided that there was no great amusement in being beaten all the time, Sab'ah shifted to another game called *nagla*. This involved using goat droppings instead of camel dung, and I had even less luck than with the first game. However, we managed to pass the afternoon and evening without too much discomfort, huddling in the lee of the crumbling walls of the fort during the night.

In spite of R'Faifan's dire predictions, the wind died down, and since it was later in the season the bitterly cold sleet and rain we had experienced a month before did not materialize. By morning the air was clear and warm and we were ready to head for Fasu'a and the railroad construction camp.

At the Fasu'a station we encountered an advance man from the construction camp, and he informed me that Doug Manson had left, either on a short leave or permanently. In any event I decided to turn westward, retracing our tracks across Bat'n al Ghūl to Khreme, where we picked up the ancient camel trail from Mudawwara, that we had followed on the last days of March into Q'a Desa and Rumm.

I searched the trail for a sign of the old Bedouin, who had haunted my memory since we passed him, sitting cross-legged on a sand dune, but there was no trace of the man. I assumed he had either been carted off by some other travelers to find his martyrdom in death, according to the Moslem gospel, or had crawled away to some nearby desert refuge he may have maintained.

The Moslem faith provides a haven for the destitute. In the Koran it is written:

Have you thought of him that denies the Last Judgment? It is he who turns away the orphan and does not urge others to feed the poor.

Woe to those who pray but are heedless of their prayers; who make a show of piety and give no alms to the destitute! (Ch. 107).

Because of this special attitude toward beggars and almsgiving, it is required that every Moslem contribute a certain portion of his income to charity, and those who die from lack of charity are favored in heaven as *shuhada,* or martyrs.

I felt again, as our camels wobbled up the embankments of the sun-scorched canyons that lead toward Rumm, along the crimson sandstone walls, that I was entering a cavern of the dead. The desolation of the desert below and around us was only sur- passed by the indescribable beauty of the colored rocks, striated in places and in others rising like rough-hewn columns toward the blue sky that hung over us, still and silent in this timeless world. I almost looked for another formation of American-made jets to roar out of the heavens, as they had on our way down to Al Jafr, to startle me out of my reverie.

At one point we crossed the tracks of several hyenas, possibly prowling out on the plains to look for the body of the old man of the desert. There are many such stories among the Bedouin; often, with that harsh cruelty that is a part of these barren lands, they will strip a dying man of any worthwhile ornaments or clothing even before he is dead, leaving the naked body of the man approaching martyrdom to shrivel in the heat of the sun.

Sab'ah seemed to have exhausted his repertoire of sage ob- servations, and he no longer veered toward me and screamed out his bits of wisdom. R'Faifan seemed depressed and silent, and I knew Dr. Mack was also tired, so we jogged along mile after mile without speaking to each other. The silence, except for the clop-clop of the camels' padded feet, began to be oppressive, and I found my thoughts begin to wander.

The story of the *ghrôl*, a female monster with one eye who lives among the rocky peaks and swoops out upon caravans to devour the living travelers, crossed my mind. I found myself looking curiously at the lofty ramparts around and below us— since we had climbed almost 2,000 feet along the black-crusted ridges leading up to Q'a Desa—wondering when the Cyclops-eyed monster would show herself. Many Bedouin insist they have seen the figure of the *ghrôl*, sometimes called Salewwa, glaring from a distance with her single ferocious eye, and as a matter of fact it would not have been hard to conjure such a fanciful image in this broiling oven of black and reddish rocks.

The intrinsic character of Bedouin, probably because of their environment in the desert, lends itself to belief in the super-natural. The night we had camped near the crumbling ruins of Qasr at Tūba, watching the bats roar out of the ancient court-yard, I had had the feeling that we were somehow witnessing a visible link with the past. The ghosts of caravans lost in history had marched across these arid lands, and I was sure R'Faifan felt this as much as I did. Sab'ah may have been too cynical and realistic to admit it, but he must have felt it, too.

There are no civilized or primitive peoples in the world that do not somehow link themselves to a past that is beyond life; save for a few hard-shelled psychologists, like my friend Dr. Mack, most Americans, I suspect, agree with Hamlet that "there are more things on heaven and earth, Horatio, than are dreamt of in your philosophy."

The casting of spells, for example, is widely accepted as a supernatural phenomenon, not only among the primitive tribes-men of Africa, but also among the farmers of Pennsylvania, as well as among Bedouin. The powers of the *sahara*—the woman who casts these spells—is neither primitive nor sophisticated; it is simply a belief they have held throughout ages of history, and they accept it as naturally as they accept the teachings of the Koran.

A belief in the supernatural among Bedouin runs the gamut from witchcraft to parapsychology. One of the most astonishing examples of the latter was provided not by a Bedouin but by no less an authority than H. R. P. Dickson, a representative of His British Majesty's Government in Kuwait, whose massive tome, *The Arab of the Desert,* is probably the foremost work on Arabic customs and traditions.

Dickson tells the story of a dream which occurred to him at a time when the British were boring for oil in Kuwait early in this century. In this fantasy he saw a body being carried from a tomb broken open by a storm. The body was that of a woman, once beautiful but now rotten with age, and as she was carried out, the signs of life reappeared. Her skin changed from a parchment-like, deathly pallor to the sudden freshness of living flesh; she sat up and asked for warm clothes and something to eat, complaining that she had suffered from "thousands of years of cold." Then she cried: "I am in danger!" and asked to see the British consul, an anachronism that probably is intelligible only to the English. In any event, a white-haired Sufi, with a long knife, appeared and demanded that the woman be buried alive.

Dickson awoke and, according to his recollection, was so impressed by the clearness of the dream that he consulted a woman of Kuwait, known for her interpretation of supernatural events. The desert seer advised him to tell the English engineers boring for oil to shift their location to a *sidr* tree, some distance away. The tomb in Dickson's dream was near a *sidr* tree, and there was only one such tree in the area. The woman explained the meaning of the dream: the corpse of the once beautiful lady represented oil which the British hoped to bring to life, or at least to the surface; the *sidr* tree was the place where the oil was to be found; the old Sufi was the hostile influence trying to keep the English engineers from finding oil!

According to Dickson, the drilling was shifted to the area of the *sidr* tree and they struck oil! Whatever the validity of this

265

slightly commercialized account may have been—and it was vouched for by Dickson—it was widely repeated throughout Arabia and has assumed the character of established fact.

Possibly the best-known story of the casting of spells occurred in the burgeoning reign of ' Abdul ' Assiz ibn Saud, the father of the present king of Saudi Arabia, who climbed the walls of Riyadh, the sacred capital of Nejd, to take over the city and cement his rule over all the Arabian Peninsula. The governor of Riyadh, Emir Ajilan, was killed in the capture of the city, and his widow prepared a mattress to be presented to ibn Saud. It was filled with a witch's concoction of needles and strands of colored thread obtained from a practitioner of *sahara,* and by good luck—for King Saud—one of his tribal henchmen flung himself first on the mattress and immediately fell ill and died. Ibn Saud, out of compassion or relief at his narrow escape, did not have the woman killed—as he might well have done—but exiled her to Hail.

However true these strange tales may be—and Dickson's account of the manner in which the British found oil in Kuwait must be classified as slightly suspect, if only on the grounds of economic self-interest—the influence of forces that seem to lie beyond the limits of life is as ingrained in the Bedouin character as is their faith in the gospel according to Mohammed. In fact, there is some reason to believe that faith in the existence of supernatural forces such as *jinns* not only antedated the Koran but has outlasted it.

As we climbed along the ascending trails over narrow gulleys worn hard by intermittent rains and the subsequent baking of the soil by the blazing sun, we could see the signs of graves by the roadside, undoubtedly of pilgrims who had once used this back road between Guweira and Mudawwara. In most cases a stone or two marked the last resting place of some poor soul who had been unable to endure the hard journey to Mecca and back.

Again the paradoxical aspects of Moslem faith struck me:

these people, hardened to life on the barren steppe, could dispose of a fellow mortal with no more ceremony than a roadside burial if death occurred on the desert; they simply dug a hole, laid the body in it, and left a few stones to mark the grave and possibly to discourage the hyenas. Yet in more settled Bedouin encampments farther south, mourning after death was an established ritual. It would continue for three or four days with lamentations and recitations from the Koran. Why the difference?

It occurred to me, as I rode along, that these strange conflicts might actually be the logical result of the very realism of desert life. The Bedouin has for centuries lived by the sword, and perhaps he is ready to die by the sword. In the Koran it is written:

On the day when the Trumpet sounds, all hearts shall be filled with terror. They will say: "When we are turned to hollow bones, shall we be restored to life?" A fruitless transformation! (Ch. 79.)

The whole question of existence, for the Bedouin, seems to have been answered in these few grim and despairing words.

3

At Desa, although our time had been shortened by several delays, Dr. Mack and I decided to pay a short visit to Rumm and see Sheikh Sudan, the "mayor" of Rumm, and other old friends who had contributed to the information about Lawrence, and perhaps pick up a few anecdotes that had been overlooked on our earlier visit.

As Lawrence noted, there is a certain fascination about Rumm that is like a siren, drawing desert travelers back to its canyon floors and rusty cliffs. For centuries not only Bani-Atiyah but tribesmen from Syria and from the south had ridden across Rumm Valley, with only a few remaining as permanent inhabitants. In the lore of the Bedouin it seems to have been a kind of thieves' paradise, where desert pirates lay in wait to prey upon caravans traveling north from the Hijaz or southward from Damascus and Ammān. There was plentiful water on the Ain O'rens with which to water their camels and irrigate small patches of the desert for growing grain and raising goats and sheep.

Sheikh Sudan was at the fort when we arrived. Knowing that Dr. Mack had to depart early the next day to return to Ammān, he arranged an interview with my septuagenarian friend, Sheikh Aid, although as far as I could discern the two *sheikhs* did not address each other. The next day Dr. Mack left, and Sheikh Sudan then insisted that before I left for Guweira and Wádi Araba, we should visit another *sheikh* who lived on the rim of the Ra's an Naqb, above Desa. His name was Sulman ibn Motlug Zuweida, and according to Sheikh Sudan he would have much to tell about Lawrence.

I felt I had about covered the Lawrence task, having turned over all my material to Dr. Mack, but it would have been impolite to refuse Sheikh Sudan's request, and the following day we rode through the tiny settlement at Desa, where bursts of green patches had grown around the pumping station, and on across the desert for several kilometers to Sheikh Sulman's *bait sha'ar*. He was a grand-looking man, dignified, courteous, and possessed of that strange combination of sadness and wisdom that seemed to be engraved on the faces of so many of the older people of the desert, particularly the tribal chiefs.

He greeted me effusively, and I recalled that I had met him on a previous journey into Rumm. But he seemed far too young to have been an associate of Lawrence or the chiefs of the Arab Revolt.

When we arrived we caught him in an unfortunate moment of personal hygiene. He was crouched behind his tent, stark naked, taking a bath from an iron pot from which he splashed himself with warm water. He looked up and smiled when he saw us, with no embarrassment whatever, and concluded his ablutions quickly. He then came over to shake hands, half-running as he wrapped his *thōp* around his body. He immediately shouted to the women in the *muharram*: "Quick! Prepare the coffee!"

He turned to me, his dark eyes lighting warmly, and added: "We will have a *mansef,* and you will all accept my poor hospitality!"

He waved his hand casually, as if to include all of time in his invitation.

Sheikh Sulman was quite fussy, and he personally arranged the pillows in his *raba᾽ a* so that everyone would be comfortable. He was equally meticulous about his attire, and when I suggested later in the afternoon that I would like to take a few pictures, he immediately retired and spent twenty minutes combing his beard and getting his *kaffiyah* and *thōp* to fall in exactly the right folds.

I mentioned my pleasure at observing the rapid improvement of the little agricultural establishment at Desa, and he nodded, as if it had been his own doing.

Both *sheikhs* were proud of these small indications of organized agriculture. Although they form only microscopic dots on the face of the vast plateau of barren and waterless steppelands, these efforts of the Jordanian government to establish agricultural centers in remote parts of the Bedouin country were evidence of the slow emergence of modern methods of living among the desert nomads.

To Bedouin from the southern parts of Arabia, where there are many fertile *widyán* with green patches of grain and tufted date palms and even engineered complexes to provide irrigation, the tiny signs of modernized agriculture in the hinterlands of Jordan might seem pitiful, even ridiculous; but to the Jordanian tribesmen they were of great significance. Whether the age-old habits of the nomads, moving from one natural grazing ground

269

to another, will ever absorb these artificial efforts of a modernized society is, of course, problematical. They never have and perhaps they never will.

My first question to Sheikh Sulman—who frequently traveled north to Ma᾿ān and even Ammān—had to do with the reports of border fighting.

"Is it possible to go over into Wádi Araba?" I asked him. He stroked his tufted chin, and finally shook his head.

"The *badia* must decide," he said. "You have papers permitting this?"

I explained that I had a letter from Colonel Nayef at Ammān, giving me passage through all lands of the Eastern Desert, but nothing specifically relating to Wádi Araba. In fact, I said, Colonel Nayef himself had been hesitant about the wisdom of going there.

"The border is not well defined," the *sheikh* then told me. "And there are military movements in the area."

Whether this was a warning, or simply precautionary advice, I could not very well determine.

Sheikh Sulman prepared an elaborate *mansef,* the first feast for R᾿Faifan, Sab᾿ah, and me in nearly three weeks of traveling. The desert provides either a feast or famine, and I looked forward with a gourmand's anticipation to the cascades of butter and animal fat that would pour down over the greasy mound of goat's meat and rice while we sat around the board, readying our hands like claws to dig into the repast.

The customs of people, including eating habits, seem to be little more than garments they wear for a time. For Westerners like myself, these garments are easily changed. I could hardly have imagined myself sitting down to a dinner in New York, ready to claw with my bare hands into a pile of mixed rice and meat in the center of a table, yet I found no difficulty in suiting myself to Bedouin table manners. I wondered what might be the secret of fixed and transitory customs. What is the source of innovation? Why do nomads and Eskimos, for example, remain unchanged in their habits while the rest of the world moves on? What is the reason for what Arnold Toynbee calls an "arrested society"?

That evening, after gorging ourselves on the *mansef,* Sheikh Sulman tugged at the sleeve of my *thōp* and pulled me to one side. We sat on the great cushions in the corner of his *raba'a,* while the others gathered around the fire pit where the coffee was bubbling away, and he said to me in slow Arabic, and in a serious way, as if he wanted to be sure I understood: "You must take great care if you go near the border. There may be activity. Since you are a friend of our people, there must be no trouble for you."

I understood his meaning. My own experiences among the people of Jordan, Arabs who lived in the cities as well as those who roamed the desert, was one of genuine friendliness. Jordan faced the West rather than the East; she looked to America rather than to Russia for support. Syria, her neighbor to the north, was oriented toward the Slavic people and the Soviet bloc, but the oppression of the Turks had fallen more severely upon the Syrians and Iraqi than upon the nomads of the Steppe, and perhaps they were more readily influenced by threatened power. Jordan was a border state, so to speak; her small kingdom lay between the two walls of power, and she had to steer a careful course. But the Jordanians have never lost their deep spirit of independence.

Sheikh Sudan, sitting on the other side of the fire pit, watched me with sharp eyes, and I assumed he and Sheikh Sulman had discussed with each other the perils that might be building up for my little expedition. It is neither wise nor safe for any Jordanian to discuss such matters with a stranger, and I was sure Sheikh Sulman was trying to give me good advice without compromising himself.

We passed the evening in fairly lively conversation, discussing

271

routes and watering places, but I had the feeling that my two friends, Sudan and Sulman, were anxious that I avoid traveling any farther westward toward the Israeli border than was absolutely necessary. In retrospect, knowing now how little the Jordanians were prepared for the burst of open warfare that occurred later that summer, I doubt if they had anything specific in mind. It was merely a growing feeling that there was trouble along the border, but this was nothing new to the Bedouin. It has been growing in varying degrees of intensity since the times of Moses.

X. *The Rose-Red City of Petra*

1

Our tiny expedition, reduced again to R'Faifan and me with our two camels, rode out across the desert early the next day, following the upper rim of Ra's an Naqb rather than the fairly well traveled road to Guweira along the canyon floor below. Sab'ah had decided to return to Rumm.

The upper trail followed the hard, flinty edge of the plateau over which we had traveled with the wild-driving Bedouin chauffeur sent down by Sheikh Faisal a few weeks before. I could hardly help comparing the speed at which we took off then in a high-powered Land Rover with the sedate pace now set by our camels.

I was actually in something of a hurry to reach Guweira. The assortment of reports and rumors of border fighting had been increasing steadily. The previous evening I had asked Sheikh Sulman if he had any report of the border incident in the north, in which Syrian and Israeli troops presumably had clashed, but he professed to know nothing about it. However,

I detected a wariness in his tone that made me realize that he must suspect something was afoot.

This was in mid-May—less than a month before the sudden eruption of violence that is now recorded in history as the Six-Day War. Every Jordanian I had talked with, at Ammān and in the *badia* forts, seemed to be completely confident of the outcome of any full-scale escalation of border fighting. Jordan's compact little air force was prepared to handle any contingency, but as yet there seemed no indication on the part of those with whom I had talked about the situation that Jordan would ever strike first at the Israelis.

The real trouble seemed to be rising from a confrontation in the south, where Nasser had made his first move to close the Strait of Tiran, Israel's access to the Red Sea. This would also mean that Jordan's only port, Aqaba, would be under Egyptian control.

I had been in Aqaba many times. Lying at the southern end of the King's Highway, it is an old port town of mud-walled buildings and piers of nineteenth-century vintage, green with date palms and other shrubbery that lend an almost tropical flavor to the place. Aqaba spreads over a flat shoreland which ascends gradually to the base of mountains almost barren of vegetation. These rise into the rim of the great Arabian Steppe which stretches 800 miles to the east and 1,500 miles to the southeast. Under plans of the Jordan government, the old structures are rapidly being replaced by modern buildings and port facilities.

A scant half-dozen miles west of Aqaba is the Israeli port of Elath, on the southernmost point of the great Negev Desert allotted to the Israeli in the division of Palestine. For centuries the Negev had been the homeland of Bedouin who were driven out by the political partition. Large, oceangoing vessels have access to both ports through the Strait of Tiran and the Gulf of Aqaba.

The Rose-Red City of Petra

Aqaba is probably more vital to Jordan than Elath is to Israel, since the latter holds a number of large ports on the Mediterranean such as Tel Aviv and Haifa, but the military and political importance of interruption of traffic through the Strait of Tiran into the Gulf far outweighed its economic significance.

As we rode toward Guweira, the last important junction on the King's Highway leading southward to Aqaba, I turned over in my mind the various alternatives that might confront me if there was real trouble along the border. First, I would have to decide whether to attempt the journey I had planned into Wádi Araba, which lies astride the Jordan-Israeli border. It is an area of tumultuous mountains, dry and barren of plant life in most places. Parts of these limestone hills are covered with a thinly laid garment of soil, with green plants bursting from scraps of what seem to be solid rock. I had previously seen only the fringe of Araba, never having traveled west of Guweira, which lies in a flat, red valley between Ra's an Naqb and Wádi Araba. Beyond this valley to the west were tumbling mountains with sharp ridges and great cliffs carved by windswept rain. This was the mountain fastness where Lawrence reported he first organized guerrilla raids along the Hijaz-Medina railroad.

However, I had no intention of trying to evade any "out of bounds" limits set by the *badia* and perhaps finding R'Faifan and myself suddenly isolated in a wild land where border patrols from either side might use us for target practice. On the other hand, I had the option of turning back into the Eastern Desert, crossing the lands of the Bani-Atiyah and the 'Arab al Howeitat and reaching Bāyir again.

As a kind of sudden compromise, I made a quick decision and yelled it out to R'Faifan: "If we cannot go into Araba, we will go to Petra!"

He stared at me in some surprise. Petra, the ancient citadel of the Nabataean Arabs, was a place of mystery to most Bedouin.

Few traveled there, since there was little commerce and obviously no caravans to prey upon, and it was widely believed that *jinns* lived among the craggy passes beyond Wádi Músa, the old gateway to Petra. As I have noted, I had been to Petra several times, but I never tire of its fantastic beauty and ancient memories.

"Only if we cannot go into Araba," I added, grinning under my covering mask of the *kaffiyah*. R'Faifan still looked puzzled, but he nodded. Perhaps he thought the desert heat had overcome me. Petra was not only senseless to the Bedouin, but in a spiritual sense it might be dangerous because of the *jinns*.

We continued along our course, high above the old trail which I could see dimly defined in the reddish sand below us. About midafternoon we rode straight toward the setting sun and down into the flats of Guweira. The red-and-green flag flew from the masthead of the compact little fort standing out against the pink background of the flats on the far side of the pale gray ribbon of the King's Highway. We had taken a full circle from the road since leaving Ammān. Except for the one brief excursion to Sheikh Faisal's *bait sha'ar*—which offered little opportunity for inspection of the paved road, since we were off it most of the time—we had seen nothing but camel trails for three months.

Guweira (sometimes spelled Queira or Kaira) is a more modern town than Mudawwara and in fact was the largest place we had visited since leaving Al Jafr nearly two months before. Our camels had difficulty finding firm footing as we rode down a sharp incline from the high rim of the plateau into the valley through which the King's Highway followed the route from Ammān to Aqaba.

It was almost like returning to civilization. Since Guweira is an important stopping station on the main route along which all heavy traffic passed, it had more than the normal collection of government buildings and mud-walled houses such as we

276

had seen at Mudawwara and Al Jafr. Beyond the gray ruins of an old Turkish fort—an inevitable landmark—which lay against a sharp sandstone hill at the intersection of the trail from Rumm and the King's Highway were the elements of a fairly modern town, including a schoolhouse and a football field.

As we plodded down the steep trail, I could see on the far side of the highway the outline of the military road westward into Wádi Araba, which I hoped to follow, Allah willing! Along the blacktop King's Highway were a succession of small stores, a café, and the *badia* post. On the near side of the highway there were two fairly sizable apartment houses. These had been constructed during the past few years and bore un- mistakable signs of the invasion of modern architecture into the ancient desert. They were all one-room affairs, more in the manner of a motel than an apartment complex. Beyond was a cluster of some of the older houses of Guweira and another café. Across from these lay a scattering of Bedouin tents, spread out on the pinkish flats, and behind these the granite mountains rose against the western horizon, guarding the Jordanian side of the Wádi Araba.

One physical aspect of Guweira, missing from other outposts of the Eastern Desert and something I had not seen since the wild ride to Sheikh Faisal's home in Wádi Hasa, was a line of telephone wires running through the town. This made it quite certain that I would have not only definite news of what was going on along the border but also a direct answer to my current question: Would I be allowed to go into Araba?

We rode through the gate into the fort, and the corporal in command came out to greet us with the usual warmth. I showed him my letter from Colonel Nayef, and he seemed to have full knowledge of our expedition and its purpose.

Once we were settled in the guest room, I wasted no time bringing to a head the one question that concerned me most.

"We wish to make a short journey into the Shafat," I said,

277

in slow Arabic, using the Jordanian designation of its own side of the Wádi Araba. This region of deep gorges and hills some 30 kilometers to the west was plainly visible from Guweira. "Is this possible?"

The corporal frowned and finally shook his head.

"It is now a military area," he told me, also speaking slowly in Arabic. R'Faifan stood beside me, listening carefully. I had an impression he was not as enthusiastic about making the trip into Araba as I was, and this was confirmed when he grinned widely at the corporal's words. "I do not have the authority to permit you to pass," the *badia* commander added. "It is to protect you and avoid an incident."

I understood. The presence of a lone American, with a Bedouin guide, might easily provoke an "incident." It could be interpreted in various ways, particularly if we wandered into an Israeli patrol. The probability is that we would be shot, and this would pose an even more serious problem for the Jordanians, let alone its effect upon R'Faifan and me.

I finally nodded and took back my letter, folding it and putting it in the pouch I carried under my robe. The corporal's face, which had been clouded with uncertainty, now was wreathed in a smile. Bedouin seem to glean more understanding from facial expressions than from words, and I realized that the corporal was greatly pleased when I accepted his decision without dissent. After all, who would know what great people I might know in high places? Protocol and the fine nuances of patronage are not unknown among the Bedouin, particularly in the Desert Patrol.

I was disappointed, but there was little that could be done. I seemed to be definitely barred from the Wádi Araba. The weather had suddenly turned bad, so we led our camels into the compound and prepared to bed down for the night.

2

The distance from Guweira to Wádi Mūsa, the gateway to Petra, is about 60 kilometers along the King's Highway; by camel it is a bit farther, due to detours which must be made to avoid close proximity to the highway and its intermittent traffic. Camels, either through fright or personal annoyance, are likely to spook when a car or truck roars by, and we had to follow old trails that ran parallel to the highway, but some distance off, from half a mile to more than a mile away from the pavement.

The schedule R'Faifan and I had drawn required making about half the distance the first day. By nightfall we hoped to reach the old Ra's an Naqb station, which at one time was an important stop for southbound caravans heading for Aqaba. The route lies over a twisting terrain, ascending from the red-colored flats around Guweira to high chalk-colored cliffs that form the western rim of the Eastern Desert and the plateau of Ra's an Naqb.

Less than 100 years ago the plains were alive with game: wild oryx and ostriches, roaming down from the forests of Karak which once covered the mountains east of the Dead Sea; gazelles from the great Wádi Hasa (the River Zeid of the Old Testament). But within the memory of many Bedouin living in the area today, the entire aspect of the land had changed, due largely to the devastation of forests and destruction of wildlife wrought by the Turks.

The trail over which we climbed slowly northward was at the lower end of a once fertile slope of mountains, dropping down toward the depths of the Jordan Rift and the Dead Sea— a shift in altitude from more than 2,000 feet at the top of the plateau to 392 feet below sea level in the middle of the salt sea. The highway, usually within sight, along which we paced was the modern version of the old Roman road linking Damascus with Egypt.

The sensation of traveling over this ancient highway is not easily described. Out on the desert I had the impression of riding over trails that belonged to a people whose origins had been lost in history, but along the western side of Jordan we were riding over lands known and described in the Bible: places familiar to almost everyone in Christendom as well as to Arabic and Hebrew historians and scholars. The feeling is neither unusual nor new; many people have traveled this route between Ammān and Aqaba, and I had ridden over it quite a few times myself. But it has always created in my thoughts the sensation of telescoping time: of journeying today, among the living, into a land whose known antiquity and the details of its history extends back for at least 4,000 years to the time of Abraham. It is like turning time backward yet living in the present!

The first leg of our journey, ascending from Guweira, at an altitude of perhaps 500 feet, to the high rocky ridge of the plateau, ranging from 1,500 to 2,000 feet, was comparatively uninspiring. It was not until we reached the top and looked back upon 50 miles of desert, spread below us in darkening stains of crimson and purple and black, that the magnificence of this western corner of the Eastern Desert struck me. Far to the left were faint outlines of red gorges which I knew led into Rumm Valley; to the right cascades of broken ridges and pinkish valleys led into Wádi Araba.

The small garrison at the Ra's an Naqb post, which is literally perched on the rim of the desert overlooking the vast panorama to the south, welcomed us with unusual ardor. Apparently few people traveling by car along the King's Highway bothered to stop even for a drink of water. These were lonely watchers of the road, whose main occupation was to sit and

280

stare at the splendid desolation around them.

There was little to be learned from them, and after sitting around for a while and staring at the small fire pit, R'Faifan and I turned in. It was evident that whatever might be happening along the border, the *badia* at Ra's an Naqb had little information about these events.

North of Ra's an Naqb, in startling contrast to the arid plains across which we had ridden for so many weeks, the character of the country changed drastically. There were rolling hills, leading down toward the wide depression of Wádi Araba; most of the hills were covered with fresh green grass, and there were many fields of barley. Flocks of goats and sheep began to appear on the hillsides. I recalled the change in the landscape we had observed when we roared across these valleys a few weeks before on Sheikh Faisal's Land Rover. Our passage then had been too rapid and rough, however, to enable us to pay much attention to the passing scene. Even the slow gait of our camels was a pleasant contrast to the breakneck ride we had taken that day.

I leaned over and slapped R'Faifan on the back, and he almost fell out of his saddle.

"Is this fast enough for you?" I yelled. "Or should we get a Land Rover?"

His teeth flashed in a quick smile, and he waved. Then he screamed at his camel, and for an instant I thought he actually had taken me seriously and wanted to make a race of it. But apparently it was only a sudden burst of Bedouin humor; he turned around to favor me with another flashing smile, then settled into the steady jog that we had become accustomed to, which represented a speed of about 3 miles an hour.

Finally I rode alongside him and yelled again: "We are going north again, R'Faifan! Don't you have any friends on this side of the desert?"

He nodded and pointed to a small tent that lay half a mile

281

off our route. It was almost indistinguishable from the rocks.

"There will be a friend," he called out to me, and he headed for the *bait sha' ar.*

Whether R'Faifan knew the occupant of the tent or not I was never able to determine. But sure enough, as we rode up, an old Bedouin came out. Without performing the usual ceremony of stopping, R'Faifan rode up and greeted him warmly, as if he were an old friend. Once again, I did not know whether he knew the old man or was welcomed by a complete stranger. His name was Motlug, the family name of Sheikh Sulman, whom we had left two nights earlier.

R'Faifan spoke so rapidly that I was unable to understand what he was saying, but he waved at me and the old man grinned and bobbed his head. I assumed it was some kind of introduction. The Bedouin quickly called to his wife, who lurked behind the thin partition of the *muharram,* and in a short time we had a lunch of eggs, milk, and bread.

Our host insisted we settle ourselves for a noonday discussion. I was unable to follow his speech accurately, but I realized that he had inquired whether we had any news of the border fighting. Since we had been on the desert for three months, we were hardly a source of news, but knowing the Bedouin passion for gossip I told him the border had been closed at Guweira. He quickly engaged R'Faifan in a spirited discussion I could not follow.

After we had started off again, intending to reach the *badia* post at Ail near Wádi Músa that evening, I asked R'Faifan what the old man had said.

"There has been more fighting," he said, his thin features contracting into a frown. This expression of worry was unexpected, since R'Faifan seldom showed any trace of anxiety, regarding all things cheerfully as the "will of Allah." However, he quickly explained that the old man had merely heard over the radio that numerous engagements had broken out along the border, and in each case the Jordanians had thrown back their adversaries.

"Jordanians!" I exclaimed. "Isn't the fighting on the Syrian border?"

R'Faifan shook his head. He explained that this was what worried him. Up to now only Syrian patrols seemed to have been involved in the border clashes. The possibility that Jordanian troops were engaged in these skirmishes seemed to bring the matter closer to home for him—and for that matter, it did the same for me. It struck me that I had a new concern: I could not very well ask R'Faifan to accompany me back across the Eastern Desert if there was likelihood that these border clashes would spread to the area around Ammān, where his family lived.

That night as we sat in the *badia* station at Ail, a small junction town from which the road branches off to Wádi Mūsa, the entrance to Petra, I began to add up various elements of my problem. Finally I said to R'Faifan, as we sat in front of the fire pit in one of the tents, the only shelter they could offer us, "If there is trouble, R'Faifan, you must go home! I will go on to Bāyir and you can join me later."

He had been watching me with narrowed eyes. Now he shook his head firmly.

"No, Abu Ghaith! You are my little brother—I cannot leave you! My son is at home, and if there is trouble, the other son will come, also. There is no problem!"

We argued at some length, and finally I decided there was no point trying to reach any decision until we knew how serious the border trouble had become. There was no real indication, after all, that this was anything more than one of the periodic escalations of friction along the frontier. It did not seem possible that the trouble arising between Nasser and the Israeli over the

Strait of Tiran could create a more serious problem with Jordan. Of all the Arab statesmen, King Hussein had stood most firmly against submission to Nasser's control. In fact I had read a news report in Ammān in which Radio Cairo had called Hussein a "Hashemite harlot" because he had failed to support Nasser's position with sufficient strength and seemed favorable to the West.

Our host, whose name was Hussein, apparently spoke no English and did not understand all we had been saying; but as we turned in for the night he advised me in Arabic that the next day I would have the great privilege of meeting the governor of Esh Shara, the regional area in which Wádi Mūsa and Petra are located.

"He is a great man!" the corporal, whose wizened features seemed tired from many years of service, told me. "He will be of help to you!"

I was not sure what sort of help I needed, but I thanked him profusely. My own thoughts were disturbed at this point; I was not sure whether I could possibly justify keeping R'Faifan away from his family for a longer period. He was obviously being faithful to his commitment to me, but was I being fair to him? Even if the border fighting turned out to be nothing more than a rising tempo in a chain of events, there was still the matter of R'Faifan's family to be considered.

In the course of this mental meandering, I thought also about my own home, and little Ghaith, as R'Faifan called my son. I presume I was being afflicted temporarily with an old-fashioned case of homesickness, which by necessity should not be an occupational disease of anyone engaged in exploration.

I caught R'Faifan looking at me again in a worried way as I went to bed, and I decided we would settle the matter immediately after his morning prayers. But in the morning the problem was somehow reduced in size. As I looked over the fresh green valley that lay between Ail and Wádi Mūsa my thoughts turned to the "rose-red city of Petra, half as old as time."

R'Faifan continued to look with troubled eyes as we rode down the sloping valley leading into the entrance to Petra. I suddenly realized that he was probably concerned not with one but with two matters. First, he must be worried about the possibility of fighting along the northern border, near his home; second, he must have assumed we were approaching a region notoriously inhabited by *jinns*. However, my Bedouin friend was seldom given to extended periods of depression; he was soon smiling cheerfully and yelping at his camel as we rode down the valley toward the Red City.

3

The trail into Petra is one of the most spectacular I have encountered in my travels through Arabia, not excepting Rumm. It is a scant 5 kilometers from Wádi Mūsa to the entrance to a deep gorge, known as the Siq, which winds through a cleft in the hills into the mountain fortress from which the Nabataean Arabs once ruled an empire larger than Jordan. The walls of this crevice rise sheer from the canyon floor, which in some places is not more than 100 feet wide, into towering precipices of solid rock that loom over the eastern gate to Petra.

Just before entering the gorge on a descending trail, a spring can be seen gushing from rocks beside the road. This is Ain Mūsa, the Spring of Moses (Wádi Mūsa means Valley of Moses in Arabic), and it is one of the most important places mentioned in the Bible. This was the fabled spot where Moses "lifted up his hand, and with his rod he smote the rock twice: and the water came in abundance, and the congregation drank, and their beasts also" (Num. 20:11).

It was also at this point that Moses asked the king of the Edomites to permit his people to pass over their lands without "turning to the right or to the left," saying: "Thus sayeth thy brother Israel, Thou knowest all the travails that hath befallen us" (Num. 20:14). As previously mentioned, the harsh rejection of this request by the king of the Edomites, who threatened to come against them "with the sword," was probably the first incident in 30 centuries of intermittent quarrels between Arabs and Jews.

However, my thoughts at the moment were not on the current outbreak along the border of Jordan, or even my exclusion from Wádi Araba because of that quarrel. My mind was filled with anticipation of the fantastic region I was entering, which, at a much later date than the time of Moses, had been the hidden citadel from which these ancient desert traffic cops apparently controlled commerce along the King's Highway. The mystery of this fragment of the Arabian nomads, who seemed to have appeared out of nowhere for a few fleeting centuries and then vanished into the silence of the desert, had always intrigued me. Although the Aramaeans under the Abbasid caliphs claimed descent from the Nabataeans, there is no established link between them beyond the common Semitic origin of both peoples. Rumm had been awe-inspiring, but Petra was like opening a page of the Bible and looking into a half-forgotten period in history.

Early in the afternoon we reached Wádi Músa, where I met the governor of Esh Shara, Abdul-Halim Awwad. I discovered to my surprise that he had some interest in a small store dug deep in the walls of the city of Petra, which was operated by a relative named Awwad, whom I knew. I recalled Hussein's remark that he was "a great man" and would provide me with help. The governor's greatness and the help he might give me were obscured in the mists of my inadequate grasp of Arabic, but I assumed it meant I could do business with his relative. We spent a pleasant hour sipping tea with him and carrying on a sporadic conversation in which quite probably neither of us knew what the other was talking about.

After tiffin, we took off again on our camels, heading down a winding valley filled with plots of growing grain. Shrub oaks, the first extensive tree life we had seen since leaving Azraq, dotted the hillside. The deeper gorges leading into the valley were covered in places by stumps of ancient trees, once part of a forest that spread down from the Wádi Hasa that leads into the southern end of the Dead Sea.

The trail across the valley, into the Siq, was the only entrance to Petra. As the valley narrowed, the round hills became steeper, rising toward the towering mountains that completely surrounded the city. No desert hideout could have been more completely insulated from attack, and one wondered why—if these early Bedouin were really desert pirates, swooping down on the caravans—they had ever given up their lair. Nevertheless, for more than 1,000 years the place had been almost empty, since Bedouin seldom traveled there. Most visitors to Petra now come from other countries on sight-seeing trips or for archaeological purposes. I had been told that Diana Kirkbride, a noted English archaeologist, had established a "dig" on the far side of Petra, and I was anxious to visit her excavations.

The approach to the cleft in the mountains led through a deep, pleasant *wádi* with a sprinkling of Bedouin tents on the slopes of the hills and flocks of goats grazing in the green pastures. In the center of this fertile valley we passed a tiny settlement where a few Bedouin horse traders carried on an intermittent business, renting horses and donkeys to travelers who preferred to ride into the gorge.

As we neared the entrance of the Siq, R'Faifan rose close beside my camel and tugged at my *thōp*. I looked at him and observed a wolfish grin on his face. He jerked his thumb backward, and I looked back. I was surprised to see four girls riding donkeys a short distance behind us.

"Are they following us?" I yelled at him. He shrugged.

"Who knows? It is an old custom."

I was both relieved and disappointed when I saw them turn off toward the hills. I had no desire, of course, to involve myself in a local incident. The Bedouin girls were apparently gathering fuel from the mountains, and I suppose I watched them with mixed feelings as they dismounted and busied themselves collecting pieces of wood and dried camel dung for their fires. I wondered whether R'Faifan's sudden action had frightened them off. It probably is inherent in the male ego, particularly after three months of enforced estrangement from the opposite sex, to theorize about such matters and to wonder what encounters of this sort might have produced. As we rode along, and particularly as I observed R'Faifan's knowing glance in my direction and his rather unsympathetic grin, I comforted myself with the thought that probably nothing good would have come of it anyway, even if the Bedouin girls had overtaken us.

I quickly became enthralled with the approach to Petra, as I had many times before. It was like entering a tomb of the past. Along the narrow opening there were caves that may have been homes of tribal nomads many centuries before the Christian era. They were pockmarked in the solid face of limestone cliffs and probably were of prehistoric origin. Since archaeology has not been able to penetrate much beyond the beginnings of the Nabataean rulers of this place, it would be virtually impossible to find out much about the earlier occupants of Petra, but the very character of this place indicates it must have seen civilizations long forgotten or obscured in history.

There were also visible remnants of a modern tragedy in the Siq. Only a few years before, a group of French nuns, visiting the ruins of Petra, had been trapped in this gorge by a cloudburst. The water came rushing through the canyon so swiftly, pouring into the Siq, that only two members of the group were able to survive by climbing the bare face of the gorge above the torrent and clinging to rocks until the flood subsided. The rest, on horseback and afoot, were carried through to their death; their bodies were found later in the mud-filled rubble at the bottom of the canyon.

I had read of this tragic event in Guy Mountfort's *Portrait of a Desert,* and as R'Faifan and I rode down the trenchlike channel we saw marks of floods, both recent and ancient, that had raged through the funnel of rock. I observed the area where the nuns were swept to their death and wondered how many people had perished in this terrifying place, either drowned in floods or perhaps killed by defenders as they tried to gain an entrance into the mountain fortress. There seemed to be an overwhelming menace in the dark passage, as if the ghosts of thousands of dead—and perhaps even *jinns*—were silently forbidding our entrance.

Along the walls of the Siq, darkened by overhanging cliffs, we saw ruins of an old aqueduct which once carried water from the Spring of Moses into the valley where the city of Petra was built out of solid rock. Part of this conduit apparently was constructed by the Romans, but the original must have been the work of the Nabataeans, or perhaps Edomites who lived there centuries before.

As we rounded the last turn, after riding for half an hour down the twisting trail at the bottom of the gorge, worn hard and smooth by thousands of feet of men and animals that had passed this way, the sky suddenly opened above us and we saw the magnificent facade of Al Khazneh, known as the Treasury. It faces northward from a recess in the solid wall of a mountain, the reddish face of a building that extended into the rock and probably was originally a tomb of early Nabataean kings. The front consisted of two stories, with the lower roof supported by six columns which bore traces of Greek origin. Above the roof were three separate structures, all carved like a gigantic bas-

289

relief in the rock, surmounted by the beetling brow of the mountain itself.

There was an impression in this building of something so old and enduring that it had defied the erosion of time and weather. Opening into the building itself was a huge door, leading into an interior vault which—according to the Bedouin—had been used as a depository for gold and other treasures collected from caravans that passed along the King's Highway under the shadows of the mountain citadel.

Beyond the Treasury was the inner city of Petra, and here the coloring changed from reddish to orange and saffron. Huge blocks had fallen from the ancient buildings and now lay in massive rubble, scarred and pockmarked from centuries of wear. Some bore traces of Roman design, but most were of Greek origin, or perhaps earlier. The crumbled walls of the city covered a space of perhaps 1,000 feet in each direction, beginning with an old Roman theater in which spectators' boxes were carved out of the mountain wall. On the far side of the city was an immense tomb, badly broken by erosion, which apparently had housed the remains of Nabataean kings.

The queer mixture of caves dug into the mountains and palatial homes that lay in ruins within the walls testified to the emergence of this place from prehistoric times to the luxuries of pre-Christian Rome. There must have been a large population living there, even before the time of Moses, but unfortunately neither archaeology nor legend have been able to probe very deeply into Petra's past. The Edomites were the most powerful people east of the Jordan Rift, but whether they actually lived in Petra has never been determined. The land surrounding Wádi Mūsa was once covered with dense forests, flourishing gardens, orange groves, and vineyards, and it is probable that the early people of Petra participated in those ancient extravagances, possibly as brigands raiding the

290

The caves of Petra: the ancient homes of early Nabataean Arabs, dug out of the solid walls of rock in the old city.

The Monastery: the magnificent face of Al-Deira, a pre-Roman building carved out of the walls of Nabataean Petra.

Edomites. I hoped Miss Kirkbride's diggings might produce useful information on this point.

As we rode along the paved road toward the western edge of the city walls, I could see the square stone building known as Nazzal's Rest House, where there is accommodation for transient visitors who wander into the place. At the foot of a huge scarp of mountainside, the top of which seemed inaccessible, were several rounded tombs with quadrangular obelisks mounted over an open gateway. They seemed to be pre-Grecian in design. The face of this massive pile was worn smooth by centuries of erosion, and I could not help marveling at the engineering feat which enabled these ancient people to carve it out of the mountain.

This was known as the Palace Tomb, and beyond it, against the western wall, was another magnificently carved building known as Al-Deira, the Monastery. It also was supported by carved columns and was so massive that a man standing on the roof would be almost lost from view from the ground. The means by which these structures were cut from solid rock must have been lost in antiquity. The actual age of Petra has never been determined, but it is believed from formations of the rock that there was human habitation in the area at least 10,000 years ago. Even the Roman theater, which could seat at least 3,000 people and was literally cut out of the side of a mountain, appeared to have been built on the ruins of a more ancient theater, in the style of the Greeks. Within the area bounded by the city wall, much of which lay in crumbled ruins, we saw temples, tombs, and even caves in which people probably of a much earlier age than the Nabataeans or Edomites had lived. Most of the Roman buildings were in ruins, having collapsed long before the more ancient structures began to give way.

While there have been valiant efforts on the part of many historians and scholars to view Petra as the eagle's perch from which powerful dynasties of Nabataeans ruled an empire stretching from Syria to the Arabian Steppe, most recent writings on Arab history seem to agree that it was a kind of desert pirates' lair, from which Bedouin marauders sallied forth to interrupt caravans traveling the main highway from Damascus into Arabia and gather spoils, much as Lawrence's raiders seem to have done at Mudawwara.

After Pompey entered Palestine in 63 B.C. and deposed the last of the kings of Petra, Aretas III, the final disposition of the Nabataean kingdom was effected by Trajan 200 years later. The Nabataeans were dissolved into historical oblivion for a period of more than 1,500 years, and it was not until 1812 that a Swiss explorer, Burckhardt, penetrated the Siq, redis-covered the ancient city, and made the site of this mountain fortress known again to the world.

Since then the place has become a playground for biblical scholars, archaeologists, and curious people like myself.

4

We rode up to the square stone hostelry which was part of the Arab settlement in Petra. After tethering our camels, we went over to the small store operated by my friend Awwad, a relative of the governor of the province. This small compound is all that is left of what was once a teeming marketplace filled with shops and trading places.

Awwad's store was in a cave, dug several thousand years ago and once inhabited, according to Bedouin tradition, by Christians fleeing from persecution in Palestine. Now it is a trading post, full of small trinkets and supplies for the traveler.

The manager of Nazzal's Rest House, Zaki abu Zayyad, whom I knew from previous visits to Petra, was in the store, and while Awwad began to prepare tea for us, Zaki motioned for me to speak privately with him. His expression was grave and slightly secretive, arousing my curiosity. When Arabs wish to talk quietly and personally, they speak of it as "between four eyes," and I had a feeling Zaki wanted to talk with me alone.

"What is it?" I asked after he led me to a corner of the room. His reply, as I had expected, was evasive. This is the custom of the Arabs in general and of Bedouin in particular. He shrugged. "Business is bad," he said. "There are few visitiors these days, and we have very little trade."

I nodded, although I was quite sure Zaki had not called me into a corner to inform me that business was not good. I could see that it was not; there were no visitors in the place but R'Faifan and me. So I waited for Zaki to continue. He spoke in English, in which he was not very proficient, so I was sure this would really be "between four eyes."

After a few more or less aimless remarks, he said, "Many people believe that activity along the border may increase. This is bad for visitors, is it not?" I agreed that it was. Zaki nodded sagely.

"You will not be traveling toward the border, of course."

It was half a question, but I quickly assured Zaki I would be heading eastward, probably toward Bāyir. He seemed quite pleased and said, "You will see many of your friends near Shaubak on the road to Bāyir. May Allah guide you!"

Zaki's remarks, which seemed to be almost a warning, disturbed me more than I was willing to admit, even to myself. I realized that he was conveying a message, even though his discourse seemed to be rambling. Arabs will seldom comment on government policy, particularly to an outsider, but I was fairly sure Zaki had information about border trouble, probably through the desert grapevine. I was equally certain that before the day was over, R'Faifan would know all about this information and would disclose it to me. Therefore I did not pursue the subject.

I told Zaki I wished to climb the mountain behind the Monastery, if possible as far as Beida, the site of a smaller city, probably older than Petra. I hoped to visit the caves where altars could be seen upon which human sacrifices had been made. Zaki nodded and promptly informed me that one of his boys, Mifleh, would accompany me to carry my camera and other gear.

Early the next day I set out with Mifleh. The narrow trail leading up from Petra to Beida can be negotiated only on foot, since horses or camels cannot pass through some of the narrow slits in the rock. It is about 5 kilometers to the top. There the remains of a stone-age village, probably of Neolithic time, led into deeper caves. There were marks of Bedouin fires along the walls, which might have been even later than the Nabataeans. Arabs today seldom visit the area outside Petra itself. I saw excavations near the trail where Miss Kirkbride had unearthed many old pieces of pottery and some very ancient Neolithic tools and flints. This place was called Seylaqat, and I later was told the village uncovered in the dig was inhabited at least 9,500 years ago. It is a miniature Petra, approached by a narrow canyon similar to the Siq, and there were evidences of occupation by farmers, since the tools were mostly for plowing.

Mifleh and I arrived back in Petra only a few minutes before a rainstorm swept down over the surrounding mountains. Since I had experienced this kind of weather in Petra before, I decided to hole up for at least another day, drinking coffee with Zaki and finding out as much as I could about happenings in the outside world. However, he steered clear of such sensitive subjects as fighting along the border, and we chiefly discussed the weather.

Before we left, Awwad made me a present of two unbroken pieces of pottery which he assured me were as old as Petra itself, and as a reciprocal gesture I bought a new *kaffiyah* from his meager store—probably the only piece of business he had transacted in a month.

XI. *The End of the Trail*

1

The point on the King's Highway from which we planned to turn eastward into the desert again was Shaubak, the ancient site of a Frankish fortress built during the Crusades, following the capture of Jerusalem. It was a huge, gray-walled castle—known as Monte Reale—on the crown of a sandy hill from which it reared its forbidding head over the countryside.

The scenery, of course, had changed since then. Once this area was matted with forests of oak and cedar. It was the beginning of the highlands where the mountainous country sloped downward to the Jordan Rift and upward to the Steppe. This land may have antedated every other region in the Holy Land in the antiquity of its original inhabitants. It was at one time one of the most fertile parts of the desert southeast of the Dead Sea, but in recent centuries it had been overrun by the Turks, who despoiled it of the great oaks and cedars: in fact, they had built a railroad spur from the main line of the Hijaz-Medina railroad, some 25 or 30 kilometers to the east at a junction called Uneixa, for the purpose of transporting the wood as fuel for their steam locomotives. This line of old rails could be seen in its abandoned state, running eastward over the dun hills toward the rising plateau of 'Arab al Howeitat. By the time of the First World War the Ottomans had denuded most of the hills of trees, and it now lay naked of vegetation, a monument to the spoiling process of the conquering Turks.

As we rode into Shaubak, we could observe many of the new works of the Jordanian government, who sought to restore the agriculture which had flourished in this region as far back as the time of the biblical Edomites. There were scattered farms around the small settlement, and a modern agricultural school, housed in new buildings. The entire aspect of the place was another illustration of the Jordanians' strenuous effort to use Western and chiefly American methods and equipment to lift their country from the medieval setback it suffered under the Turks.

The farmers, called *fellahin* by the Bedouin, were a separate segment of the Arab population, as different from the desert nomads as the city Arabs. They had well-kept stone and wooden houses surrounded by green fields, with sheds sheltering farm machinery, and they had formed a settled community.

We rode along the dirt road toward the *badia* fort under a sudden deluge of pelting rain, and by the time we reached the gate we must have looked like half-drowned monkeys perched on our camels. My *nága,* growing old and probably tired from having traveled several hundred miles across the desert, managed to slip on a patch of mud and went to her knees as we rode up. I pitched off the saddle in an unceremonious entrance to the Desert Patrol compound.

The police station was built around an old Turkish fort, and we were given quarters for the night in a stone-walled room. By the early hours of the next morning we had passed beyond the farmlands, and in place of the *fellahin* farms, Bedouin tents began to appear on the hillsides. One of the

The old and the new: Sheikh Debshi is in center, with his sons on either side and grandchildren wearing baseball caps.

herders directed us to the *bait sha'ar* of an old friend, Sheikh Slaman, whom I had seen at the feast for Emir Hassan at Sheikh Faisal's place, about 30 kilometers to the north.

The *sheikh,* recognizing me from a distance, came out to meet us, and once again I had the happy feeling of being back in the warm hospitality of the desert. R'Faifan behaved with his usual reticence, hanging back as we neared the tents, but the *sheikh* remembered him from the feast at Sheikh Faisal's *bait sha'ar* and invited him to join us in the *raba'a.* There is always a curious mixture of regal authority and democratic simplicity of manners among Bedouin which Westerns often find difficult to understand; yet this same direct simplicity characterizes the Moslem faith, and Bedouin have no difficulty understanding it. A wealthy man with large herds of sheep and fine camels has an obligation under the Moslem code to be considerate of his less fortunate neighbors, and this extends to his personal feelings as well as his actions. I cannot remember having observed a Bedouin act harshly or unkindly toward anyone purely on the grounds of social or economic superiority.

This combination of dignity and personal compassion is a trait of character that only those who have lived among the Bedouin can comprehend. It is, in essence, the *noblesse oblige* of desert aristocracy.

Sheikh Slaman, as a gesture of friendship, gave me three old coins. I have since checked them with archaeological experts and found they date back to Byzantine days. They were so well preserved that one appeared to have just come out of the mint! I am certain they were among his prized possessions, and I hesitated to accept them, but I understood clearly that my refusal to accept a gift would, in the tradition of Bedouin, be equivalent to insulting the giver.

We stayed long enough with Sheikh Slaman to enjoy another feast of roast lamb and rice, and he tried to prevail upon us to stay over a second day, but my schedule was becoming tighter and I still was worried about getting R'Faifan back to his family. Our next stop would be at the desert homes of two *sheikhs* I had known from earlier days—Mamdooh al Jazi and Debshi Guftan al Jazi, both relatives of Sheikh Faisal and powerful members of the Howeitat clan. Their camps would be found about 15 kilometers north and east of the Slaman tents. We rode upward over the brown hills and down into a pleasant *wádi* where about a dozen tents—all part of the community of the two *sheikhs*—stretched over about half a mile.

Sheikh Debshi had already prepared a feast, and it struck me that Slaman had probably sent a courier ahead of us to inform him of our impending arrival. No visiting *emir* could have been given a more royal welcome. Almost at the moment I climbed down from my camel, Sheikh Debshi came forward and presented me with a gift that is one of my greatest treasurers of the desert: a sword his father had carried in the campaigns with Lawrence! The blade was of fine Damascus steel, and the handle was laced with gold filigree. It seemed to me that the closer I got to the point at which I would have to make a decision to return to Ammān with R'Faifan or head out into the open land to the east by myself, the more these heartwarming incidents conspired to lure me again into the ancient plains of the Eastern Desert!

The sensation of antiquity one has when passing through this region is difficult to put into words. Mandooh's and Debshi's encampment lay just southeast of the Dead Sea, below the Wádi Dana, where battles were fought back into the second millennium before the Christian era. There is a feeling of treading soil that has been the scene of some of the mightiest events in history. Thousands of years ago this was the area where Neolithic man passed from the age of stone to the age of iron and bronze, where primitive peoples living in caves in the cliffs that face toward the Jordan Rift first began to shape metal into cutting tools with sandstone rocks.

It was in this area north of Wádi Dana that the king of the Moabites was besieged by the combined armies of Israel, Judah, and Edom in the tenth century B.C., and where Isaiah placed a curse on the Moabites. This was also the hilly country where Arab tribesmen under Khalid, the field commander of the Omayyad caliph, raided and disorganized the Byzantine armies during the siege of Damascus A.D. 635 and five centuries later it was the battlefield of Crusaders who fought off the intermittent attacks of the Abbasid caliphs in their desultory efforts to drive the Christian invaders from Jerusalem. There are a number of massive castles in the area, erected by the Crusaders in the tactical style of the Middle Ages to hold territory east of the Dead Sea during the Second Crusade.

North of Dana was the site of the ancient city of Karak, now a modern Jordanian town. This place, standing on the rising hills that ascend upward to the high plateau almost 5,000 feet above sea level, has been a fortress guarding the surrounding domains for more than 3,000 years under the successive rules of Moabites, Nabataeans, Byzantines, the Damascene and Baghdad caliphs, the Ottoman Turks, and finally the Hashemite Kingdom of the Jordan.

During our stay at the *bait sha'ar* of Sheikh Debshi I asked many questions about the early history of the place, but Bedouin are notoriously vague about such matters, mixing post-Mohammedan times with earlier legends in a kind of potpourri of miscellaneous and largely apocryphal information.

Sheikh Debshi was a quiet, soft-spoken man, about fifty years old, with gray hair and a gray tuft of beard. His deeply tanned face had the regal dignity of a desert *emir*. After he presented the sword with great ceremony, he seemed to retire from personal contact with R'Faifan and me, busying himself with orders to his servants while R'Faifan tended our camels and I lay in luxurious comfort among the deep piles of pillows and rugs scattered over the floor of the *raba'a*. At first I thought he was annoyed and perhaps did not want me as a guest in spite of the extraordinary gift of the sword, but one of the lesser functionaries in the place, who was quite convivial and talked easily about everything, explained that the *sheikh* was so delighted at my pleasure at receiving the sword he did not want to embarrass me by speaking of the gift, and had deliberately secluded himself.

During the hot evening, with the humid pressures of summer already beating upon the *wâdi* where the tents were located, the *sheikh* seemed to have lost some of his reserve and chatted amiably with me, trying to answer my numerous questions. We had a second *mansef* that evening, and I lay deep in the pillows, as completely satiated with food as I had been at any time since the extraordinary day of feasting during the ceremonies of Id-al-Adha at Al Jafr. Since Sheikh Debshi's father, whose sword I had been given, also was a member of Auda abu Tayi's band of Bedouin raiders, the *sheikh* told me something of their exploits. Again I was both interested and amused to note that the role of Lawrence was made quite subordinate to that of the Howeitat tribal chief.

We left the following morning for the *bait sha'ar* of Sheikh Faisal ibn Jazi, a few miles to the north.

2

On the way to Sheikh Faisal's camp we passed through the tiny town of Jurf, little more than a way stop on the camel trail. It had once been a station on the old Hijaz-Medina railroad, known as Darawash, and there still were a few mud huts and the ruined remnants of the old station house. The local "store," which seemed to have little more business than that of my friend Nassar at Bat'n al Ghūl, provided some fresh cheese and tea, and it was cool inside, so we lingered for about an hour chatting with the proprietor.

As we were finishing our lunch, Sheikh Jidoor and Mohammed ibn Jazi, Sheikh Faisal's younger brother, walked into the little café.

I sensed immediately that they had known in advance that we were traveling through Jurf, and had come down from their homes a few miles northwest to meet me. Sheikh Jidoor, who had only one good eye, the other being crossed inwards so that it gave him a fierce expression, came over and spoke quietly to me.

"You must come directly to our tents," he said. "We will speak there."

Later he indicated that R'Faifan should ride westward ahead of us on the trail to Tafila, the location of their community of *buyút sha'ar* and the center of the Jazi family, while I should ride in a Land Rover with Mohammed and himself. On the way we overtook R'Faifan, laboring along on the big bull camel, Mohammed abu Brahim, and leading my female, Al-Gazala (the gazelle). I felt sorry for him in his hot, lonely ride, but R'Faifan smiled cheerfully and waved at us. Possibly he knew more at the time than I did about the reason for Mohammed and Jidoor's intercepting us.

However, I was not long in doubt. Mohammed told me, as we bumped along over the winding trail, that his older brother, Faisal, had sent word that they must be prepared for war any day. Later Mohammed's younger brother, who had just returned from school at Ammān, repeated the same thing, and I realized that a crisis was developing along the border.

We reached the encampment where the tents of Sheikhs Faisal, Jidoor, and Mohammed were located, and I was taken immediately to the former, where I was led into the spacious *raba'a,* extravagently furnished with many decorations, rugs piled four and five deep on the floor, and cushions of every size and hue packed around the sides.

Sheikh Faisal was not at home. I was told by the younger brother that great events were taking place, and the accelerating

304

tension between Israel and the Arab states required him to remain in Ammān.

That evening a band of Nuwar, desert gypsies, came by, their possessions and musical instruments piled on white donkeys. Two boys ran up to the *bait sha' ar* and began beating a drum and twanging at a *rabába*—the square, violin-type instrument of desert nomads—but after a short discussion, Sheikh Mohammed sent them away. Their price for entertainment was too high, he explained, and besides the dancing girls were too fat!

The Nuwar are held in fairly low esteem by Bedouin. They do not herd sheep or goats and have no camels as a rule; except for white donkeys, which they seem to breed with great success, they have no particular virtues. I observed the Bedouin around the tent winking at each other, and I gathered they were exchanging some earthy viewpoints about the fat girls. The girls looked at the men of the encampment with uninhibited interest as they rode by on the donkeys. I caught R'Faifan appraising one of them, and told him I would report the matter to Um Jizar, his wife. R'Faifan grinned and assured me with an evil leer that he would contact Tony Hallec when we were back in Ammān and have him dispatch a letter to my wife in New York, describing my interest in the plump Nuwar girls.

Mohammed walked out to meet the chief of the group and handed him some money. Whether this was a standard honorarium for gypsies passing through the camp, or advance payment against services that might be expected of the Nuwar girls later in the evening, I obviously could not determine at the time, but I suspected it was the latter. The Nuwar are notorious Bedouin camp followers, and their women often provide forms of entertainment not readily available in the austere environment of desert homes. Lawrence, in *Seven Pillars of Wisdom,* comments on the need of desert men occasionally to "slake their thirst" on sexual fare other than that normally provided in the seclusion of the *bait sha' ar* with legitimate wives, and hints that this need is sometimes satisfied with personal associations between the young men of the desert. This is a viewpoint that I suppose is widely entertained by Westerners as a result of Lawrence's book, but there has been nothing in my observations of desert life that would support the notion. Bedouin men, like all males everywhere, have their miscellaneous methods of satisfying physical needs, but the desert does not breed strange abnormalities in this respect any more than the cities, and perhaps not as much!

In any event, R'Faifan and I reached a compromise in the matter at hand: each would keep his thoughts to himself, and if his wife has any notion that he was ogling the Nuwar girls, she received it from him!

During the evening I was able to get a radio, and I tuned it in to the Ammān station for news. The Arabic newscast was not particularly illuminating, since I understood little of it, but there was a brief broadcast in English announcing that the United Nations inspection team had been withdrawn from the Gaza Strip! This was ominous news, since it brought the tension closer to the Jordan borders. I said little to Sheikh Mohammed about this, but his younger brother talked quite freely, using excellent English, and I gathered that the popular feeling in Jordan was becoming more intense as a result of the growing problem of Palestinian refugees.

"They are our people," the young boy said. "We cannot forget them merely because of political actions of people who are not deeply concerned with our problems."

I gathered from his remarks that Jordan wanted to remain aligned with the Western bloc of nations and did not intend to follow the course of Syria and Egypt by aligning itself with the Soviets, but that in a conflict involving Jordanians in Israeli lands —such as the Negev—they would fight as one man to protect their people.

It appeared that this little country—the modern version of the old Hashemite kingdom—was caught in a kind of pincer move-

306

ment between its age-old Arab loyalties and the onrushing wave of alien influences which were engulfing them the way a huge wave sweeps over pebbles on the beach. The Arabs of the desert had survived successive invasions of foreign influences from the time of the Romans and had retained their own identity after each wave of conquest. Would this be another episode in the long chain of survivals, or would it be the beginning of the end of a 4,000-year-old era, the final chapter in the story of the nomads of the Arabian Steppe?

It seemed to me I was standing on the brink of history. As a matter of personal choice, I was not sure which way I should turn—whether to go back into the desert and complete my expedition while the beginnings of war flamed or flickered along the border, or return to Ammān to await the outcome of the present situation and possibly go home.

While I was debating my own problem, I saw a strange-looking boy standing near the front of Sheikh Faisal's tent. Everyone else seemed to be sleeping in the heat of the midday, but this boy, dressed in white, stood alone, looking off into the distance. He had a young, smooth face, and seemed almost ascetic. I found later that he had ridden his camel alone all the way from Sakakha, in Saudi Arabia, returning from a personal pilgrimage. He wore a long, white *kaffiyah* over his head, without an *agál* to bind it, and his dark eyes seemed to be looking into another world. There is no priesthood among the Moslems, but if there were, this boy would seem to have been a novitiate.

He was a member of the Sinai Howeitat, the largest of the northern tribes, with branches extending through and into Saudi Arabia. In Jordan the Howeitat occupy all lands south of Al Qatrana as far as Rumm, the borderland of the Bani-Atiyah tribes.

I wanted to take a picture of the youth as he stood looking into the distance, but there is a sense of privacy among Bedouin that one familiar with their customs never violates. A picture may not

307

be taken without the approval of the one whose picture is taken, and I forbore to interrupt the young man's reverie merely to ask him, like a tourist, if I could snap his picture.

On the following morning I made my decision: R'Faifan and I would return as rapidly as possible to Ammān and await the outcome of the present crisis. My trip into the Eastern Desert, which had become a consuming desire—now that I had finished the task of tracking down available information on the personality of T. E. Lawrence—would have to be delayed until there was a more settled and politically defined situation between Israel and the Arab states.

I totd R'Faifan what I planned to do, and although he did not display any marked emotion, I realized that he was relieved at my decision. He would have gone back with me into the Eastern Desert, but it would have been under pressure of worry about his family, and I would not have asked him to go.

Under these circumstances, it seemed to me to be the best decision. If the current crisis subsided, we could always head eastward again on a shortened schedule, and if the trouble increased, I would be able to get out of the country.

3

At the crack of dawn R'Faifan and I set off for the north. He had said his morning prayer, and from the lively look in his eyes I realized that he was glad to be speeding homeward to his people in the *bait sha'ar* near Jiza. By noon we had reached the tents of another member of the Jazi clan, Sheikh Haditha Mohammed al Jazi, whom I had met in Ammān. After a short stop, in which he welcomed us to his tent for lunch, we set out again over the desert. I knew our camels were rested from the two days at Sheikh Faisal's camp, although they were fairly well worn down by three months of almost steady traveling. We had 150 kilometers to travel to Ammān, passing the length of the Dead Sea, and I hoped to reach Jiza in three days.

That night we passed near the *bait sha'ar* of Hussein abu Tayi, a relative of the leader of that clan who, as I have noted, was a direct descendant of old Auda abu Tayi. In the tent was an ancient Bedouin, Gobalan abu Tayi, another member of the Abu Tayi clan. I was told he was ninety years old. When I brought out the sword Sheikh Debshi had given me, his old eyes lighted up and he promptly clamped the sword belt around his waist, drew the sword, and began what seemed to be a warlike dance.

For an instant I thought the old man was going to attack me with the sword, as he swung it around in circles, but he grinned at me, waving at my camera, which was slung from my shoulders. I realized he was inviting me to take his picture, which I did. That night, with the aid of R'Faifan's slower Arabic, old Gobalan abu Tayi told me of his exploits with Auda, and I felt transported back once more in my imagination to the fascinating sessions I had with Sheikh Aid in Rumm on much the same subject.

The tales of these aging desert warriors all had slight variations as to detail, and all were undoubtedly an accumulation of things that happened and things they heard about. But in retrospect, they all had a similar theme: the recapturing of memories of the past.

In order to record the whole business, I turned on my tape recorder as the old man talked. The results may have lacked significance as historical material, but to me they were true portraits of the Bedouin of the desert: wild and bold, poetic and ardent, and above all as changeless in the hardness of spirit and unyielding confidence in themselves as the Bedouin of more than 1,000 years ago, when they came charging out of Arabia to establish the Islamic empire.

When we left Sheikh Hussein's tent the following morning, the entire top had been stripped off and they were preparing to move to another location. The disassembling of the tent and its contents had been going on since midnight, carried on dutifully by the women of the camp while the men slept.

By this time R'Faifan and I were pressing our camels, traveling at a rate of 45 to 50 kilometers a day, and by the following afternoon we were deep in the Bani-Sakhr country, among R'Faifan's old friends and fellow tribesmen. That night we slept near Qatrana Station, at the northern line of the Howeitat tribal area, in the small *bait sha'ar* of Sheikh Slaman Hamdar of the Hejaiya tribe. This family was scattered over both Howeitat and Bani-Sakhr lands. He was an old friend of R'Faifan, and although his circumstances obviously were poor in comparison with the elaborate *buyût sha'ar* of the powerful and wealthy Jazi tribesmen we had just visited, he provided grain for our camels and food for ourselves, and talked volubly about the impending confrontation with Israel. He had no doubt the Jordanian air force would crush the Israeli in a matter of days.

We had by this time traversed half the distance to Jiza, since making the decision not to head out over the Eastern Desert. The land was high and dry, and the trails were over hard-packed sand and gravel. While the going was smoother over flat country, the pace was hard on the camels. Nevertheless, we were pounding across the desert at the fastest clip we had set on the expedition, not exactly like the Arabs of old under Khalid, when they were racing toward Damascus, but still a lot faster than the plodding gait of our earlier jaunt down the Eastern Desert. There was also much to distinguish us from the galloping pace of the Bedouin warriors on their finely bred steeds in the days of Mohammed: our *jamal* camels wheezed and labored over the endless sandy ridges, snorting with disgust when we urged them to faster speeds. But in the main, I felt that with our white-checked *kaffiyahs* flying in the wind, our sun-darkened faces set with grim determination, we must have resembled to some extent those old Bedouin raiders, at least from a distance.

Now and then R'Faifan, sensing the nearness of home, would

utter one of his spasmodic yelps that used to startle me out of my reveries. On the final day's journey we rode 17 hours, from dawn until almost ten o'clock, stopping only for lunch and R'Faifan's regular prayers in the afternoon and at sundown. As we pulled up in Jiza, I sought a telephone to call Tony Hallec in Ammān but found that all service was off. There was an air raid drill at Ammān!

The storekeeper, from whom I had bought supplies before we left Jiza, remembered me and provided food, for which he would take no money. By eleven o'clock I was able to reach Tony Hallec. The air raid alert was over, and he said he would drive down from Ammān and pick me up.

R'Faifan was left to assemble our two camels and herd them over to his *bait sha'ar,* where his wife, one son, and two daughters were anxiously awaiting his return. I asked him to fatten up the camels, either for our next dash into the desert or in order to sell them.

Tony Hallec greeted me warmly, but his expression was grave.

"It is good that you have come back," he said quietly as we drove through the night in his Volkswagen. "The events of the last few days have brought things to a head."

That night I wrote in my diary: "The crisis continues, but I think the end is in sight. Mr. Nasser seems to have won a victory. Hope to be back in action tomorrow."

How widely this missed the mark is a matter of history. This was May 29, 1967. When I awoke late the next morning in my room at the Continental Hotel, I heard a rumbling outside and looked out into the street. A column of tanks was roaring by, with hundreds of Jordanese lined along the streets, waving at the soldiers in their trim, olive-drab Jordanian uniforms as they headed for the Israeli border. I knew that Nasser had closed the Strait of Tiran, and I felt the mobilization of troops along the border was a prelude to the end of Israel.

During the day I learned from the radio that King Hussein

had gone to Cairo to confer with other Arab leaders. There appeared to be a united front among all Arab and Afro-Asian countries, including non-Moslem and non-Arab peoples, supporting the Arab stand. I hoped fervently that there would be a settlement short of war, and I would then be able to return to Jiza and head into the desert with R'Faifan to complete my expedition. The entire Palestine issue was going before the United Nations in New York. It seemed to me it would only be a matter of hours before everything would be cleared up.

That night there was a blackout in Ammān. The entire city had suddenly been aroused into the fever of war. Crowds milled along the streets until the sudden intervention of the security police dispersed them and the streets were closed by curfew. Overhead the planes of the Royal Jordan Air Force roared across the sky, and I thought of the sudden appearance of jet fighters in the sky above Bāyir the afternoon R'Faifan and I rode into the desert watering place.

By Sunday morning, June 4, I was becoming uncertain as to my future plans. It was impossible to make any decision until this sudden confrontation was ended. That afternoon I visited the Tourism Authority at the Foreign Ministry, which was open, and was able to dispatch my pictures to New York. Everyone seemed quite calm, and I was advised to remain in close touch with the American Embassy.

On the morning of June 5, Monday, I awoke to the realization that all the Middle East was at war. An air raid siren shrieked while I was having lunch with Tony Hallec, and we were suddenly told to go down into the basement. A few minutes later I heard the roar of planes and the crash of explosions. An Israeli air attack on the Ammān airport had been repulsed within an hour, with little damage to the city, but there was no question that the war was at our doorsteps.

That night Tony Hallec and I went to his nightclub, but everyone —including the dancing girls—was so nervous no one seemed to enjoy anything. Rumors were all around us. An oil refinery at Haifa had been bombed by the Jordan Air Force. An Israeli plane had been downed over the airport. An English woman, sitting at a table next to ours, kept leaning over and explaining that she had gone through this kind of thing in London during the blitz. The only thing to do was to keep calm and keep on drinking.

The next day I tried to contact R'Faifan, who was to have come into Ammān to make plans for our departure, but he did not show up. I left money with Tony Hallec to pay him if I was not at the hotel when he arrived. I went over to the American Embassy and talked with the United States consul at Ammān, Dave Mack (no relation to Dr. Mack). He was quite calm and told me to wait at the hotel, where I would be advised what to do.

During the evening we sat in darkness at the hotel. The entire city was blacked out. I was informed from various sources that the Jordanian forces were holding their own, but there was fighting in the Arab sections of Jerusalem. Soon the news began to trickle in, and it was all bad from the Jordanian point of view. Egypt was falling, or had fallen, under crunching Israeli attacks by air, land, and sea. The Israeli forces were on the eastern side of the Suez Canal, near Ismailia, driving columns of tanks into the Egyptian flank. By Thursday, June 8, the United Nations had ordered a cease-fire on the Israeli-Jordan and Egyptian fronts. Syria, which had been shelling across the border, also agreed to the cease-fire, but on the morning of June 9 we heard that the Syrians were still fighting.

The Six-Day War of course is recorded history. On the afternoon of June 9 all Americans were brought together in a downtown hotel, and arrangements were announced for our immediate departure from Ammān.

I had not seen R'Faifan since I left him a week before at Jiza. I told Tony Hallec to hold his money for him, and left for New York.

* * * *

Many sons and brothers of Bedouin clans I had known were engaged in the latest Middle East conflict. Even R'Faifan's second son, Mansour, whom I had never met, was at the front around Jerusalem.

A few weeks after my return home, I learned in a letter from Tony Hallac that R'Faifan and his family were safe, in the desert hills east of Jiza. Mansour was still with his unit, now on the east bank of the Jordan River.

R'Faifan looks forward to the day that I return to Jordan and once again we ride off together into the vastness of the desert we love. I have yet to see the remote regions east of Bāyir!

Glossary

There is no common spelling in Arabic due to the use of six throat consonants (kh, gh, h, ', h, and '), which are not readily translatable into English alphabetical sounds, and the "emphatic" consonants (t, d, s, and z) which influence pronunciation of the surrounding vowels. The spelling of the words here is therefore somewhat arbitrary and may differ from other English alphabetical variabtions in Arabic.

agál: head cord
'arab al'ariba: a true Arab; descendant of Yarab
'arab al masta'áriba: one who "becomes an Arab"
badia: Desert Patrolman
bait sha'ar (pl., *buyút sha'ar*): tent
bani (pl. of *ibn*): sons
bátiniyah: special breed of camel
bedu: Bedouin
burqa: heavy face veil
dhalla: women's litter basket for camel
ghôr: mud flat

háram: sacred place for women (harem)
he-shee: tobacco
jabal (pl., *jabál*) : peak
jamal (pl., *jamál*) : pack camel
kaffiyah: burnous
khalifa: caliph ("successor")
leban: camel buttermilk
mansef: feast
masjid: mosque
milfa: veil
muharram: section for women in tent
nága: female camel
q'a: a place; usually a mud flat
q'ata: screen between tent sections
raba'a: men's section in tent
rabába: one-string musical instrument
rayat al bait: mistress of the tent; wife
salám: peace (as, *Salám 'alaikum*: Peace be with you!)
shaūd: martyr
sheikh: chief of calm; literally "old man"
thōp: riding robe
um al' ayál: mother of the house
'umaniyah: highly bred camel
wádi (pl., *widyán*) : valley or gulch
wāsm: camel brand

316

Notes

Preface
1. Edward Gibbon, *The Decline and Fall of the Roman Empire,* Vol. II, ch. 50.

Chapter I
1. T. E. Lawrence, *Seven Pillars of Wisdom* (New York: Doubleday & Co., 1926). Page numbers in note references are from the Dell paperback edition (1962). P. 37
2. Joel Carmichael, *The Shaping of the Arabs* (New York: Macmillan, 1967), p. 5.
3. *Ibid.*

Chapter II
1. Lawrence, *op. cit.,* p. 29.
2. Carmichael, *op. cit.,* p. 39.

Chapter III
1. John Van Ess, *Meet the Arab* (New York: John Day, 1943), p. 89.
2. *Ibid.,* p. 17 fn.

Chapter VI
1. Translation of Bat'n al Ghūl varies; it means both "hollow belly" and "belly of the ghoul." Béled al- Araba means "road into Arabia proper." See Charles Montagu Doughty, *Travels in Arabia Deserta* (London: Jonathan Cape), quoted by Lowell Thomas, ed., *Great True Adventures* (New York: Hawthorn Books, 1963), p. 201.
2. Lawrence, *op. cit.*, p. 351.
3. *Ibid.*, p. 352.
4. *Ibid.*
5. *Ibid.*, p. 356.
6. *Ibid.*, p. 353.
7. *Ibid.*, pp. 366–67.

Chapter VII
1. H. R. P. Dickson, *The Arabs of the Desert* (London: George Allen & Unwin, 1949), p. 395.
2. Lawrence, *op. cit.*, p. 356.
3. *Ibid.*, p. 376.

Chapter VIII
1. Lawrence, *op. cit.*, p. 366.
2. *Ibid.*, p. 128.
3. *Ibid.*, chs.98–107.
4. *Ibid.*, p. 64.
5. *Ibid.*, p. 361.
6. Hallat Ammár is a depression near the Mudawwara wells, from which vapor or steam is exuded, appearing like smoke; this may have confused Lawrence. It is believed to be the site of an ancient city. See Doughty, *op. cit.*, and "Arabian Odyssey," in Thomas, *op. cit.*, p. 212. See also Lawrence, *ibid.*, pp. 365–67.
7. *Ibid.*, p. 362.
8. *Ibid.*, p. 363.
9. *Ibid.*, p. 370.
10. Carmichael, *op. cit.*, p. 111.
11. Gibbon, *op. cit.*, ch. 50.
12. Carmichael, *op. cit.*, p. 129.
13. Herodotus, *The History.*